Media Skills for Middle Schools
Strategies for Library Media Specialists and Teachers

Second Edition

Lucille W. Van Vliet

Edited by

Paula Kay Montgomery

1999
LIBRARIES UNLIMITED, INC.
Englewood, Colorado

To Alexandra and Victoria,
soon to be middle school students

LIBRARIES UNLIMITED, INC.
P.O. Box 6633
Englewood, CO 80155-6633
1-800-237-6124
www.lu.com

Production Editor: Kay Mariea
Copy Editor: Louise Tonneson
Proofreader: Eileen Bartlett
Indexer: Linda Bentley
Design and Layout: Pamela J. Getchell

Library of Congress Cataloging-in-Publication Data

Van Vliet, Lucille W., 1926-
    Media skills for middle schools : strategies for library media
specialists and teachers / Lucille W. Van Vliet ; edited by Paula
Kay Montgomery. -- 2nd ed.
    xv, 231 p. 22x28 cm. -- (Library and information problem-solving skills
series)
    Includes bibliographical references and index.
    ISBN 1-56308-551-8 (pbk.)
    1. Library orientation for middle school students--United States.
2. Middle school libraries--Activity programs--United States.
I. Montgomery, Paula Kay. II. Title. III. Series.
Z711.2.V36   1998
027.8'222--DC21   98-33898
                                                              CIP

Media Skills for Middle Schools

Library and Information Problem-Solving Skills Series

Paula Kay Montgomery, Series Editor

CUES: Choose, Use, Enjoy, Share: A Model for Educational Enrichment Through the School Library Media Center. Second Edition. By Phyllis B. Leonard.

Media Skills for Middle Schools: Strategies for Library Media Specialists and Teachers. Second Edition. By Lucille W. Van Vliet.

Library Information Skills and the High School English Program. Second Edition. By Mary H. Hackman.

Information Literacy and Information Skills Instruction: Applying Research to Practice in the School Library Media Center. By Nancy Pickering Thomas.

Contents

Part Two

Part Three

Foreword

Preparing middle school students to attain and master the skills necessary for continued academic success and lifelong learning is a continuous challenge to any middle school teacher or library media specialist. Middle school students are undergoing physical and emotional changes that alter them from day to day, hour to hour. The challenge is to use multiple methods to motivate students, capture their attention, and impart necessary skills. This book, *Media Skills for Middle Schools*, is one of a series of books that looks at those library and information skills that are essential for independent use of resources whether in books or on the Internet.

Media Skills for Middle Schools presents an integrated approach to the teaching of library and information skills. When used as the author has demonstrated in her own practice, it is an effective method for imparting those essential skills. The library media specialist and teacher are partners or collaborators in the delivery of instruction to students. They are co-facilitators of learning or co-mentors for students. Instruction is provided in a variety of ways by either of the instructors. Learning is the normal outcome of the unified library media program. Students learn through a variety of methods and formats in situations that are meaningful to them. This book provides a model for this type of instruction. It identifies more than 45 sample learning situations that might be useful to the middle school teacher or library media specialist.

Lucille Van Vliet focuses on integrating library and information skill instruction into all areas of the curriculum. She gives attention to the efforts necessary to plan with teachers. She shows specific examples of support from the principal, and she suggests the tools needed for instructional planning. A portion of this book is devoted to lesson plans and instructional units. Each lesson and unit prescribes the content and the library and information skill goals or objectives to be taught. The learning situation, materials and resources, and activities are suggested.

Reproducible activity worksheets appear throughout the book. Among the most helpful ideas are the suggestions for the roles that the teacher and library media specialist might play. Every effort has been made to balance the type of role that each might play.

The author, Lucille Van Vliet, has been a library media specialist and educator for more than 30 years at both the middle school and junior high school levels. While teaching, she put these ideas into practice in an exceptionally successful manner. She earned the admiration and respect of students, peers, school faculty, and administration. Her school library media program at Hammond Middle School, Howard County Public Schools, Ellicott City, Maryland, was awarded the Mae I. Graham Award from the Maryland Educational Media Organization for Outstanding Media Program of the Year. The author is now retired from the school system but continues to substitute in library media centers. She is actively involved in public library programming for children.

The many examples provided in this book should assist library media specialists who are just beginning their careers and motivate those already in the profession who need new ideas. The lessons encourage team efforts between teachers and library media specialists.

Paula Kay Montgomery

Preface

The purpose of this second edition of *Media Skills for Middle Schools: Strategies for Library Media Specialists and Teachers* is to update goals, objectives, learning strategies, and resources to encompass the Information Age. The rapid growth of technology permeates all of society. The world of work is changing at a dramatic pace on a global basis. Students must have the technical skills, knowledge, and attitudes necessary to meet the demands of the twenty-first century.

The organization and focus of this book provides a framework for collaboration among library media specialists, teachers, and administrators in middle schools. Part One contains five chapters that lay the foundation on which the lesson plans are based. A thorough knowledge of middle school philosophy and goals is inherent to a successful middle grade program. Characteristics and needs of middle grade students are addressed.

Part Two contains 45 lesson plans with specific library media skills and objectives, as well as competency goals and objectives. Planning procedures and teaching strategies are delineated. Resources that reflect new technologies are suggested as tools for teaching the lessons. Resources of suggested print materials include familiar reference sources and up-to-date materials.

The lessons are designed to be used by library media specialists and teachers to promote the teaching of information and computer skills as an integral part of the school curriculum. The theories behind the lessons advocate the involvement of students as self-directed learners, creative thinkers, problem solvers, and group participants. Many student-related activities are included in the lessons to provide enjoyable, stimulating, and meaningful experiences. Additional suggestions help facilitate family, home, and community connections.

Acknowledgments

GENERAL ACKNOWLEDGMENTS

Grateful acknowledgment and thanks are given to the following people and organizations:

Thanks to middle grade students with whom I have worked and who have enriched my life. As I revised each lesson from the first edition of *Media Skills for Middle Schools: Strategies for Library Media Specialists and Teachers*, I recalled the exciting times we shared at the schools where I served as library media specialist with our class activities, multiethnic festivals, booktalks, productions, parties, field trips, outdoor education, and film festivals. I still proudly wear my sweatshirt inscribed "Coach Van Vliet."

Thanks to the Howard County Public Schools in Ellicott City, Maryland, for permission to use curriculum guides in the preparation of lessons. The Howard County School System provided innovative school facilities, abundant resources, supportive administrators, teachers committed to the middle school concept, flexible scheduling, and clerical assistance. Thanks for the opportunity to have six months of intensive preparation and travel as groundwork for my position as library media specialist in the model middle school. Thanks to Dr. H. Thomas Walker and Celeste Smalkin for administrative and professional services. Specific thanks to David Oaks, principal; and Phyllis Weller, media aide; all well as to the teachers, administrators, and clerical staff at Hammond Middle School, with whom I worked for 15 years.

Thanks to the Maryland Educational Media Organization for honoring me with the Mae I. Graham Award and a lifetime membership.

Thanks to Dr. Paula Montgomery, my mentor and my friend, for her guidance and support. She enlisted me as a columnist for *School Library Media Activities Monthly* magazine and has been my series editor for three professional books. We have attended professional conferences and made joint presentations at the American Library Association (ALA) and American Association of School Librarians (AASL).

Thanks to Dr. Margaret Denman-West for the opportunity to supervise student teachers and to teach Children's and Young Adult Literature at Western Maryland College in Westminster, Maryland.

Thanks to the North Carolina Department of Public Instruction for permission to use information from curriculum guides. A special thanks to Dr. Elsie Brumback, director of Media and Technology Services, North Carolina Department of Public Instruction, and to Frances B. Bradburn and Gerry Soloman of the Information Technology Evaluation Services. The review and evaluation center was a great help, as was their publication, *InfoTech.*

Thanks to Moore County Public Schools, Carthage, North Carolina, for permission to use curriculum guides and a profile of West Pine Middle School. A special thanks to Dr. George D. Griffin, assistant superintendent of Moore County Public Schools, and to Dr. Kaye Richards-Beale, director of Middle Grades Education.

Thanks to Peggy Olney, Media Services director, Moore County Public Schools, for her professional services and friendship. She granted me access to Moore County Public Schools Library Media Centers, the media specialists, and the professional library. She also invited me to attend professional conferences and introduced me to library media professionals in the state. Her staff has been especially helpful.

Thanks to Mr. William E. Moore, principal, Aberdeen Middle School, and the faculty and staff for their cooperation and willingness to share teaching experiences with me when I substituted as the library media specialist. A specific thanks to Dixie Reynolds, assistant in the media center, and to Mr. Peter Pezzi and his "stay gold" young men.

Thanks to Mr. Nathaniel Jackson, principal, Southern Pines Middle School, Audrey Moriarty, media specialist, and Rhonda Slocum, teacher, for allowing me to use their resources and to share some skills lessons with them.

Thanks to the Gamma Sigma Chapter of Delta Kappa Gamma for their support and encouragement. A particular thanks to Dr. Celia Dickerson.

Thanks to Lynn Thompson, Southern Pines Public Library director and special friend; Lynn Bowness, assistant director; Jeane Rinker, Public Services librarian; and the staff for their valuable assistance with research. A specific thanks to Kaye Brown for inter-library loan assistance.

Thanks to Sandhills Community College library staff and the Continuing Education Department, Computer Division for their assistance.

Thanks to the members, staff, and the church library committee of First Baptist Church, Southern Pines, North Carolina, and Community Bible Study members for their interest and moral support.

Thanks to friends Becky and Bob Hudson, Alfreda Martino, Carolyn Warren, Doris Kirby, and Iris Burnett for inspiration and encouragement.

Thanks to my daughter, Jo Ann Van Vliet, and her husband, Dr. Hans-Jürgen Guth, for their influence as scholarly writers; to my son, Alan Van Vliet, his wife, Elaine, and my granddaughters, Victoria and Alexandra, for their love, support, and interest; and to my husband, Robert Van Vliet, for his love and quiet acceptance of the many days spent in my home office and at libraries, conferences, and conventions.

ACKNOWLEDGMENTS FOR PERMISSION TO REPRINT MATERIALS FROM PUBLICATIONS

Grateful acknowledgment to the following for permission to reprint materials from their publications:

American Library Association. Grover, Robert. Fall 1996. *Collaboration.* Lessons Learned Series.

Berger, Sandy. 1997. Having fun with your computer. In *How to Have a Meaningful Relationship with Your Computer.* Fairfield, Iowa: Sunstar.

Board of Education, Howard County Schools, Ellicott City, Maryland. David Oaks, principal, Hammond Middle School. 1984. Curriculum Guides and Committee Reports used in preparation of lessons taught jointly by Lucille W. Van Vliet and teachers at Hammond Middle School appearing in *Media Skills for Middle Schools: Strategies for Library Media Specialists.* First ed. Littleton, Colo.: Libraries Unlimited.

Davies, M. 1992. Are interdisciplinary units worthwhile? Ask students. In *Connecting the Curriculum Through Interdisciplinary Instruction.* Edited by J. Lounsbury. Columbus, Ohio: National Middle School Association.

Keller, Eve. 1997. Walking the copyright wire: How one county keeps its balance. General Conference Booklet. Paper presented at NCAECT annual conference, 5-7 March.

Moore County Schools, Carthage, North Carolina. 1994. *Computer Skills Curriculum, 6th grade, 7th grade, 8th grade.*

North Carolina Department of Public Instruction. 1992-95. *Learning Connections: Guidelines for Media and Technology Programs,* 1992. *Information Skills Curriculum* and *Computer Skills Curriculum,* 1995.

ACKNOWLEDGMENT OF CONTRIBUTIONS

Grateful acknowledgment to the following for contributions:

Andrea Stuart, graphic artist of Southern Pines, North Carolina, for her contribution of graphics.

Dianne Sanchez, Spanish teacher, for providing information on Spanish festivals.

Alfreda Martino, library media specialist, Elkridge Landing Middle School, Elkridge, Maryland, for information for an essay "Profile of an Exemplary Middle School."

Vickie McKenzie, library media specialist, and Joan B. Frye, principal, West Pine Middle School, West End, North Carolina, for information for an essay "Profile of an Exemplary Middle School."

Kaye Richards-Beale, Ph.D., director of Middle Grades Education, Moore County Schools, Carthage, North Carolina, for information for an essay "Profile of an Exemplary Middle School."

PART ONE

CHAPTER ONE

The Middle School

DEFINING THE MIDDLE SCHOOL

The middle school is a specially designed transitional school that provides for the education of early adolescents between elementary school and high school. Based on the nature and developmental needs of these students in transition, the middle level school ideally supplies a suitable environment for 10- through 14-year-old students. A student-centered program offers the opportunity for academic, personal, and social growth. The middle school has an awesome responsibility of preparing students for the role they will play in the twenty-first century.

THE MIDDLE SCHOOL MOVEMENT

The middle school movement gained momentum during the 1960s as educators became increasingly dissatisfied with the junior high school. Many people felt that the junior high school was not accomplishing its originally intended purpose of providing a school especially for the young adolescent. However, little was done to prepare special courses of study based on the learning requirements of early adolescents. In fact, some junior high schools had become a mere imitation of the senior high school in instructional methods, curriculum, and social activities. Another problem was that junior high schools did not contain those pupils of compatible physical, social, and emotional maturation.

The middle school concept was promoted in the 1960s and 1970s by such prominent educators as William Alexander, Mary Compton, Donald Eichorn, Paul S. George, John H. Lounsbury, Conrad F. Toepfer Jr., Gordon Vars, and Emmett Williams. Their ideas on the philosophy, goals, and program had a profound effect on the development and growth of middle schools.

The recent death of William Alexander, noted as an educational visionary who sparked the middle school movement, prompted this editorial tribute in the January 1997 issue of *Middle School Journal:* "Thousands of middle school educators are laboring daily to create his vision of a school in the middle, built around the notion that a school should offer a personally relevant, developmentally appropriate curriculum" (Erb 1997, 2).

Many other educators contributed to the middle school movement through books, journal articles, research studies, and conference reports. They stressed the need for a student-centered school developed along a pattern that would serve students who have similar intellectual, physical, and emotional needs. Of special significance was the organization of the National Middle School Association, which holds an annual middle school conference and publishes the *Middle School Journal* and a number of professional books.

The growth of middle schools has been phenomenal, with new middle level schools being established throughout the United States each year. The structure varies, but the most common organization includes grades six through eight. Other middle schools include grades seven through eight, four through eight, and five through eight. Just as middle schools vary in organizational structure, some middle schools vary in their potential for implementing an exemplary middle school program; however, the middle school concept offers many possibilities for achieving its mission.

Middle School Standards

The report of the Task Force on Education of Young Adolescents: *Turning Points: Preparing American Youth for the 21st Century* by the Carnegie Council on Adolescent Development sets standards for all middle level school programs (Carnegie 1989). It identifies the middle level schools as potentially society's most powerful force to "recapture millions of youth adrift, and help every young person thrive during early adolescence."

In 1988, the American Association of School Librarians (AASL) and the Association of Education Communications and Technology (AECT) prepared far-reaching guidelines entitled *Information Power: Guidelines for School Library Media Programs.* These joint associations are currently preparing a new set of standards and guidelines for school library media programs and other professionals containing information literacy standards for student learning. A "vision" committee on these standards has gathered research, incorporated multiple reviews, and solicited responses and feedback from members of AASL and AECT and other professionals. The new standards are divided into three categories: Information Literacy, Independent Learning, and Social Responsibility (AASL and AECT 1996). The completion of these new standards and forthcoming guidelines will greatly enhance the entire library media and informational skills program. All library media professionals are encouraged to "latch on to these standards" and put them into practice.

Exemplary Middle Level School Practices

An exemplary middle level school "builds from a foundation of student-centeredness that places learners first and enables them to feel safe, secure, and successful." (Allen, Splittgerber, and Manning 1993, 1). Teams of teachers and students work together to achieve academic and personal goals for all students. "Making a Difference in the Middle: High Standards, High Expectations for All" was the theme for the March 1997 National Middle Level Education Month, as publicized in the *Middle School Journal.* The high standards and high expectations became goals for educators, students, parents, and the community.

Exemplary middle level schools are those that prepare students for active participation in a culturally and ethnically diverse society in today's world and in the twenty-first century. They have clear mission statements. They use a variety of methods to establish goals and priorities. They endorse the concept that all students are capable of achieving success. They have planned and implemented effective discipline standards. They work toward integration of the curriculum and the declining of boundaries between disciplines (Ogden and Germinario 1994, 213).

The use of the technological tools of the Information Age to provide instruction in the process and application of high-level thinking skills required for information literacy is paramount in exemplary middle level schools. State-of-the-art lab facilities with a high technology profile provide the impetus for promoting information literacy. The multimedia approach, with its wide range of accessible instructional materials and variety of activities, is consistent with the intellectual and physiological scope of middle school age students (Romano and Georgiady 1994, 12).

Other exemplary practices in middle level schools include interdisciplinary team organization, flexible scheduling, ongoing staff development, core academic programs, exploratory elective programs, differentiated programs for students of all abilities, a developmental guidance program, flexible grouping, varied instructional methods and strategies, and high impact parental and community involvement.

PHILOSOPHY AND GOALS

The philosophy of a middle school must be derived from the overall philosophy of its educational system. The broad statement of beliefs subscribed to by many educational systems includes important concepts relevant to middle schools: To develop self-potential, to achieve success, to understand themselves and others, to achieve proficiency in basic skills, to respect the dignity of work, to grow in the range of cognitive abilities, to respect all individuals of different cultures and races, to become responsible citizens, to obtain the skills needed for effective living, and to develop lifelong interests for leisure activities. The middle school faculty and staff must be committed to its philosophy.

The paramount goal of a middle school is to provide programs designed specifically to meet the physical, social, emotional, and intellectual needs of young adolescents. These programs should be student-centered and activity-oriented and have clearly defined measurable objectives. In support of this goal, a middle school should strive to:

1. initiate a continuous progress program allowing students to move at their own rate toward the mastery of skills;

2. provide training for teachers to help them understand their role as middle school educators;

3. promote an outstanding library media/informational skills program as an integral part of the total school program;

4. provide a wide assortment of instructional activities such as games, field trips, festivals, and audiovisual projects;

5. teach students basic process skills;

6. develop higher level thinking skills in students;

7. provide for flexible scheduling and flexible grouping of students;

8. use a variety of learning materials and strategies;

9. promote team planning and team teaching of interdisciplinary units;

10. include a strong program of health and physical education classes;

11. provide for remedial instruction;

12. promote ideas that involve students in exploration and discovery;

13. plan programs of study for the gifted and talented students;

14. plan programs of study for the less able students;

15. emphasize the development of communication skills;

16. plan continuous methods of evaluation and reporting;

17. involve students in coeducational programs in home economics and industrial arts;

18. provide instruction and enrichment activities in art and music;

19. institute an advisor/advisee program;

20. provide a well-developed guidance program for individuals and groups;

21. accept the differences in each student;

22. initiate a special interest or activities program for students;

23. provide many opportunities for students to interact with peers;

24. help students develop a commitment to their own education;

25. provide social experiences designed for middle school students;

26. give students the opportunity to develop creativity and self-expression;

27. emphasize the development of responsibility, self-respect, and self-discipline;

28. provide an extensive intramural sports program;

29. plan and implement sound communication between the elementary school and middle school, as well as between the middle school and high school;

30. provide for use of innovative programs and new technology;

31. provide the necessary tools, both hardware and software, for every student to reach the optimal education experience in this technological age; and

32. promote a strong PTA organization involving the parents and community.

Implementation of Goals

The implementation of the goals of a middle school is the joint responsibility of the local school system staff members and the individual school. All staff members involved with middle schools should be committed to the middle school concept and should understand the needs and capabilities of middle school students. The members of the board of education, the superintendent, the assistant superintendent, the director of middle schools, and the supervisors and specialists play key roles in providing policies, services, financial support, lists of appropriate texts and materials, curriculum guides, and workshops. They also assist in the improvement of instruction by direct involvement in the instructional program.

Staff Commitment

Additional school system resources include human relations services, pupil personnel workers, psychological services, research and development services, and staff development services. The success of a middle school program depends ultimately on the effectiveness and commitment of the staff. The principal and assistant principal provide the leadership and vision to design a viable organization for the instructional program. They formulate and implement policies and procedures, coordinate school activities, and provide a continuous assessment of the program. By creating a communications network composed of the staff, students, parents, and community, they can involve these groups in the decision-making process.

A well-prepared, cooperative teaching staff participates in program planning and evaluation. They strive to use the teaching strategies that meet the needs of middle school students by emphasizing process skills and activity-oriented experiences. The guidance counselor coordinates programs dealing with the affective needs of students and plans individual and group guidance activities. The guidance counselor is also responsible for promoting career awareness and improving human relations. The library media specialist or information specialist participates in the instructional program of the school by collaborating with teachers in making library media and information skills objectives an integral part of the curriculum. As a teacher, library media center administrator, computer specialist, literacy advocate, and provider of services, the library media or information specialist contributes to the total school program. A courteous, friendly, and helpful secretarial, cafeteria, and custodial staff who relate to middle school students can provide many services to ensure the efficient operation of the school. They can become the students' role models of the everyday work force.

ORGANIZATIONAL PATTERN

The organization of a middle school determines its educational program. Some form of team teaching is basic to the middle school concept. Team teaching is a flexible process of grouping students for instruction by two or more teachers who plan together the lessons' specific objectives and activities. Teams may be organized as disciplinary, interdisciplinary, or a combination of the two. Using guidelines from the school system, the principal and staff jointly plan for the use of space, time, and personnel. A flexible schedule is necessary to accommodate team teaching, independent study, advisory groups, minicourses, and many other activities.

The teaching strategies in a middle school include a wide variety of methods that allow for student activity, movement, and interaction. Successful strategies employ learning centers, games, field trips, experiments, lectures, demonstrations, role playing, and programmed instruction.

Evaluation is a necessary part of the middle school program. Reporting student progress and performance has changed from just relying on grade equivalents of A, B, C, to providing a broader spectrum of student performance and behavior. Frequent communication and dialogue between the school and the home is now the norm. The teacher uses a wide variety of strategies to assess a student's progress

or performance. This progress is reported to parents through report cards, conferences, telephone calls, and efficiency/deficiency reports. Parent/teacher conferences are scheduled to accommodate the parents. Students are taught self-assessment procedures and are encouraged to communicate with teachers concerning grades and evaluations. Special recognition and encouragement is given to students through displaying their work or giving them certificates, congratulations, or a special honor. Pictures of students who are selected as chef-of-the-week, super-reader, or media quiz winner are prominently displayed.

The observation and evaluation of all middle school teachers and staff focus on the attainment of goals and objectives. Periodically, all staff members should be a part of a schoolwide assessment of the philosophy, goals, and programs of the school.

FACILITIES

The facilities for a middle school should be appropriate for the program and goals of that school; however, the facilities do not make the program. Traditional buildings can house a progressive middle school program; innovative open space buildings can house a traditional program. Ideally, the facilities for an exemplary program provide for flexible grouping. Moveable partitions and large group instructional areas help to provide this flexibility. Special planning is needed to accommodate laboratories for computers, science, home economics, industrial arts, foreign language, remedial subjects, and production areas. Study carrels throughout the school offer places for independent study.

It is important for the library media/information center and computer labs to be accessible to all parts of the school. Adequate space is needed for individual and small group work as well as for large group instruction and media activities. Space should be provided for reading, listening, viewing, studying, teaching, planning, and producing audiovisual programs.

Comfortable furnishings, pleasing colors, interesting learning centers, exhibits, displays of student reports or artwork, and decorations contribute to the atmosphere of middle level schools. Students respond well to bright and cheerful surroundings.

CURRICULUM

The middle school curriculum and instructional practices vary according to school systems and individual schools. Curricular opportunities depend partly on the size of the school, the grade-span, the student/teacher ratio, the type of community, the socioeconomic conditions of the families served by the community, and the ethnic composition of the student body (Becker 1990, 450). Many middle schools use a developmental skills program as a broad, general base for the education of all students. State departments of public instruction publish standard courses of study in separate curricular frameworks.

The middle level curriculum is defined as an integration of learning experiences organized in a given school around knowledge, commonly shared concerns of young adolescents, and global social issues experienced by students and the world (Allen, Splittgerber, and Manning 1993, 151). Interdisciplinary and multidisciplinary curriculums are an essential part of an integrated curriculum approach.

Media and Technology

The middle school curriculum is changing to meet the challenges of the twenty-first century. This is especially true in the area of media and technology. For example, in January 1992 the Division of Media and Technology Services, North Carolina Department of Public Instruction, published an extensive guide *Learning Connections: Guidelines for Media and Technology Programs* which is aligned with the national guidelines entitled *Information Power* as well as with the 1992 *North Carolina Computer Skills Curriculum* and the *North Carolina Information Skills Curriculum*. Committees to review, revise, and develop 1998 curriculums for each of these areas were established in September 1996 and January 1997, under the leadership of Martha Campbell, Information Skills and Computer Skills consultant, Instructional Services, NC Department of Public Instruction. Teachers were invited to share their ideas on key curriculum issues relating to the content of the revised documents. The North Carolina State Board of Education approved the *1998 North Carolina Computer/Technology Skills Curriculum* in May 1998 for use by all teachers in the North Carolina school system. The *1998 North Carolina Information Skills Curriculum* was adopted in the summer of 1998. Classroom teachers, library media specialists, and computer resource teachers will collaboratively use these curriculum guides to prepare students to gather, process, use, and communicate information (Public Schools of North Carolina 1992 and 1998).

A Sample Middle School Curriculum

Art

Formal elements of art and composition:
  Art history
  Art criticism
  Aesthetics
  Seeing
  Enjoying
Creating art forms
Computer skills:
  Viewing
  Listening
  Word processing
  Graphics
  Production
Career concepts

Foreign Language

Introductory experience:
  Conversation
  Communication
  Cultural awareness:
      Customs
      Current events
      Geography
      Songs
      Games
Computer skills:
  Word processing
  Telecomputing
English as a second language
Development of functional skills in English
Career concepts

Health

Comprehensive health programs and
      services
Utilization of community health resources
Instruction:
  Use of audiovisual material
  Models
  Printed materials
Monitoring of personal health of students
Nutrition
Good health practices
Disease information
Assimilated substances:
  Alcohol, tobacco, and drugs
Family life and human development
Fitness and first aid
Growth patterns
Career concepts

Home Economics

Programs for strengthening family life
Food and nutrition
Clothing and textiles
Home furnishings
Home management
Consumer education
Career concepts

Industrial Arts

Qualities of good design and construction
Computer skills:
  Computer-assisted design
  Databases
  Spreadsheets
  Graphics
Robotics
Sketching, drawing, planning, and production
Woodworking, leather crafts, and plastics
Proper use of tools
Career concepts

Language Arts

Continuous progress program in literature,
      composition, and spoken arts
Reinforcement of cognitive skills
Listening skills
Computer skills:
  Word processing
  Desktop publishing
  Newsletters
  Graphics
  Databases
  Telecomputing
Genre reading
Study skills
Research
Career concepts

Math

Continuous progress/appropriate placement
General math
Geometry
Algebra
Use of manipulatives
Computer skills:
  Data processing
  Graphing
  Graphics
  Publishing

Databases
Spreadsheets
Programming
Accelerated/advanced courses
Career concepts

Music

Music literacy:
  Reader
  Writer
  Performer
  Consumer
Chorus
Instrumental:
  Band
  Strings
Rhythmic development
Positive attitude toward music
Awareness of the nature, structure, and
    meaning of music
Computer skills:
  Music applications
  Listening
Career concepts

Physical Education

Sequential developmental program:
  Team sports
  Individual sports
Body management
Locomotor skills
Manipulative skills
Water safety
Intramurals
Positive social interaction
Career concepts

Reading

Developmental:
  Sight vocabulary
  Functional word attack skills
  Comprehension skills
Judging quality, accuracy, and usefulness
    of resources
Challenging higher level thinking processes
Enjoyment of reading:
  Reading, listening, and viewing for
    pleasure
  Reading, listening, and viewing for
    information
Corrective
Diagnostic and prescriptive

Individualized instruction
Computer programs:
  Literature enrichment
  Literature comprehension
Career concepts

Science

Activity-oriented:
  General science
  Life science
  Physical science
Laboratory safety
Laboratory experiments
Observation techniques
Tools of science
Metric system
Exploratory activities
Computer skills:
  Word processing
  Databases
  Spreadsheets
Computer resources:
  Interactive video
  Laser discs
  Telecommunications
Research using technology:
  Accessing, assimilating, and producing
Career concepts:
  Nontraditional careers

Social Studies

Preparing students for productive and
    effective citizenship
Fostering positive attitude and values:
  Belief in democratic government
  Dignity and self-worth of individual
  Equality of opportunity
  Interpersonal relationships
  Diverse cultures
Data collection
Computer skills:
  Word processing
  Database and spreadsheets
  Graphing
  Publishing
  Interactive videos
  CD-ROM research
Maps and globes
Research and problem solving
Working collaboratively
Career concepts:
  Nontraditional careers

SPECIALIZED PROGRAMS AND ACTIVITIES

The regular instructional program of a middle school may be enhanced by specialized programs and activities. A program for the gifted and talented can provide many opportunities for students with great potential to participate in varied activities related to academics or the performing arts. A program for at-risk students and students with learning or behavior deviations or other special needs is met with lessons adapted to the visual, auditory, and tactile kinesthetic learner. Instructional strategies are multisensory and activity-oriented and include audiovisuals and technology tools. Developmental assistance for special needs students is often provided by resource specialists in regular classrooms.

A program of independent study emphasizes the student's role in developing personal competencies by allowing the student to select and plan a course of study or project in a special field of interest. A teacher serves as a consultant or advisor. The organizational structure, types of programs, reporting, and supervision may vary.

Another program designed to meet the special interests of middle level students and to provide an introduction to a wide range of activities is the minicourse, club, or special activities program. Students and teachers can interact in a nonacademic setting and share happy rewarding experiences in such activities as Chinese cooking, bridge, chess, model-making, photography, reading, computer game playing, and aerobic dancing.

The advisor/advisee or home room program is essential to the development of interpersonal skills. It helps to build a closer relationship between teachers and students, students and peers, and students and family. It offers many students a caring environment where they can identify their strengths and weaknesses, learn to understand themselves and their peers better, communicate effectively, and make suitable decisions.

Appropriate social activities for middle schools allow for the development in students of diverse interests. As students participate in field trips, concerts, and festivals, they have the opportunity to socialize with one another. Multipurpose parties with games, dancing, and movies provide choices for students. Most middle school students love to eat; therefore, a wide assortment of food could be a part of each party.

The sports program of a middle school includes a basic skills program in the physical education curriculum and a well-planned intramural program. Intramurals usually take place immediately after school. Some schools provide an activity bus two days a week for a small fee to encourage student participation. Some of the successful intramurals include basketball, bowling, gymnastics, volleyball, soccer, hockey, wrestling, and softball. Middle school teachers from many disciplines should be encouraged to sponsor intramurals.

STATUS OF MIDDLE SCHOOLS

Ideally, middle level schools are responding to the special needs of young adolescents. Students are actively involved in learning, using new technologies and other modes of learning in which they can participate. They have a wider range of subjects and tools to keep them challenged. They have a faculty and staff that have a vision of the twenty-first century and are committed to guide students toward setting goals for lifelong learning and attaining success in this information-rich society.

Successful middle schools have the organization, facilities, staffing, and resources to provide a curricular and instructional program committed to the middle school philosophy. These include interdisciplinary teams, flexible scheduling, advisor/advisee programs, exploratory elective programs, physical and health educational programs, differentiated programs for exceptional students, intramural programs, varied instructional methods, and materials related to high technology. Library media and information specialists work with all teachers and staff members to integrate the teaching of informational and computer skills with all areas of the curriculum. Teachers, administrators, and other school employees participate in ongoing staff development. Parents and community leaders are directly involved in their local schools.

Yet many middle level schools do not have the financial resources and trained personnel to implement the middle school policies, procedures, goals, and objectives required to attain the status of a true middle school. But changes are being made with the help of the government. The Federal Communications Commission approved the implementation of discounted telecommunications services in the nation's schools and libraries beginning in January 1998. Carol Henderson, executive director of the ALA Washington office, stated: "We look forward to working to make universal service an effective policy and to assure that the new age of telecommunications and information becomes a reality for all" (Flagg 1997). Many parents, communities, local governments, students, and the general public are backing educational reform and asking that exemplary middle schools be made available to all middle level students.

If middle level students are to be successful citizens in the twenty-first century, they must be given the tools to accomplish this goal. An exemplary middle school status can only be achieved through the joint efforts of a dedicated staff, informed parents, an involved community, and receptive students.

REFERENCE LIST

Allen, Harvey, Fred L. Splittgerber, and M. Lee Manning. 1993. *Teaching and learning in the middle level school.* New York: Macmillian.

American Association of School Librarians (AASL) and the Association of Education Communications and Technology (AECT). 1988. *Information power: Guidelines for school library media programs.* Chicago: American Library Association.

——. 1996. *National Guidelines Vision Committee: Information literacy standards for student learning.* Draft #5. Chicago: American Library Association.

Becker, Henry J. 1990. Curriculum and instruction in middle-grade schools. *Phi Delta Kappan* 71: 450–57.

Carnegie Council on Adolescent Development. 1989. *Turning points: Preparing American youth for the 21st century.* The Report of the Task Force on Education of Young Adults. New York: Carnegie Corporation of New York.

Carson, Ben B., and Jane Bandy Smith, eds. 1993. *Renewal at the schoolhouse.* Englewood, Colo.: Libraries Unlimited.

Erb, Tom. 1997. Crossing over a watershed. *Middle School Journal* 28 (3): 2.

Flagg, Gordon. 1997. FCC approves telecom subsidies for libraries, schools. *American Libraries* 28 (6): 12.

Ogden, Evelyn Hunt, and Vito Germinario. 1994. *The nation's best schools: Blueprints for excellence.* Vol 1. Lancaster, Pa.: Technomic.

Public Schools of North Carolina. 1992. *Computer skills curriculum.* Raleigh, N.C.: North Carolina Division of Media and Technology, Department of Public Instruction.

———. 1992. *Information skills curriculum.* Raleigh, N.C.: North Carolina Division of Media and Technology, Department of Public Instruction.

———. 1998. *1998 North Carolina computer/technology skills curriculum.* Raleigh, N.C.: North Carolina Division of Media and Technology, Department of Public Instruction.

Romano, Louis G., and Nicholas P. Georgiady. 1994. *Building an effective middle school.* Madison, Wis: W. C. Brown and Benchmark.

CHAPTER TWO

The Middle School Student

CHARACTERISTICS OF MIDDLE SCHOOL STUDENTS

The middle school student is a special person who requires a special depth of understanding and acceptance. On the threshold of adulthood, each student has a unique pattern of physical, social, emotional, and intellectual growth. These differences are reflected in the varied interests, abilities, attitudes, and social and emotional adjustments of each individual. It is important to remember that these characteristics interact with each other. They are not separated by boundaries but are intertwined with each other and may overlap (Milgram 1992, 17–25). Educators need to understand the complexities of this age group in order to provide for the diverse personal and academic needs of each student.

Physical Development

The physical characteristics of individual middle school students differ widely. In fact, the physical growth of students varies most in grades 7 and 8 (McKay 1995, 19). Many adolescents experience rapid physical development in height and weight. Others mature physically at a slower rate of speed. "Growth spurts" on the average come two years earlier in girls than in boys. Girls are usually taller and more physically developed than boys for the first few years of early adolescence. Growth patterns are also irregular. For instance, bone growth is faster than muscle development, resulting in awkwardness and lack of coordination (Forte and Schurr 1993, 26). Fluctuations in basal metabolism cause restlessness, anxiety, apathy, and indifference. Many students who overexert can tire easily. Such physiological changes can cause students to work less efficiently.

The biological changes that occur at puberty produce dramatic and visible changes in young adolescents. These changes usually occur between the ages of 10 and 14. The most important physiological change of young adolescents is the development of the sexual reproductive system (Allen, Splittgerber, and Manning 1993, 46). A wide range of diversity in these pubertal changes is present in both girls and boys. This diversity in maturation creates marked differences in physical characteristics and is interrelated with the physical, emotional, and social development of middle school students.

The uneven growth patterns of students often affect their self-image. This is especially true for those students who develop very early or very late. Because they may become confused about their physical changes, students need to be taught about body systems and human development.

Students can also express anxiety in regard to health issues. They are very concerned about contemporary health issues such as AIDS, anorexia nervosa, drug abuse, alcoholism, and teenage pregnancy. Middle school educators need to accept the responsibility of planning a curriculum that addresses these concerns. A systematic approach that provides sufficient accurate and factual information is imperative. Together, administrators, teachers, guidance counselors, health educators, and advisors need to provide direct instruction, informal interactions, and appropriate literature on these subjects. Guest speakers such as medical personnel, social workers, and personnel from other social service agencies can be invited to present relevant programs.

Middle school students are concerned about their physical appearance. Many desire to be exactly like their peers and are constantly comparing themselves with others. A skin blemish, a scar, or the gaining of a few pounds can be devastating to their egos. Their level of maturity is often erroneously judged by their physical appearance.

Social Development

The social characteristics of middle school students revolve around their desire to understand themselves and their relationships with peers and teachers. Students may ask themselves:

- Who am I?
- How do I compare with others?
- Why am I different?
- What do others like/dislike about me?
- Do I belong?
- Why are friends so changeable?
- Do my teachers like me?

- Why do they pick on me?
- Why are my parents so hard to please?

Students are frequently troubled by their answers to these questions.

Most middle school students desire recognition and acceptance by their peers. These students tend to accept peer group values and standards and enjoy socializing with their peers. Generally belonging to a group provides high self-esteem; not belonging to a group produces low self-esteem and dejection. However, some young adolescents are loners. They prefer to work and play alone. They may be shy, absorbed in a fantasy world, engrossed in watching television, or interested only in playing video games. Some are avid readers, while others are ardent computer and Internet users. These students may be scholars, slow learners, or have no interest in the traditional learning styles.

Friendship for many middle school students is changeable as students are in and out of favor with friends almost daily. Best friends who are inseparable one day may not be on speaking terms the next day. They may have one best friend or prefer to be with a group of friends. Gender plays an important role in selection of friends at this level. Same-sex friendships are the norm at least for the first year of middle school. Generally girls become interested in boys long before boys are interested in them. As middle school students mature, their interpersonal relationships change. They may value friendships and set new standards for maintaining these friendships.

A transition takes place in the family relationships of many middle school students. Students become more independent and are able to stay away from home for longer periods of time. They resist parental guidance and authority and may even be rebellious. Although they feel their parents do not understand or appreciate them, most middle school students are still very dependent on their parents. In fact, most of their behavior and values are patterned on the standards and models set by their parents.

Parents hold diverse opinions and standards for their children. Some may be overindulgent and reluctant to accept the changes they observe in their children, feeling that their "little darlings" can do no wrong. Other parents label their young adolescents as moody, impatient, impulsive, demanding, lazy, and sloppy. They complain about sibling rivalry and the teasing, fighting, and arguing between members of the family.

Many times, changes in the family status greatly affect the middle school student. These changes include divorce, illness, and death. Middle school students are also affected by changes in economic status, moving to another community, and various other family problems. Regardless of these changes, parents should try to build a sense of family togetherness that involves mutual love, respect, communication, and understanding. Instilling moral and spiritual values and ethics is an important part of parental responsibilities.

A great many middle school students desire social interaction with teachers and other staff members. They want to talk about their problems, concerns, successes, failures, and goals and seek support, acceptance, and special considerations. They enjoy meeting with teachers and staff members on an informal basis at parties, club activities, home room or advisory programs, lunch, intramurals, and field trips. In fact, students who display antisocial behavior toward teachers and staff members are often seeking special attention. Positive interactions between students, teachers, and staff members can help to promote better relationships among these groups.

Emotional Development

The emotional characteristics of middle school students reflect the changing nature of early adolescents. On the one hand, they are likable, cooperative, responsible, sensitive, and trusting and show interest, motivation, and ingenuity. On the other hand, they are disagreeable, troublesome, egocentric, and avoid responsibility and can also be prejudiced, insensitive, and intolerant. Some may demonstrate erratic and inconsistent behavior and boredom, while others may struggle with sex-role or ethnic identification. These characteristics are a product of the students' need for approval, acceptance, and self-confidence.

Intellectual Development

A wide range of intellectual characteristics is present in middle school students. All students should move from concrete thinking operations to transitional thinking operations to formal thinking operations. Concrete thinkers focus on the tangible, usually ignoring inferences, assumptions, and systematic methods. Transitional thinkers are able to handle more abstract ideas while still relying on some concrete experiences. Formal thinkers can deal with abstract concepts, problem solving, the scientific method, sequences, and long-range planning. Slow-rate and fast-rate learners grow toward mental maturity at their own rates (Romano and Georgiady 1994, 30).

E. D. Hirsch Jr. details an extensive program of academic knowledge in the subject areas traditionally taught in the sixth grade in his book *What Your Sixth Grader Should Know* (Hirsch 1993). His Core Knowledge curriculum program affects intellectual development and provides specific examples of instruction. For the most part these instructional examples can be incorporated into a curriculum integrated with the library media skills curriculum.

In *The Unschooled Mind: How Children Think and How Schools Should Teach,* Howard Gardner conceptualizes the development of the mind (1991, 6–7). He presents insights and clues of three types of learners, from the intuitive learner to the traditional student or scholastic learner to the disciplinary expert or skilled person. The progression of learning matures from the young child to the individual who has mastered the concepts and skills to apply knowledge. He bases his scholarly theories and practices of educational reform on cognitive research and human development. He stresses that during the years of middle childhood, students should have opportunities to engage in apprenticeships, participate in projects, and interact with appropriate technologies in which they can cultivate and develop literacy, numeration, and scientific skills (225–26).

The middle school should provide a flexible, continuous progress program to help meet the students' intellectual abilities, while paying special attention to the at-risk and academically gifted students.

NEEDS OF MIDDLE SCHOOL STUDENTS

Middle school students have many personal needs. They need to be accepted as individuals, to be treated fairly, and to be heard. They also require affection, security, understanding, acceptance, positive role models, and moral support from teachers, family, and peers. Teachers, guidance counselors, advisory group leaders, and other staff members can provide guidance in helping students foster values and ethics and become responsible for self-development.

Middle school students have many academic needs. Since they often become bored with routine assignments and drills, activities that allow manipulation and movement are desirable. Students need the opportunity to learn how to use the latest technological tools and to be introduced to a variety of literary resources.

Middle school students need to work with trial and error situations where grading is not a factor. Because they are curious and inquisitive, middle school students enjoy opportunities to experiment and time to explore and discover. They should be challenged to stretch their imaginations, develop creativity, and increase self-expression. By interacting with peers, middle school students try out new ideas and strategies and search to find their own answers. Opportunities for success, recognition, and rewards are an important part of the middle school students' academic life.

Middle school students need to be encouraged to read and to know the joy and pleasure of this activity. The library media specialist and teachers can nurture reading by opening up to all students the treasure-house of knowledge in books and related media. Students travel to imaginative worlds, face and conquer human experiences, discover adventures, expand interests, and find meaning in their lives through the enchantment of books. When used effectively, electronic media can greatly enhance literature and reading programs (Van Vliet 1992, 3–4).

Students not only need to experience reading for pleasure but also to experience reading for information. Regardless of the present and future technologies, reading skills of locating, selecting, interpreting, and analyzing data will be necessary. Students must be taught a process approach to utilize information effectively. They must question, reason, doubt, judge, create, and become independent learners (Van Vliet 1992, 5).

MIDDLE SCHOOL STUDENTS IN TRANSITION

The middle school student can successfully make the transition through the stages of pre-adolescence to adolescence and achieve realistic goals if administrators, teachers, staff, and parents recognize and analyze the student's individual characteristics. The library media specialist uses this knowledge and cooperatively plans lessons integrated with the curriculum, providing learning experiences that are relevant to the student's needs. The sample lessons in this text have been developed by the library media specialist and teachers using the characteristics of middle school students as an underlying factor.

REFERENCE LIST

Allen, Harvey, Fred L. Splittgerber, and M. Lee Manning. 1993. *Teaching and learning in the middle level school.* New York: Macmillan.

Forte, Imogene, and Sandra Schurr. 1993. *The definitive middle school guide: A handbook for success.* Nashville, Tenn.: Incentive Publications.

Gardner, Howard. 1991. *The unschooled mind: How children think and how schools should teach.* New York: Basic Books.

Hirsch, E. D., Jr., ed. 1993. *What your sixth grader needs to know.* New York: Doubleday.

McKay, Jack A. 1995. *Schools in the middle: Developing a middle-level orientation.* Thousand Oaks, Calif.: Corwin Press.

Milgram, Joel. 1992. A portrait of diversity: The middle level student. In *Transforming middle level education,* edited by Judith L. Irvin. Boston: Allyn & Bacon.

Romano, Louis G., and Nicholas P. Georgiady. 1994. *Building an effective middle school.* Madison, Wisc.: W. C. Brown and Benchmark.

Van Vliet, Lucille W. 1992. *Approaches to literature through genre.* Phoenix, Ariz.: Oryx Press.

CHAPTER THREE

The Library Media Specialist

THE CHANGING ROLE OF THE LIBRARY MEDIA SPECIALIST

The role of the library media specialist is changing in response to the changes in education, teaching procedures, and resources. Site-based management, year-round schools, resource-based learning, interdisciplinary instruction, cooperative learning, core academic programs, team teaching, and continued progress instruction require changes in the duties and responsibilities of the library media specialist. The information explosion and technological advances also necessitate an expanded role for the library media specialist. In this global information society the library media specialist is a catalyst in leading administrators, teachers, and students to search for information electronically. The automated library media center has electronic card catalogs and circulation processes, bar code readers, CD-ROMs, and computer-assisted instruction. Networks or telecommunications systems include telephones, facsimile machines, computers and modems, instructional telecomputing resources, and video-based resources. In addition to these resources are print and nonprint materials and the equipment necessary for productions and presentations that support the instructional program.

To facilitate these changes at the middle school level, reorganization in staffing patterns to include professional and support staff, who possess specialized skills, is employed in many school districts. The library media specialist, as director of the library media program for the school, plays a key role in coordinating the instructional program with all related staff members.

TERMINOLOGY

Not only has the role of the library media specialist changed but so have the titles and names for those who hold this position. Leandra Sunseri, in her article, "By Any Other Name," discusses the change in the title "librarian" to "media specialist" and how it was made in an attempt to encourage the acceptance and use of audiovisual resources in the curriculum (Sunseri 1994). She promotes the use of the title "librarian" for those who provide resources to students in public and academic libraries. New standards encourage the return to the term "library" in reference to the school library media center and the school library media specialist. The roles identified for the library media specialist in *Information Power: Guidelines for School Library Media Programs*, the joint publication of the AASL and the Association for Educational

Communications and Technology (AECT) (1988), include teacher, information specialist, and instructional consultant. Titles currently in use include:

- Media Coordinator
- Resource Manager
- Computer Specialist
- Instruction Technology Specialist
- Information Specialist
- Instructional Consultant
- Teacher

Regardless of the title, the library media specialist plays an important part in implementing a school media program that is an integral part of the total instructional process. He or she is a provider of services and materials, resource person, planner, innovator of instructional technologies, curriculum designer, communications expert, and team member.

MISSION, GOALS, AND VISIONARY ACTION PLANS

Mission

The mission of the library media specialist is to work together with the administration and staff to support the total instructional program, to prepare students for lifelong learning, and to assist students and staff in attaining the ability to manage and use information in various formats.

Goals

The goals for a library media skills program that is integrated with the instructional program are based on the educational philosophy, goals, and objectives of the system and district levels and the individual school. These goals can be adapted to meet the needs of an individual school and community through the combined efforts of the instructional supervisors, the principal, the teachers, and the library media specialist. Inherent in these goals are the following responsibilities:

- To develop independent learners by teaching the skills of locating, analyzing, interpreting, and utilizing all forms of media.
- To teach informational skills and reinforce them within the school's instructional program.
- To assist students in developing the ability to manage and use information to solve problems.
- To aid students in becoming discriminate users of information obtained from various sources.
- To encourage students to seek out and discover new ideas and to explore new concepts.
- To promote good communications skills of listening and speaking.
- To foster the love of reading and the lifelong enjoyment of books.
- To promote cooperative learning and the ability to work in groups.
- To instill in students a vision for the future.

Visionary Action Plans

The visionary action plans of the library media specialist provide the greatest latitude for creative expression in the area of curriculum design and implementation. It is essential that the library media specialist be knowledgeable about the schoolwide curriculum. This knowledge can serve as a framework for writing, developing, and implementing library media skills into all areas of the curriculum. By reading curriculum guides, observing classroom instruction, and discussing needs with teachers and supervisors, the library media specialist can discover many possibilities for designing lessons and units that extend, enrich, and supplement the existing curriculum.

LEADERSHIP

The library media specialist has the primary responsibility for leadership for the instructional planning and implementation of an integrated library media program. This key leadership function is expanded to include the cooperative roles of additional professional and support staff. With additional technology programs prevalent in many schools, technology coordinators or computer specialists are being hired. In these cases, the balance in the division of responsibilities is clearly delineated in job descriptions and assignments, as determined by the administration. The professionals should function as a team and communicate regularly in order to ensure consistency through a coordinated, cohesive plan that serves the entire school population.

The desirable qualities of a good leader include the following:

- excellent organizational ability
- dedication
- mutual respect
- cooperation
- consistent behavior
- flexible practices
- sense of fairness
- good communication skills

To provide this leadership, the library media specialist should have thorough knowledge of the structure and purpose of the educational system, the advances in educational theory and practice, and the new and expanding role of technology in education. The library media specialist should also know the curriculum, the learning abilities and needs of students, and the strengths and capabilities of the teaching staff.

To prepare for this expanded role, the library media specialist should be involved in a continuing educational program, professional organizations, and in-service programs. In addition, the library media specialist gains knowledge and experience by attending national and state conventions and seminars, serving on curriculum committees, and participating in team planning sessions. Reading curriculum guides and participating in planning sessions prepares the library media specialist for work with team leaders, individual teachers, and students in coordinating the teaching of library media skills that are integrated with the curriculum.

MANAGEMENT AND OPERATION PROCEDURES

The management and operation of a quality media library program is the responsibility of the library media specialist. It must be built on a foundation of effective administrative procedures. The efficient daily management of library media center routines necessitates well-defined operations for the circulation of media materials and equipment, scheduling of classes and productions, orderly conduct of business, and organization of resources. In many schools, the automation of the card catalog, the circulation process, and office management procedures greatly assist the library media specialist. Budgeting, evaluation, selection of resources, inventory, and maintenance of equipment are necessary functions. A flexible monthly schedule for administrative tasks is a helpful tool.

SELECTION AND UTILIZATION OF RESOURCES

The selection and utilization of materials and equipment to support the instructional program is a major responsibility of the library media specialist. Based on the school system's selection policy, the library media specialist should use a variety of selection aids. By using the established criteria for the evaluation of instructional materials, the library media specialist and teachers can preview and evaluate many materials that meet the learning needs of students. The library media center collection should provide a broad range of materials with a vertical and horizontal continuum of subject matter that supports the students' inquiry process, concept formation, and intellectual and emotional growth.

Meaningful classification and organization of all materials will extend the usefulness of the collection. A yearly inventory with emphasis on weeding and replacement will greatly enhance the collection.

Students, teachers, and administrators must be invited and welcomed to the library media center. Every effort must be made to facilitate the use of resources and facilities. The library media specialist should establish flexible guidelines for the loan of books, materials, and equipment. An up-to-date, well-organized collection that is easily accessible and available is the key to successful utilization. The use of telecommunications to locate and acquire the latest information on a given subject is of the utmost importance in this technological age.

The evaluation and assessment of the library media program should be an ongoing process for the library media specialist. From the evaluation and selection of resources and equipment, the review of the collection, and the assessment of services to the teaching and evaluation of lessons and units, the procedures for assessment should be built into the prescribed activity through well-defined objectives. The standard of performance set by the objectives becomes a measure of accountability. Using the data formulated from assessments, the library media specialist can revise, restructure, and improve many aspects of the library media program.

THE SERVICE ROLE OF THE LIBRARY MEDIA SPECIALIST

The service role of the library media specialist includes a wide range of reference, bibliographic, and production services to teachers and students. The extent of these services should be determined by establishing service preferences and priorities. The multimedia and interactive multimedia approaches drastically change teaching and learning for the library media specialist, the teacher, and the student. The library media specialist must be a catalyst in providing information services such as using full-text resources on compact discs, accessing bibliographic databases through online computer catalogs, using data-based management practices, and linking to networks outside of the school. To implement these services the library media specialist, computer teachers, and technology specialists must carefully select the essential hardware and software.

With the strong emphasis on the involvement of the library media specialist in the instructional program, the role of the library media specialist should include formal and informal teaching, inservice training, and reading guidance. As a teacher, the library media specialist should prepare general instructional objectives and specific competency goals for units and lessons. Using a variety of teaching strategies and instructional materials, emphasis should be placed on developing information skills and the process of research in this technological age. Students can participate in global networks by connecting to the Internet, making a school Web site, publishing a classroom newsletter, using e-mail, working in large and small groups, preparing media presentations as individual and group projects, and enjoying many exploratory activities. These activities should promote the students' intellectual and social development.

The library media specialist's role in promoting reading and the use of print resources is still an important part of the library media program. Evelyn Hunt Ogden and Vito Germinario (1994, 218) in *The Nation's Best Schools: Blueprints for Excellence* state that the use of technology does not reduce the importance of books. They also claim that the best schools have pride in their book collections and in their high level of circulation. Reading guidance and the appreciation or love of books can be incorporated not only in booktalks and annotated reading lists but also in lessons and units jointly taught by the library media specialist and teachers. For example:

Unit	Books
Social Studies: Our Legal System	Aaseng, Nathan. 1996. *The O. J. Simpson Trial: What It Shows About Our Legal System.*
Art: Biographies	Pescio, Claudio. 1995. *Rembrandt: And Dutch Painting of the 17th Century.*
Science: Insects	*Familiar Insects and Spiders.* 1995. A National Audubon Society Pocket Guide.
Social Studies: European Exploration	Fritz, Jean. 1994. *Around the World in a Hundred Years: From Henry the Navigator to Magellan.*

COOPERATIVE PLANNING

Cooperative planning with the staff and the community is essential for the achievement of a successful library media skills program that is integrated with the curriculum. *Learning Connections: Guidelines for Media and Technology Programs* (North Carolina Department of Public Instruction, Division of Media and Technology Services 1992, 3, A1–A3) is an excellent resource book that addresses many facets of the entire media library program. Of special note are the guidelines for the establishment of a media advisory committee.

Media Advisory Committee

This committee functions on the premise that an integrated program is the joint responsibility of media and technology professionals, administrators, teachers, support staff, students, parents, and community representatives. They work together to translate the mission and goals of the school into plans of action. The committee should be under the leadership of the library media specialist, and members should be appointed by the principal. The system or district level media supervisor serves in an advisory capacity. The functions and responsibilities of the media advisory committee may vary from school to school but may include the following:

- Examining the curriculum and objectives of the school.
- Encouraging the integration of information skills into all areas of the curriculum.
- Establishing guidelines to assist in this integration process.
- Providing for the needs and interests of the students.
- Promoting flexible scheduling and easy access to the library media center.
- Furnishing input into maintaining a well-balanced media collection.
- Reviewing and evaluating materials based on the approved selection tools.
- Setting priorities for expenditures.
- Initiating public relations activities that promote the library media program.

The media advisory committee assists the library media specialist by modeling the effective use of the library media center and its facilities.

In addition to cooperative planning with the media advisory committee, the library media specialist should plan with key individuals and groups to provide the structure and support for the instructional design of an integrated library media skills program. These individuals and groups include supervisors, the principal, teachers, students, and parents.

Supervisors

At the school system or district level, the supervisors or directors provide the impetus for the planning and development of an integrated library media program. The supervisor of library media services, in accordance with school board procedures, generates the policies, goals, and objectives that provide the framework for the program. A curriculum guide containing library media skills with objectives and recommendations for their integration into specific curriculum areas will greatly facilitate the implementation of the program. The supervisor of library media services should work with subject supervisors to plan strategies for the cooperative teaching of library media skills. Support for the program by the library media supervisor, who provides in-service training, feedback and interaction, and encouragement in each library media center, is an ongoing process.

Getting to know the subject supervisors by name and talking with them when they visit in the school will help to establish a foundation for support of an integrated library media skills program. When the subject supervisor observes an integrated library media skills lesson being taught by the subject area teacher and the library media specialist, the supervisor should be asked for comments and suggestions. Additional ideas on the teaching of library media skills, the use of the library media center, and the recommendations for purchase of resources by the library media specialist should be solicited from the subject supervisor. The subject supervisors should also be asked to include a library media specialist in curriculum workshops and in-service meetings to provide input for the integration of library media skills into classroom instructional units and curriculum guides.

The Principal

The library media specialist must schedule planning sessions with the principal to discuss and evaluate the general goals and objectives and desired learning outcomes of the program.

By providing joint planning time and encouraging teachers to plan and share teaching responsibilities with the library media specialist, the principal can promote an integrated library media skills program. Active support should include allocation of funds for resources, overseeing the implementation of policies and procedures, and participation in promotional activities. By observing, analyzing, and evaluating a lesson or unit jointly taught by the library media specialist and a teacher, the principal can identify needs, facilitate communication and cooperation, appraise outcomes, and provide motivation for improving the effectiveness of the program.

The library media specialist should inform the principal about unsuccessful programs, problems, needs, and activities in the library media center. The principal should be invited to observe and participate in games, projects, fairs, news quiz programs, and productions. The importance of the principal's support and guidance in implementing, strengthening, and evaluating a unified library media skills program cannot be overemphasized.

Teachers

Joint planning by the library media specialist and teachers provides the structure and support for the instructional design of an integrated library media skills program.

The library media specialist should be a motivating force who helps teachers accept and participate in the integration of a library media skills program. Some suggestions include:

1. Getting to know teachers and inviting them to open houses, celebrations, and in-service programs.

2. Assisting teachers to learn the use of new technologies.

3. Routing professional journals to subject area teachers.

4. Preparing guidelines such as: "What the Library Media Center Can Do for You and What You Can Do for the Library Media Center."

5. Attending team planning sessions and jointly planning performance objectives.

6. Sharing ideas and responsibility for teaching.

7. Offering to work with small groups or individuals.

8. Suggesting ideas for and assisting with student productions.

9. Assisting with locating information through the Internet, inter-library loans, public and college or university libraries, and community resources.

10. Volunteering to go to team or class areas for large or small group presentations.

11. Jointly evaluating lessons or units and offering to read, correct, and grade part of the students' work.

Students

Students should be included in the planning process by incorporating their ideas and suggestions obtained from class discussions, individual conferences, and lesson or unit evaluations. If students are part of an independent study program, they will meet regularly with their advisor and the library media specialist to plan strategies, review and evaluate progress, judge the adequacy of resources, and receive guidance.

One example of this cooperative teaching procedure follows: Two students would like to work on an independent project for science class. They write a proposal to research and explain the theory of plate tectonics and present the proposal to the science teacher. The library media specialist is asked to become a part of the planning team, along with the science teacher and students. Together they meet to plan objectives, assign responsibilities, design the project, determine the schedule, and define evaluative criteria. The library media specialist discusses and reviews the selection, location, and utilization skills with the students, who meet in the library media center during their independent study time. The students successfully use the library catalogs, encyclopedias and courseware on CD-ROM, and the *Reader's Guide Abstracts* on WilsonDisc, as well as many reference books and indexes. They use the Internet to request information from the Smithsonian Institution and National Geographic headquarters. Their additional resources are requested through the inter-library loan network. After consulting many sources, the students analyze data, which involves discriminating between relevant and irrelevant facts, summarize and draw conclusions, and prepare an outline to submit to the science teacher. Next, they obtain suggestions and approval from the science teacher. The students write a report and consult with the library media specialist concerning the format for citing references and making a bibliography. With the assistance of the library media specialist, the students apply the information gained through research by planning and producing a videotape incorporating computer-generated graphics and photographs from a digital camera. Using a computer, they also produce a hard copy of their report, complete with graphics. The science teacher and library media specialist jointly evaluate and critique the project. The students share their production experience during a large group presentation.

Middle school students enjoy helping to plan activities and creating projects. Include their input when planning media-related field trips, celebrations, festivals, and productions. They can get valuable information through the Internet, e-mail, pen pal programs, the National Geographic Kids Network, interactive videodiscs, and other telecommunications applications.

When activities in the library media center include small or large group participation, students may use alternative methods to reach their subject-related objectives. Students delight in participating in the production of graphics and audiovisual materials using the latest technological advances available to them. Joint planning between the teachers, the library media specialist, and students is important for the creation of these productions. Student research and reports are greatly enhanced by student-generated transparencies, filmstrips, audiotapes, computer graphics, slides, videotapes, signs, posters, photographs, and maps.

The library media specialist works with the students and assists them in planning a storyboard or production guide, preparing visuals, filming, editing, and evaluating the production. During this process, students are allowed the freedom to express themselves. The library media specialist serves as a resource person and technical advisor. Developing the ability to plan cooperatively and work with students is one of the goals of a library media specialist.

Parents

Communication is the key to cooperative planning between the library media specialist and parents. By informing parents about the general goals and objectives of the library media skills program, the library media specialist activates the communication process. An orientation meeting for the parents of incoming students, a library media center open house during the PTSA Back-to-School Night, a survey of service needs, an invitation to schedule a visit during parent-teacher conference periods, and a library media center newsletter sent to parents are some suggested activities designed to gain the interest and support of parents.

Parent volunteers of the library media center assist the library media specialist by performing clerical duties, helping with book fairs, assisting with audiovisual productions, and participating in field trips. An explanation of the goals and objectives of the library media program is included in the training session for volunteers. These parents may also become members of the media advisory committee. Because of their firsthand experience in the library media center, parent volunteers become strong advocates in support of the budget, acquisition policies, and overall library media program.

THE KEY ROLE OF THE LIBRARY MEDIA SPECIALIST

The role of the library media specialist is constantly and will continue changing with the introduction of new teaching techniques and technologies. Library media specialists play a key role in this Information Age. New guidelines for the library media program and the role of the library media specialist are now being developed at the national, state, and local levels. Library media specialists must be prepared for these changes if they are to continue in their key role as leaders and participants in the educational process.

REFERENCE LIST

Aaseng, Nathan. 1996. *The O. J. Simpson trial: What it shows about our legal system.* New York: Walker.

American Association of School Librarians (AASL) and the Association of Education Communications and Technology (AECT). 1988. *Information power: Guidelines for school library media programs.* Chicago: American Library Association.

Familiar insects and spiders. 1995. A National Audubon Society Pocket Guide. New York: Alfred A. Knopf.

Fritz, Jean. 1994. *Around the world in a hundred years: From Henry the Navigator to Magellan.* New York: G. P. Putnam's Sons.

North Carolina Department of Public Instruction, Division of Media and Technology Services. 1992. *Learning connections: Guidelines for media and technology programs.* Raleigh, N.C.: North Carolina Department of Public Instruction.

Ogden, Evelyn Hunt, and Vito Germinario. 1994. *The nation's best schools: Blueprints for excellence.* Vol. 1. Lancaster, Pa.: Technomic.

Pescio, Claudio. 1995. *Rembrandt: and Dutch painting of the 17th century.* New York: Peter Bedrick Books.

Sunseri, Leandra. 1994. By any other name. *Wilson Library Bulletin* 68: 64–66.

The Teacher and the Library Media Specialist

COLLABORATIVE ROLE

The process of planning and designing an integrated library media skills program that encompasses the information and computer skills curriculums requires a commitment from the teacher and the library media specialist. Both must invest a great deal of time and effort in jointly planning teaching units and lessons. Teachers who may have been reluctant to share lesson plans and teaching responsibilities with the library media specialist may be enticed to do so with the availability and uses of new technologies and the library media specialist's specialized knowledge of the information field. Teachers know the value of students' access to a wide variety of information through the Internet, electronic networks, computer graphics, CD-ROMs, and telecommunications. Library media specialists know the value of teaching students how to access, analyze, interpret, synthesize, and apply computer technologies. A collaborative effort on the part of the teacher and the library media specialist can be the impetus to integrate the technologies and information skills into specific subject fields throughout the curriculum.

As an instructional consultant, the media professional collaborates or networks with others in planning the integrated library media skills program. Administrators, teachers, and the library media specialist must join with students to nurture young adolescents and empower them with the necessary information skills that reach beyond the walls of the school. Students must be taught how to use the constantly changing technology resources as they face the twenty-first century (Lewis 1993, 50–51).

The Role of the Teacher

A factor that influences the cooperative effort of the teacher and the library media specialist is based on the role of the teacher in the middle school. Middle level teachers function in many different roles. They are decision makers, human relations specialists, classroom managers, counselors, technologists, and evaluators. These roles help to prepare them for meeting the personal, academic, and social needs of the young adolescent (Allen, Splittgerber, and Manning 1993, 113). Specific middle level teacher preparation is a great asset in shaping the teacher's commitment to the philosophy of middle schools. The quality of this preparation is improving in colleges and universities throughout the United States. A number of studies on this issue have been conducted, including a joint study by the

Center of Early Adolescence and the National Middle School Association, which provides recommendations for strengthening middle level teacher preparation (Scales and McEwin 1994, 6). A survey by the authors as a follow-up to their 1991 study reported that 93 percent of the respondents felt positive about their career choice to teach young adolescents. One reason the teachers gave for this choice was the challenge and opportunity to make a positive difference in the lives of young adolescents (44).

An effective middle school teacher recognizes the unique physical, social, emotional, and intellectual needs of students and uses a variety of techniques to meet these needs. The development of reading, writing, listening, and computation skills is practiced in the context of content areas. The processes of reasoning, problem solving, interpreting, applying, analyzing, and evaluating become goals for the students based on their ability. Using the levels of student achievement, the teacher plans a continuous progress program that provides appropriate instruction in many subject areas. Special attention is given to fostering a positive self-image in each student.

The teacher's support of information literacy, whether through books or technological resources, is important to the collaborative efforts of the teacher and the library media specialist. Teachers who want their students to become active learners who use many sources, as in resource-based learning, will see the value of the library media program in the curriculum and may recognize that the library media center is at the heart of such a program (Warden 1997, 17). Teachers often use technology as a springboard to assist students in using new ideas and expressing themselves creatively. These factors affect the cooperative effort of the teacher and the library media specialist in designing and implementing a library media skills program that is an integral part of the instruction program. In this program

the library media center is viewed as an extension of the classroom.

The Planning Process

The planning process varies according to the needs, circumstances, schedules, and styles of the teacher and the library media specialist. Important aspects of the planning process may include motives and stimulus, as well as procedures.

Planning may begin when:

- a science teacher schedules a planning time with the library media specialist to discuss the science fair;

- the library media specialist shares an idea for a booktalk with the reading teacher;

- an art teacher asks for help with an animated movie;

- a language arts teacher asks the library media specialist to recommend a literary work for intensive class study;

- the library media specialist invites the math teachers for afternoon coffee to discuss the computer program;

- a social studies teacher asks the library media specialist to obtain resources including electronic media, for a unit on taxes;

- a music teacher requests the use of the library media center and computer lab to locate learning centers about the musical theater;

- a science teacher sends a note asking if it would be convenient to use the video equipment the following week for closed-circuit viewing of a bug race;

- a physical education teacher comments in the lunchroom that it has been difficult to plan a theme for the gymnastic show and asks the library media specialist for ideas; and

- the library media specialist wants to have a celebration during National Library Week and asks for teacher input.

These types of experiences provide the stimulus for the joint planning and teaching of integrated library media skills and units.

Integration of Objectives

Before effective and meaningful planning for an integrated library media skills program can take place, the teacher and library media specialist must thoroughly comprehend and interpret the scope and sequence of library media, information, and computer skills objectives, as well as the curriculum objectives for the subject area. The list of library media skills objectives, and competency goals can be more readily incorporated into the annual curriculum plans when the teacher and library media specialist jointly share and analyze the objectives.

Library media skills that include information and computer skills can be integrated into a teaching unit by merging the instructional objectives and the library media skills objectives into one set of unit objectives and precise competency goals. An integrated model for library media skills instruction presented in *Teaching Library Media Skills* by H. Thomas Walker and Paula Kay Montgomery (1983) illustrates the process of combining objectives into a single instructional unit taught jointly by the teacher and library media specialist.

Fig. 4.1. Integrated Model of Library Media Skills Instruction.

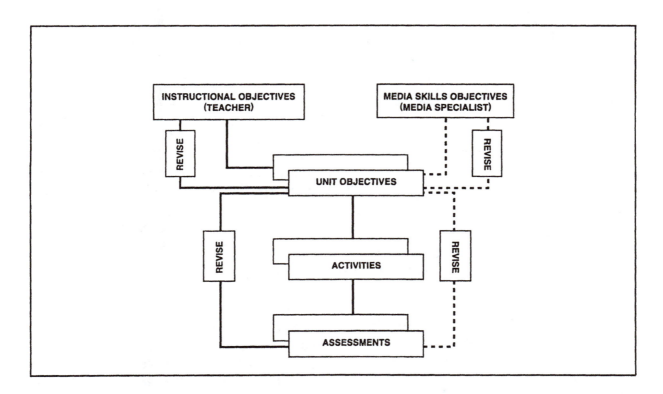

From H. Thomas Walker and Paula Montgomery, *Teaching Library Media Skills*. 2d ed. Reprinted by permission.

PLANNING PROCEDURES

The planning procedures for the teacher and the library media specialist for integrated curricular and library media skills lessons or interdisciplinary units should include the following processes:

- discussion of tentative plans, concepts, and generalizations
- outline of content
- resources
- suggested procedures
- schedules
- instructional objectives of teacher
- library media and information skills and objectives
- integrated lesson or unit goals and objectives
- competency goals and objectives
- duties and responsibilities of the teacher
- duties and responsibilities of library media specialist
- learning activities
- initiation of lesson procedures and grouping procedures
- culminating activities
- evaluation

Sample Unit

This example illustrates the process and planning of a unit entitled Introducing Shakespeare: The Man and His World. The library media specialist received a note from an eighth-grade language arts teacher stating the desire to plan research activities on Shakespeare, Elizabethan England, the Globe Theatre, and *Romeo and Juliet* beginning on November 10. The library media specialist went to the teacher's planning area during planning time and discussed the tentative plans. After collecting resources from the school library media center, the public library, and inter-library loan, the library media

specialist invited the teacher to the library media center to review resources, determine joint objectives and competency goals, and assign responsibilities. The teacher wanted to familiarize the students with the history and background of Elizabethan England and to arouse student interest in reading Shakespeare's *Romeo and Juliet.* The unit included plans for the students to view the play on television, film, or as a live production. The culminating activity was the presentation of oral reports or projects by students. Helping to plan the activities provided the opportunity for the library media specialist to incorporate many library media, information, and computer skills into the unit. As a follow-up to the Shakespeare Unit, students enjoyed reading Avi's *Romeo and Juliet—Together (and Alive) at Last* (1987). It is the story of two young people who have the leading roles in a school production of *Romeo and Juliet.* It abounds with humor by gently poking fun at young love (Van Vliet 1992, 26).

This unit can be adapted to an interdisciplinary team approach incorporating many curricular areas. *Connecting the Curriculum Through Interdisciplinary Instruction,* edited by John H. Lounsbury (1992), provides samples of collaborative planning and teaching of interdisciplinary units. Linkages between fields of knowledge may be planned using the techniques of webbing or drawing a lesson plan tree or an interdisciplinary wheel.

Examples of Cooperative Teaching Topics

The teacher should consider the library media specialist a team member who can provide unique skills to all areas of the curriculum. Cooperative teaching can use the strengths of the teacher and the library media specialist as they become partners in instructional design and implementation. Several examples of cooperative teaching topics include:

- Library Media Specialist: Filmmaking
  Art Teacher: Props, set design, titles

- Social Studies Teacher: World events
  Library Media Specialist: Online databases

- Foreign Language Teacher: Multicultural studies
  Library Media Specialist: Films and recordings

- Health Teacher: Facts about drugs
  Library Media Specialist: Research and resources for reports

- Language Arts Teacher: Dictionary skills
  Library Media Specialist: Word searches, puzzles

- Library Media Specialist: Photography
  Language Arts Teacher: Forms of poetry

- Math Teacher: Metric system
  Library Media Specialist: Metric learning center

- Physical Education Teacher: Sports heroes
  Library Media Specialist: The Internet

- Industrial Arts Teacher: Models of Colonial Americana
  Library Media Specialist: Reference books (encyclopedias, photographs, art objects, etc.)

- Library Media Specialist: Listening skills
  Music Teacher: Great composers

- Reading Teacher: Comprehension and study skills
  Library Media Specialist: Videocassette on basic research skills

- Science Teacher: Concepts and generalizations
  Library Media Specialist: Videocassette on scientific inquiry and problem solving

- Library Media Specialist: Sound slide show of travels in Mexico
  Social Studies Teacher: History and culture of Mexico

- Library Media Specialist: Techniques of debating
  Social Studies Teacher: Problems, issues, and resources

- Language Arts Teacher: Oral communications
  Library Media Specialist: Videodisc of speeches

Scheduling and Discipline

Careful attention to scheduling is vital for a successful integrated library media skills program. The teacher and library media specialist should chart as many lessons and units as possible on a monthly and/or weekly calendar. Specific days and periods can be scheduled in the teacher's and the library media specialist's plan books. Time allotments should be flexible, but good communication is necessary to ensure the best use of everyone's time. If an entire class is scheduled for a lesson in the library media center, the teacher should accompany the class and participate in the learning activities because joint teaching requires the involvement of both the teacher and the library media specialist. Of course, many times the library media specialist will work with individuals and groups in the library media center, production center, computer lab, or in other areas of the school, while the teacher remains in the classroom with other students. This requires detailed scheduling, especially when students are involved in projects and productions. After a timetable has been determined by the teacher and the library media specialist, students should be given a schedule, along with the requirements for the unit.

The standards for student behavior should be jointly set by the teacher and library media specialist based on the policies of the school. Maintaining consistent discipline, whether in the classroom or in the library media center, is of the utmost importance in implementing a quality integrated library media skills program.

INSTRUCTIONAL PARTNERSHIP

In the education process, no role is more important than that of the teacher. For it is the teacher who must bridge theory and practice, develop curriculums, diagnose and prescribe learning activities, interact with students, and effectively manage and teach students. "The new teacher becomes a professional through the support of colleagues and administrators and by cultivating positive connections with students and parents" (Dickerson 1997, 56). Teaching is an opportunity to continue learning. As competent professionals, teachers must continue to learn new strategies and methodologies gained from research and new technologies. The library media specialist can provide much-needed assistance by providing instruction in the use of new technologies and sharing some of the teacher's workload. In this instructional partnership classroom teachers and library media specialists must be co-designers of instruction. (Kuhlthau 1994, vii). The cooperative venture of planning, designing, and implementing an integrated library media skills program adds the dimension of the library media specialist's expertise to the instructional program. After the teacher and library media specialist have cooperatively planned and implemented a unit of study, they may shorten the planning process and procedures to accommodate their styles and needs.

FURTHER SUGGESTIONS

An excellent resource for library media specialists, teachers, and administrators is the booklet by Robert Grover, entitled *Collaboration,* produced by the American Association of School Librarians for its Lessons Learned Series. In August 1994, AASL sponsored a five-day institute, Meeting in the Middle. The purpose was to foster collaboration among library media specialists, teachers, and administrators. Participants from different states worked together to plan student-centered learning activities. Participants were asked to implement the teaching plans in their schools and to submit reports highlighting their experiences. An analysis of the reports is included in the publication under Lessons Learned About Collaboration. It is recommended reading. The conclusion states "Collaboration is hard work with many rewards—it's a journey, not a destination, with students as the beneficiaries of creative team efforts of library media specialists, teachers, and administrators" (Grover 1996, 6).

REFERENCE LIST

Allen, Harvey, Fred L. Splittgerber, and M. Lee Manning. 1993. *Teaching and learning in the middle level school.* New York: Macmillian.

Avi. 1987. *Romeo and Juliet—together (and alive) at last.* New York: Franklin Watts.

Dickerson, Celia. 1997. Beginning again. *The Delta Kappa Gamma Bulletin* 63 (2): 6.

Grover, Robert. Fall 1996. *Collaboration.* Lessons Learned Series. American Association of School Librarians. Chicago: American Library Association.

Kuhlthau, Carol. 1994. *From library skills to information literacy: A handbook for the 21st century.* Castle Rock, Colo.: Hi Willow.

Lewis, Carol. 1993. Developing personnel. In *Renewal at the schoolhouse*, edited by Ben Carson and Jane Smith. Englewood, Colo.: Libraries Unlimited.

Lounsbury, John H., ed. 1992. *Connecting the curriculum through interdisciplinary instruction.* Columbus, Ohio: National Middle School Association.

Scales, Peter C., and C. Kenneth McEwin. 1994. *Growing pains: The making of America's middle school teachers.* Columbus, Ohio: National Middle School Association and Center for Early Adolescence.

Van Vliet, Lucille. 1992. *Approaches to literature through genre.* Phoenix, Ariz.: Oryx Press.

Walker, H. Thomas, and Paula Kay Montgomery. 1983. *Teaching library media skills.* 2d ed. Littleton: Colo.: Libraries Unlimited.

Warden, Milton. 1997. Technology and educational standards: Crossroads in the media center. *North Carolina Libraries* 55 (1): 15–18.

Integrated Library Media and Technology Programs

LIBRARY MEDIA PROGRAMS

The process of planning and designing a library media and technology program that is integrated with the curriculum requires a commitment from the system-level and building-level staffs. An integrated program is one in which the media skills program is incorporated into the content subjects or curriculum and is jointly taught by library media specialists and teachers. Media skills that are taught solely as skills lessons are not as meaningful and not as easy for students to apply to learning situations. The integrated media and technology programs expand, support, and complement classroom learning. Information skills and computer skills are an important part of the media skills program. Many school systems are enlarging their professional and technical staff positions at the system level and building level to promote the use of new technologies. The staffing patterns and titles of media personnel at both levels differ in most school systems across the country.

Library Media Programs at the System Level

At the system level, the media director provides leadership in implementing the information and computer skills curriculum by developing an effective, unified program in each school. Responsibilities include providing a vision of the twenty-first century's evolving technologies and offering a skills program that promotes students' successful use of these technologies. This entails providing a strong staff development program for all media personnel, who will in turn provide strong staff development programs in their schools. The media director works with media personnel in each school in planning, implementing, and evaluating techniques and strategies to accomplish the goals and objectives of the unified program. To meet these goals and objectives the media director works to provide each school with the necessary facilities, resources, and tools. The media director also plans with other system-level directors and supervisors to promote the inclusion of media personnel on curricular and planning committees. This affords support for including the teaching of information literacy in all areas of the curriculum.

Library Media Programs at the Building Level

Media and technology professionals at the building level have the primary responsibility of implementing a media program that serves as an integral part of the instructional program. These include the library media specialist or media coordinator, computer teachers, instructional technology specialists, and information specialists. Also included are clerical and technical support staff. The significant relationship of the media, information, and computer skills to the curriculum content must be communicated to the teachers and staff to ensure that the media instructional techniques are used in all content areas. A thorough knowledge of the curriculum in all subject areas, including the subject's competency goals and objectives, provides the media professionals with the framework for planning ways to incorporate the media program into the instructional program.

Research shows that the curricular and instructional roles of library media specialists are often related to teacher and administrator expectations. The school principal plays a key role in promoting the instructional role of the library media specialist (Winstead 1993, 11). The attitude of teachers toward the library media specialist operating within the instructional program is changing. Many teachers recognize the valuable contribution that library media specialists can make with their wide range of knowledge, skills, and abilities. New opportunities are provided through school-based management for the library media specialist and teachers to share in making decisions that affect the whole school. Media specialists must have the necessary technological skills to access information in a variety of formats to provide instruction to teachers and students. Teachers and students are taught the process of finding, analyzing, synthesizing, and producing data from the most appropriate sources (Lewis 1993, 51).

At the building level, team planning and teaching is emphasized. The library media specialist working with the media advisory committee decides on the mission, goals, and objectives for library media programs and services. An example of team planning is afforded through resource-based teaching, in which students are actively involved in the learning process. This approach brings the classroom teacher or team of teachers who are content specialists and the library media specialist or information specialist together to plan and implement a single lesson or a unit. A variety of materials and strategies are used that are aimed toward a common instructional objective. The library media center, resource center, or a computer lab become the core of the instructional program.

IMPLEMENTING TECHNOLOGY IN LIBRARY MEDIA PROGRAMS

Technology is the popular term today to signify the sweeping information gathering, storage, and retrieval changes in society in general and in education and businesses in particular. School library media specialists and information specialists know the importance of technology in providing access to information gathering and processing. The teaching of information literacy skills and ethical standards for their effective use is a mandate for school media personnel. They must become leaders in schools and communities in mastering and teaching new technologies. Students need to learn how to express their needs, to find accurate and appropriate information, to analyze and evaluate information, and to use that information. Proper use of technology greatly enhances students' ability to produce polished demonstrations of their learning (Stripling 1997, 1–2).

Implementing technology in library media programs begins with using technologies to improve the administration and utilization of media resources. Electronic catalogs, automated circulation, CD-ROM indexes, cable television, integrated media systems, computer networking, telecommunications, Internet, fax, and e-mail are being used extensively in library media centers and computer labs throughout the country.

New standards are being developed to deal with technology and the role of the library media specialist and the school media program. These standards emphasize teaming, cooperative learning, problem solving, real-life applications of knowledge, individualized instruction, and a broad base of learning resources. One set of standards dealing with technology and the role of the media program was produced by the National Association of Secondary School Principals. The teaching of information skills and their application to all areas of the curriculum is inherent to the school library media program (Warden 1997, 15–17).

For technology to be integrated with classroom instruction, technology facilitators are at work in many counties in North Carolina, as well as in many other states. Technology facilitators spend time at individual sites assisting in the implementation of new programs. This may involve putting a technology plan into action by cabling voice, video, and data information networks in classrooms and connecting all classrooms to the Internet.

Technology presents many challenges to library media professionals. The North Carolina Department of Public Instruction, Division of Instructional Technologies, offers a variety of professional development opportunities for school media coordinators in the state. The Video Conferencing Center provides services to media coordinators and teachers. They also publish numerous documents, including *Infotech: The Advisory List*, which provides updated information reviews for school librarians. Also available is the innovative program, STAR Schools, which is a federal distance learning enterprise, aimed at integrating technology throughout the curriculum (Kreszock 1997, 10).

Implementing technology into education demands time, effort, resources, and support from the administration, teachers, students, parents, and the community. It should be used by teachers and library media specialists as a tool to provide students with knowledge of the information search process that leads them to access, evaluate, and use information in a variety of formats.

New Technologies for Education: A Beginner's Guide by Ann Barron and Gary Orwig (1993) is an excellent resource book for library media specialists, teachers, and administrators. Its overall purpose is to improve the instructional process through the appropriate use of new technologies by presenting benefits and issues of technology integration. Information and educational applications are presented for technologies such as CD-ROM, videodisc, digital audio, hypermedia, networks, telecommunications, and teleconferencing.

Projects for New Technologies in Education: Grades 6–9 by Norma Heller (1994) is another highly recommended resource. Student projects are presented in worksheet format and involve technology-based activities such as searching library catalogs, understanding databases, using computer programs, producing audiovisual reports, traveling via telecommunications, and using information networks. Worksheet activities are also provided for using specialized dictionaries and reference resources, multimedia encyclopedias, and *Readers' Guide to Periodical Literature*.

One technology that may have a profound effect on education is virtual reality, the fascinating technology that allows one to experience another world. According to *Merriam-Webster's Collegiate Dictionary* (1996, 1320) virtual reality is "an artificial environment which is experienced through sensory stimuli (as sights and sounds) provided by a computer and in which one's actions partially determine what happens in the environment." It is a bold new technology with many implications for the future. Students might watch simulations of historical events, student athletes might receive advice from great coaches, and historical figures might be interviewed. Children might be networked with children from all over the world into the same simulations. The possibilities are endless, as delineated in *Virtual Reality: A Door to Cyberspace* by Ann Weiss (1996, 86–87, 111–16). The development of virtual reality, with its potential and problems, is also discussed by the author.

INTERDISCIPLINARY INSTRUCTION

Interdisciplinary instruction is a mandate for the '90s, according to John Lounsbury, a nationally known leader in middle level education. He states that educators must broaden their roles to unify learning and connect the curriculum through interdisciplinary teaming. A prerequisite for interdisciplinary instruction is a common planning time and block scheduling (Lounsbury 1992, 1–2).

Connecting the Curriculum Through Interdisciplinary Instruction (Lounsbury 1992) contains informative and useful articles on various aspects of interdisciplinary instruction, many of which appeared previously in the *Middle School Journal.* "Are Interdisciplinary Units Worthwhile? Ask Students," by Mary Davies (1992, 37–41) provides insights on student perceptions of this program. Five years of student evaluations validated the use of the units. Students responded favorably with the following statements:

1. "The topic was interesting to me."
2. "I felt I learned something."
3. "I felt I learned something from the sharing of the projects."
4. "I worked well with others."
5. "I learned that I like(d) working with myself and other people."
6. "I enjoyed this unit."

Students were asked to rate their own project or participation as the last item on the evaluation. The five-category rating scale ranged from poor to excellent. The ratings by students for all units ranged from good, very good, to excellent.

Team planning and team teaching emphasizes using the teachers' strengths through common and collaborative planning experiences. Interdisciplinary and integrative learning affords opportunities of appropriate student learning strategies. Provisions are made for individualized instruction and exploratory programs, and a variety of student groupings are available depending on learning activities involved (McKay 1995, 42–43).

INTEGRATING THE CURRICULUM

A number of approaches have been proposed for integrating the curriculum of the middle level school. Models have been developed by such leaders in middle level education as Eichorn, Alexander and George, Wiles and Bondi, Lounsbury and Vars, The California Model, and Beane. These proposed theories stress that the young adolescent should be the focus of all middle level curriculums. Integrated units serve as means to connect the personal needs and social concerns of young adolescents to the academic content of a middle level curriculum. "While knowledge is considered important in each type of curriculum, it should not dominate the middle level curriculum design" (Allen, Splittgerber, and Manning 1993, 160, 167, 202).

John McKay states in *Schools in the Middle: Developing a Middle-Level Orientation:* "The curriculum should consist of thematic units whose organizing centers are drawn from the intersecting concerns of early adolescents and issues in the larger world. If the middle-level school curriculum is to prepare youth for the future, the curriculum should develop intellectual skills and an understanding of human-kind that will permit the student to gather information, organize it in a meaningful fashion, evaluate its utility, form reasonable conclusions about it, and plan for individual and collective action" (McKay 1995, 17).

The successful integration of intellectual and social skills in middle level schools creates a solid developmental program in skill and content areas, with opportunities for remediation (Toepfer 1992, 216). "Interdisciplinary teams naturally lend themselves to integrated instruction if teachers will avail themselves of this opportunity. Teachers can design themes to study that are of interest to young adolescents. Content can be taught and the processes of reading, writing, speaking, computing, and problem solving can be learned through this integrated instruction" (Irvin 1992, 309–10).

Integrating curriculum in which the curriculum is restructured to blend various subject areas into a common theme is developed through a process of evolution. As subject areas are dissolved through a collaborative effort, correlation of content moves to interdisciplinary curriculum, then to integrated curriculum where subject areas are replaced by common themes. There are advantages and barriers to this approach. Overcoming barriers to take advantage of the opportunities that an integrated curriculum offers requires "knowledgeable and visionary leadership" (Clark and Clark 1994, 104–6).

MIDDLE LEVEL SCHOOL CURRICULUM GUIDELINES

A comprehensive and systematic approach to library media skills instruction must start with the development of competencies and objectives for students that will enable them to acquire the necessary skills to become independent learners. The core of common learning, or competencies, is generally determined by the

state and school districts. These courses usually consist of reading/language arts, social studies, mathematics, science, the arts, and media and technology programs. Teachers and administrators have a number of ways in which they can organize the curriculum so that it is appropriate for young adolescents.

Scope and sequence requirements for curriculums are being reorganized using alternative structures. Content skills that are especially relevant in terms of early adolescent developmental characteristics are identified and emphasized. As various content areas are organized around common themes, relationships among the various subject areas are making connections that are meaningful to students (Clark and Clark 1994, 92–93).

Information and computer skills that middle level students need to be effective users of ideas and information in this information-rich society provide the framework for the scope and sequence of the library media skills curriculum. These skills must be relevant to the needs and characteristics of young adolescents, and taught in ways that have application to the lives of students. The time frame, development, and implementation of instruction should be carefully planned. Also, it is a good idea for library media professionals to work closely with the teachers and team members to ensure that the necessary information and computer skills are taught to the students in conjunction with regular classroom coursework. Skill learning is an important part of an integrated curriculum.

In *From Library Skills to Information Literacy: A Handbook for the 21st Century*, Carol Kuhlthau (1994, 3–17) states that an information-literate person organizes information for practical applications, integrates new information into an existing body of knowledge, and applies information in critical thinking and problem solving. The research process includes the need to know and becomes the motivating factor in producing a product. The process becomes real when the product is something the receiver needs. Students, teachers, and the library media specialist must be partners in the research process.

Information Literacy Standards for Student Learning, which is presently being developed by AASL and AECT (1996), will provide the standards that encompass the competency goals for information and computer skills, independent learning, and social responsibility. School library media professionals can better define their roles and responsibilities when using these standards in conjunction with program guidelines from their state and local media and technology departments.

REFERENCE LIST

Allen, Harvey, Fred L. Splittgerber, and M. Lee Manning. 1993. *Teaching and learning in the middle level school.* New York: Macmillian.

American Association of School Librarians (AASL) and the Association of Education Communications and Technology (AECT). 1996. *National Guidelines Vision Committee: Information literacy standards for student learning.* Draft #5. Chicago: American Library Association.

Barron, Anne E., and Gary W. Orwig. 1993. *New technologies for education: A beginner's guide.* Englewood, Colo.: Libraries Unlimited.

Clark, Sally N., and Donald C. Clark. 1994. *Restructuring the middle level school.* Albany, N.Y.: State University of New York Press.

Davies, Mary. 1992. Are interdisciplinary units worthwhile? Ask students. In *Connecting the curriculum through interdisciplinary instruction,* edited by John H. Lounsbury. Columbus, Ohio: National Middle School Association.

Heller, Norma. 1994. *Projects for new technologies in education: Grades 6–9.* Englewood, Colo.: Libraries Unlimited.

Irvin, Judith L., ed. 1992. Developmentally appropriate instruction: The heart of the middle school. In *Transforming middle level education: Perspectives and possibilities.* Boston: Allyn & Bacon.

Kreszock, Martha. 1997. A holistic look at professional development. *North Carolina Libraries* 55 (1): 7–11.

Kuhlthau, Carol. 1994. *From library skills to information literacy: A handbook for the 21st century.* Castle Rock, Colo.: Hi Willow.

Lewis, Carol. 1993. Developing personnel. In *Renewal at the schoolhouse,* edited by Ben Carson and Jane Smith. Englewood, Colo.: Libraries Unlimited.

Lounsbury, John H., ed. 1992. *Connecting the curriculum through interdisciplinary instruction.* Columbus, Ohio: National Middle School Association.

McKay, Jack. 1995. *Schools in the middle: Developing a middle-level orientation.* Thousand Oaks, Calif.: Corwin Press.

Merriam-Webster's collegiate dictionary. 1996. 10th ed. Springfield, Mass.: Merriam-Webster.

Stripling, Barbara. 1997. AASL: Support for leadership. *AASL Hotline/Connections* 4 (3): 1–2.

Toepfer, Conrad F. Jr. 1992. Middle level school curriculum: Defining the elusive. In *Transforming middle level education: Perspectives and possibilities,* edited by Judith L. Irvin. Boston: Allyn & Bacon.

Warden, Milton. 1997. Technology and educational standards: Crossroads in the media center. *North Carolina Libraries* 55: 15–18.

Weiss, Ann E. 1996. *Virtual reality : A door to cyberspace.* New York: Twenty-First Century Books.

Winstead, Frank Charles. 1993. Improving the program. In *Renewal at the schoolhouse,* edited by Ben Carson and Jane Smith. Englewood, Colo.: Libraries Unlimited.

PART TWO

Introduction

Media Skills for Middle Schools: Strategies for Library Media Specialists and Teachers, second edition, is designed to reflect the trends and resources of the Information Age. Part II contains examples of integrated library media skills lessons that are appropriate for middle school students as they prepare for life in the twenty-first century. The skills lessons are separated into lessons for grade six, grade seven, and grade eight. Sixth-grade skills lessons begin with orientation lessons to the world of media and progress through lessons on astronomy, classification, basic computer technology, biographies, listening skills, festivals, and lifelong reading skills. Seventh-grade skills lessons emphasize research techniques, working with computers, writing reports, creating multimedia productions, observing foreign cultures, and studying consumer education. Eighth-grade skills lessons provide more advanced research methods, a look at careers, aspects of visual literacy, copyright guidelines, independent study themes, an emphasis on reading for pleasure, and ideas for celebrating the beginning of the next millennium.

The principles discussed in Part I concerning the middle school concept, characteristics of middle school students, and the roles of the library media specialists, information specialists, teachers, and administrators provide the foundation for the skills lessons.

The sample lessons were created to assist the library media specialist and the teacher by providing a framework for a dynamic middle grade library media skills program integrated with the curriculum. Each lesson contains library media skills objectives, competency goals, and evaluative criteria. Information skills and computer skills are emphasized throughout the lessons.

Library media specialists and teachers should pay careful attention to modifying the skills lessons based on the guidelines and curriculums established by their school system and individual school. Suggested resources should also be changed to reflect the resources available at their individual schools.

Lessons are designated by grade levels and organized to run from grades six through eight. Each lesson contains the following information.

Title
Description or slogan.

Overview
Purpose and expectations.

Library Media Skills Objectives
Emphasis on information, communication, and computer skills, including search strategies, locating, accessing, devising, and using resources in all formats.

Competency Goals
Broad goals and objectives for the learner in curricular areas.

Subject Area
Curricular or content area, discipline, or interdisciplinary team.

Learning Strategy
Instructional variables—lecture, demonstration, large or small group instruction, independent study, group projects, learning centers, booktalks, production, practice, etc.

Resources
Suggested general resources, worksheets, quizzes, guidelines, and courseware. Lessons have a reference list of a variety of resources to serve as a guide to the library media specialists and teachers in preparation for teaching. The resources listed on the reference list are not intended to be a requirement for teaching the lesson. They can be supplemented by available resources. Print resources included in the lessons contain the author's name, title, and copyright date or in some cases, only the title and copyright date. Full citations are included in alphabetical order in the bibliography, which is located in the appendix. Nonprint and courseware resources included in the lesson contain the title, type of medium, copyright date, and producer. They are not included in the bibliography.

Methods
The teacher will
Suggestions, responsibilities, and teaching strategies for teachers to use in integrating curricular and competency goals and objectives with library media skills and objectives.

The library media specialist will
Suggestions, responsibilities, and teaching strategies for library media specialists to use in integrating the library media skills objectives with curricular objectives and competency goals.

The student will
Assignments, responsibilities, and activities for students.

Evaluative Criteria
Criteria of acceptable student performance.

Further Suggestions
Notes, follow-up activities, suggestions for extending or reducing lesson plans, additional resources, or examples of interesting or exemplary uses of the lesson.

Skills Lessons for Grade Six

LESSON ONE

Title
Orientation—World of Media

Overview
The purpose of this lesson is to introduce sixth-grade students to the world of media as an orientation to the library media center. Students will learn about the resources, the personnel, and the policies and procedures for using the library media center.

Library Media Skills Objectives
Orientation and organization:

Identify types of library media center resources.

Identify library media center personnel.

Identify services provided by library media center staff.

Identify policies and procedures for use of library media center.

Competency Goals
The learner will identify, explore, and apply strategies to access resources for learning.

Subject Area
Language Arts or Interdisciplinary Team.

Learning Strategy
Large group instruction—listening and viewing.

Resources
Overhead transparencies

Guidelines: Policies and procedures of the library media center

Suggested equipment: Overhead projectors with LCD panels, computers and printers, television monitor/receiver, computer with CD-ROM drive, video recorder/player, videodisc player with video projector, audiocassette player, CD audio player, projection screens, sound filmstrip projector/viewer, microform reader/printer, slide projector, listening center/jackbox, etc.

Fig. 6-1-1. Overhead Transparencies.

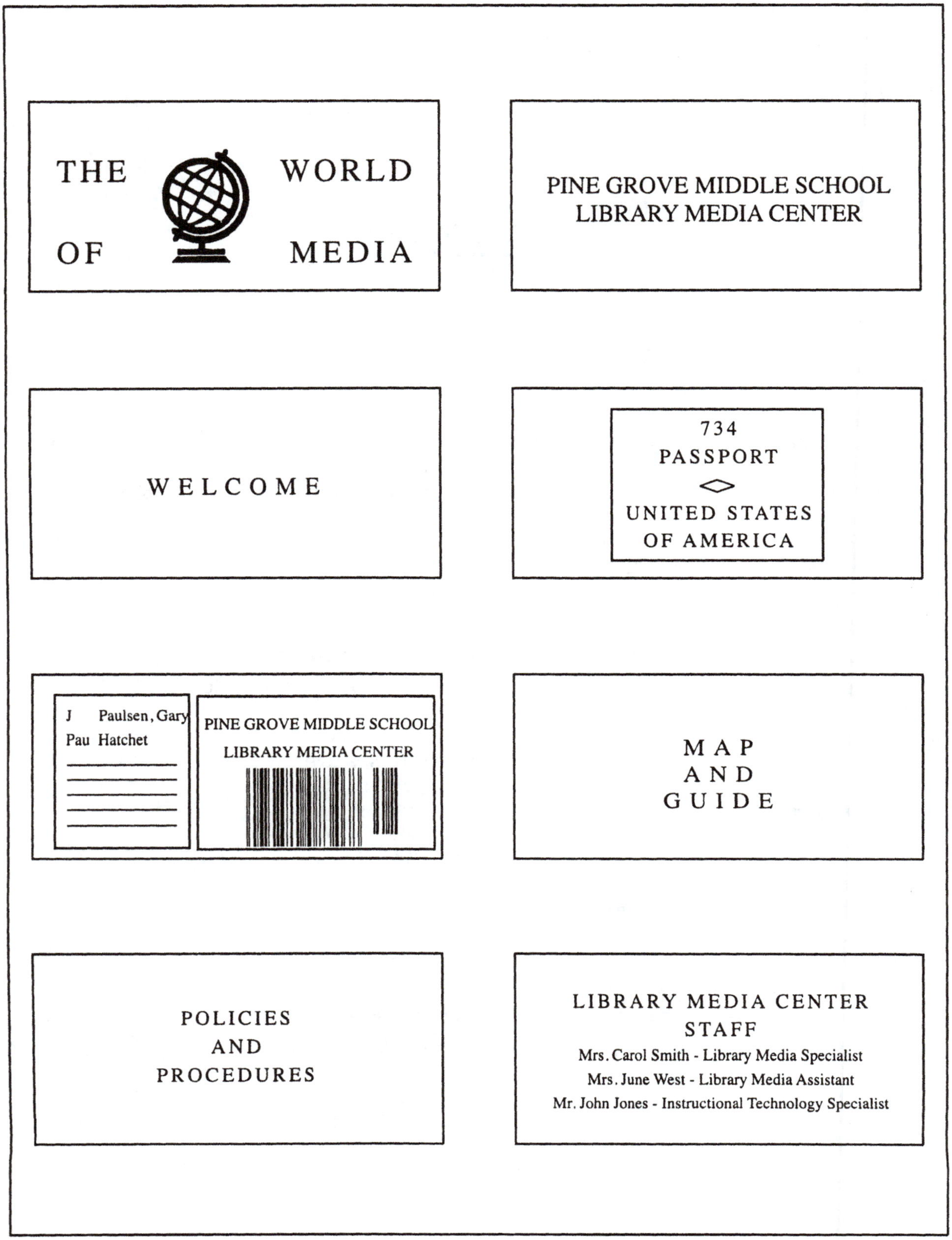

THE (globe) WORLD OF MEDIA

PINE GROVE MIDDLE SCHOOL LIBRARY MEDIA CENTER

WELCOME

734
PASSPORT
◇
UNITED STATES
OF AMERICA

J   Paulsen, Gary
Pau Hatchet

PINE GROVE MIDDLE SCHOOL
LIBRARY MEDIA CENTER

MAP
AND
GUIDE

POLICIES
AND
PROCEDURES

LIBRARY MEDIA CENTER
STAFF
Mrs. Carol Smith - Library Media Specialist
Mrs. June West - Library Media Assistant
Mr. John Jones - Instructional Technology Specialist

Print and nonprint materials and courseware: One for each piece of equipment on display.

Suggested additional resources

Maps, globe, pictures, posters, magazines, newspapers, books, models, etc.

Print

Cooper, Kay. 1990. *Where in the World Are You? A Guide to Looking at the World.*

Howard, Tracy Apple, with Sage Alexandra Howard. 1992. *Kids Ending Hunger: What Can WE Do?*

Macaulay, David. 1977. *Castle.*

Parsons, Larry. 1990. *A Funny Thing Happened on the Way to the School Library: A Treasury of Anecdotes, Quotes, and Other Happenings.*

Nonprint and Courseware

Castle explorer. 1996. Dorling Kindersley. CD-ROM.

A child's celebration of Broadway. 1995. Music for little people. Compact disc.

Madeline and the magnificent puppet show. 1995. Creative Wonders. CD-ROM.

Mammals: A multimedia encyclopedia. 1996. National Geographic Society. CD-ROM.

Mystery math island. 1995. Level 2. Lawrence Productions. CD-ROM.

The perfect beat. 1995. WGBH Educational. Videocassette.

STV: Habitat. 1996. National Geographic Society. Videodisc.

Wonders of the sea. 1986. SVE. Sound filmstrip.

Methods

The teacher will

1. Schedule the large group instruction with the library media specialist.
2. Review the lesson by conducting a class discussion the following day.

The library media specialist will

1. Prepare transparencies.
2. Gather resource materials and equipment.
3. Give large group instruction.
4. Instruct media support staff concerning duties to implement this lesson.
5. Use the following guidelines for implementation:
   - Set up large group area with overhead projector in the middle, with the transparency "THE WORLD OF MEDIA" displayed.
   - Have all equipment operating at the same time with appropriate viewing and listening resources as students are being seated.
   - Let students be bombarded with the sight and sound for approximately five minutes.
   - Loudly state: "In our library media center we have books, magazines, models, kits, televisions, computers, compact disc players, sound filmstrip projectors, and other interesting objects."
   - Show a globe, a model, and several books, newspapers, and magazines as sample holdings.
   - Turn off each piece of equipment as it is named.
   - Show the transparency with the word "WELCOME" and welcome all students and teachers to the school and to the world of media that can be found in the library media center.

- Show transparency with the words "[NAME OF SCHOOL] MIDDLE SCHOOL, LIBRARY MEDIA CENTER."
- Show the transparency with the words "PASSPORT: UNITED STATES OF AMERICA" and state: "You need a passport to gain entry into most countries of the world."
- Show transparency of a book charging card or a card with a bar code and state: "This is your entry into a world of multimedia resources. Use the computerized checkout with your bar coded card or sign the bookcards and leave them at the circulation desk."
- Show transparency with the words "MAP AND GUIDE" and state: "You will be given a map of the floor plan of the library media center by your teacher tomorrow, and library media center personnel will take you on a tour."
- Show transparency with the words "POLICIES AND PROCEDURES."
- Distribute a copy with the library media center's **policies and procedures** to each student and tell them that the policies and procedures will be discussed at a class session in the library media center.
- Show transparency with the words "LIBRARY MEDIA CENTER STAFF" and introduce the staff members.
- Show transparency "THE WORLD OF MEDIA" again and play recorded music as students return to class.

The students will

1. View multimedia production.
2. Listen to the library media specialist.
3. Read the policies and procedures.
4. Discuss library media center policies and procedures during a class in the library media center.

Evaluative Criteria

The students will correctly name the library media center personnel, five or more resources, and three or more policies of the library media center.

Future Suggestions

Special note to library media specialists and teachers: Modify the resources, equipment, and policy statements to conform to your local school library media center.

Policies and Procedures of the Library Media Center

Borrowing Rules

1. <u>Two weeks loan</u>: All fiction and nonfiction books, except REFERENCE BOOKS.
2. Books may be renewed.
3. <u>Overnight loan</u>: Many reference books, including encyclopedias, film-strips, slides, audiocassettes, kits, and games. Limited number of compact discs, CD-ROMs, and videotapes. Equipment: Cassette re-corders, filmstrip previewers, slide previewers. Special arrangements may be made to borrow additional types of equipment.
4. <u>Checkout system</u>: Computerized checkout at the main desk with bar coded card or by book cards attached to books and materials.
5. <u>Overdue notices</u>: Identified by computer at checkout of additional material or sent to section or home room.
6. <u>Fines:</u> There are no fines; however, materials should be returned or renewed on or before the due date.
7. <u>Missing materials</u>: Personal responsibility for lost, overdue, and dam-aged materials.

Hours

1. One half hour before and after school hours each day. Arrangements may be made with the library media staff for extended hours for special projects and group work.
2. At lunch break with pass obtained from a teacher or from the library media staff.
3. During all school hours. Individuals and small groups are always welcome.
4. Teachers and staff members jointly schedule the use of the library media facilities, the computer lab, media programs, and services with the library media staff.

Library Media Staff

Mrs. Carol Smith, Library Media Specialist
Mrs. June West, Library Media Assistant
Mr. John Jones, Instructional Technology Specialist
Student Media Assistants
Parent Volunteers

LESSON TWO

Title
Puzzled About Your Media Center?

Overview
The purpose of this lesson is to provide orientation and guidance to the library media center by defining terms related to the use of the library media center. Students will complete a puzzle and worksheet with explicit definitions.

Library Media Skills Objectives
Identify: Library catalogs, Dewey decimal classification system, general reference books, circulation desk, print materials, nonprint materials and courseware, and electronic communications.

Competency Goals and Objectives
The learner will explore orientation processes that meet information needs.

Subject Area
Language Arts or Interdisciplinary Team.

Learning Strategy
Puzzle, worksheet, and completing group project.

Resources
Outline of key and puzzle
Worksheet

Methods
The teacher will
1. Schedule students to continue the orientation program in the library media center.
2. Check the completed puzzles and answer students' questions.

The library media specialist will
1. Construct a large outline of a key using heavy tagboard for the base.
2. Construct an overlay for the key to make a puzzle containing media-related terms using lightweight tagboard.
3. Cut out the overlay containing media-related terms to form pieces of a puzzle.
4. Make 10 copies of the key base and the puzzle.
5. Cut the puzzles into jigsaw pieces and put them into envelopes.
6. Divide students into groups of three to complete the puzzle using the key outline as a base or background for the puzzle.

Fig. 6-2-1. Puzzle.

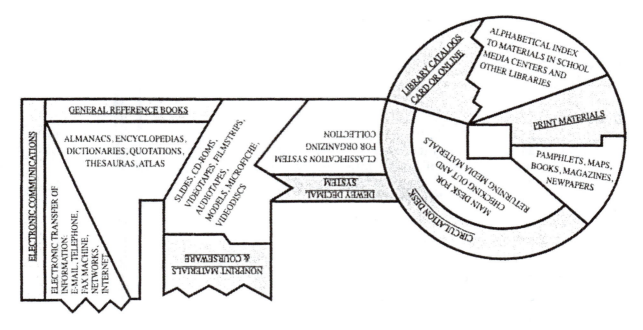

The students will

1. Complete the puzzle.
2. Complete the worksheets.
3. Ask the teacher or library media specialist to check the solution.

Evaluative Criteria

The students will correctly solve the library media center puzzle and complete the worksheet.

The Key to Library Media Center Resources

Puzzled about your media center? Use your completed puzzle to define the key terms listed here.

1. Library Catalogs
2. Dewey Decimal System
3. General Reference Books
4. Circulation Desk
5. Print Materials
6. Nonprint Materials and Courseware
7. Electronic Communications

LESSON THREE

Title
Following Directions: Mapping Your Way

Overview
The purpose of this orientation lesson is to help students understand the organization of resources in the library media center by completing a map of the physical location of resources and facilities. They will listen attentively and follow directions.

Library Media Skills Objectives
Locate fiction and nonfiction collections.

Locate nonprint materials and courseware.

Locate library catalogs (card or online).

Locate the vertical file/information file.

Locate encyclopedias and general reference books.

Locate magazines/newspapers.

Locate audiovisual equipment.

Locate library media facilities.

Competency Goals and Objectives
The learner will participate in an orientation project to identify the resources and facilities of the library media center.

Subject Area
Interdisciplinary Team, Social Studies, or Language Arts.

Learning Strategy
Lecture, individual project, and large group discussion.

Resources
Outline maps of library media center

List of library media center resources and facilities

Signs or labels in the areas (use what your center provides)

Methods
The teacher will
1. Review mapping skills.
2. Schedule classes in the library media center.
3. Take students to the library media center large group instruction area.
4. Give students an outline map of the library media center and a copy of the list of library media center resources and facilities.
5. Tell students that they are to locate the resources and facilities and list the number of each on their maps.
6. Give assistance to students in completing their maps.

Fig. 6-3-1. Map of School Library Media Center.

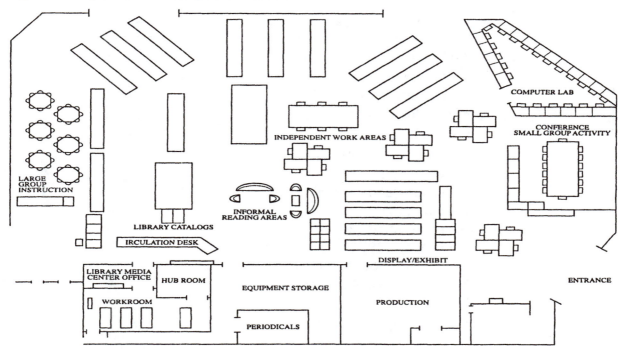

The library media specialist will
1. Make outline maps of the library media center resources and facilities.
2. Prepare a list of library media center resources and facilities.
3. Prepare signs or labels for any areas where they are needed.
4. Prepare transparencies showing location of resources and facilities.
5. Lead discussion about location of resources.

The students will
1. Complete the map of the library media center by labeling the areas where resources and facilities are located.
2. Discuss the location and purposes of the areas with the library media specialist during a large group session.
3. Check and correct map using the transparency projected by the library media specialist.
4. File the completed map and the list of library media center resources and facilities in their student handbooks.

Evaluative Criteria
The students will correctly label the map of the library media center, identifying the physical location of resources and facilities.

Further Suggestions
The map and lists of library media center resources and facilities must be prepared to match the resources and facilities of each individual school.

Library Media Center Resources and Facilities

1. Reference Books
2. Magazines/Newspapers
3. Vertical File/Information File
4. Nonprint Materials and Courseware
5. Fiction (A-Z)
6. Nonfiction: (000-999)
    Generalities (000)
    Philosophy and Psychology (100)
    Religion (200)
    Social Sciences (300)
    Language (400)
    Natural Sciences and Mathematics (500)
    Technology (Applied Sciences) (600)
    The Arts (700)
    Literature and Rhetoric (800)
    Geography and History (900)
    Biography (920, 921)
7. Circulation Desk
8. Library Catalogs (Card or Online)
9. Large Group Instruction Area
10. Independent Work Areas
11. Informal Reading Areas
12. Computer Lab
13. Library Media Center Office
14. Workroom
15. Hub Room
16. Production Area
17. Equipment Storage
18. Periodical Storage
19. Conference/Small Group Activity

LESSON FOUR

Title
Astronomy: Out of This World

Overview
The purpose of this lesson is to assist students in developing a group search strategy in the field of astronomy, in exploring research processes, and in communicating information by producing a final group project.

Library Media Skills Objectives
Develop a search strategy.

Find, evaluate, use, and create information and ideas.

Use Dewey decimal system of classification numbers relating to astronomy to locate materials.

Communicate information and ideas through projects and presentations.

Competency Goals and Objectives
1. The learner will use a variety of information skills and computer technologies to access, analyze, interpret, synthesize, apply, and communicate information.
2. The learner will devise systems and models to illustrate basic cycles and characteristics of the celestial bodies.

Subject Area
Science or Interdisciplinary Team.

Learning Strategy
Lecture, research, practice, and create project.

Resources

Print
Dewey Decimal Classification and Relative Index. 1989. 20th ed.

Gibbons, Gail. 1992. *Stargazers.*

Goldsmith, Donald. 1996. When Worlds and Comets Collide. In *World Book Science Year 1996.* 211-19.

Lightman, Alan. 1994. *Time for the Stars: Astronomy in the 1990's.*

McKeever, Susan, ed. 1993. Space. In *The Dorling Kindersley Science Encyclopedia.* 273-304.

Muirden, James. 1993. *Stars and Planets.*

NASA Educational Publications

Nicolson, Iain. 1991. *The Illustrated World of Space.*

Seymour, Simon. 1994. *Comets, Meteors, and Asteroids.*

Shapiro, Lee T., ed. 1997. Astronomy and Calendar. In *The World Almanac and Book of Facts 1997.* 440-80.

Nonprint and Courseware
Eyewitness encyclopedia of space and the universe. 1996. Dorling Kindersley Multimedia. CD-ROM.

A field trip to the sky. 1996. Sunburst Communications. CD-ROM.

Planet Earth. 1996. Macmillan Digital USA. CD-ROM.

Science navigator. 1995. McGraw-Hill Science and Technical Reference Set. CD-ROM.

Sirs photo essays: Man on the moon, the space shuttle, Hubble telescope, the solar system. 1995. Space series. SIRS Photo Essays. Poster sets.

Solar system explorer. 1996. Maris. CD-ROM.

STV: Solar system. 1992. National Geographic Society. Videodisc.

Methods

The teacher will

1. Introduce the lesson.
2. Discuss how the frontiers of astronomy have been expanded by space exploration and observations in new parts of the spectrum, as in gamma-ray and x-ray astronomy. The new observational techniques have led to the discovery of new astronomical objects such as pulsars, quasars, and black holes. Discuss the findings of the space mission to Mars.
3. Assist students with defining and analyzing the task.
4. Assign students to work in groups.
5. Review computer skills: The function of word processing utilities such as the spell checker, electronic thesaurus, grammar checker; use of a prepared database to sort records and to search for desired information.
6. Evaluate the product.

The library media specialist will

1. Present information on the Dewey decimal classification system:

    500 Natural Sciences and Mathematics
    503 Dictionaries and Encyclopedias
    520 Astronomy and Allied Sciences
    520.1-.9 Standard Subdivisions
    521 Celestial Mechanics
    522 Techniques, Equipment, Materials
    523 Specific Celestial Bodies and Phenomena
    525 Earth (Astronomical Geography)
    526 Mathematical Geography
    527 Celestial Navigation
    528 Ephemerides
    529 Chronology

2. Review the 520 classification and define terminology.
3. Give a brief overview of information on astronomy using books, pamphlets, and courseware resources such as the Internet.
4. Review the search strategies for locating information:

    Define topic: Narrow or broaden topic if necessary.

    Methods of searching library catalogs: card, book, and electronic catalogs.

    Use of specialized indexes: *Newsbank Periodical Index, Readers' Guide to Periodical Literature,* and WilsonDisc [CD-ROM].

    Government agencies to contact: National Aeronautics and Space Administration, Smithsonian Institution.

5. Assist with research and projects.

The students will

1. Plan group procedures.
2. Develop a search strategy.
3. Locate print, nonprint, and courseware materials on astronomy.
4. Interpret and use information found in resources.
5. Plan, organize, and present a group project.

Evaluative Criteria

The students will locate and use information in the field of astronomy and will produce a group project.

Further Suggestions

Numerous science resource links are available through World Wide Web sites such as NASA, *NASA Learning Technologies: Shuttle Team*, NASA Observatorium, and Data at Work NASA. Because addresses frequently change, check for the current addresses.

LESSON FIVE

Title

Tumbling On!

Overview

The purpose of this lesson is to help students improve motor skills for gymnastic routines by viewing a videotape of themselves performing selected routines. Students will plan and produce the videotape.

Library Media Skills Objectives

Plan and produce a videotape.

Use appropriate audiovisual equipment for selected presentation.

Operate a video recorder/player.

Competency Goals and Objectives

1. The learner will communicate information and ideas through products and presentation.
2. The learner will use systematic processes to create products.

Subject Area

Physical Education, Library Media Production.

Learning Strategy

Practice, audiovisual instruction, and audiovisual production.

Resources

Print

Bielak, Mark. 1995. *Teacher's Resource Book: Television Production Today.*
Bielak, Mark. 1995. *Television Production Today.*
Duden, Jane. 1992. *Men's and Women's Gymnastics.*
Gutman, Dan. 1996. *Gymnastics.*
Haycock, Kate. 1991. *Olympic Sports: Gymnastics.*

Nonprint and Courseware

Fitness and physical performance. 1991. STV. Videocassette.
Shao Ping the acrobat. 1982. Coronet. Videocassette.

Methods

The teacher will

1. Show a videocassette tape of a gymnastic team or of an individual gymnast to the class. Critique and discuss the techniques and performance.
2. Teach gymnastic routines to students.
3. Schedule videotaping sessions with the library media specialist.
4. Schedule individual videotape playback sessions with the library media specialist.

The library media specialist will

1. Review videotaping procedures with student assistants.
2. Arrange for student library media technicians to videotape gymnastic practice sessions.
3. Keep a log of names of individual students who are being videotaped and the number of the sequence on the videotape.
4. Schedule individuals for playback of videotapes.
5. Instruct each student in techniques for operating the video recorder/player for playbacks.

The students will

1. Practice a gymnastic routine and perform for a videotape session.
2. Check the log for their name and location of their routine on videotape.
3. Receive instruction in operating the video recorder/player for a playback.
4. View and critique their videotaped routine.
5. After viewing videotape, practice routine to make improvements.

Evaluative Criteria

The students will correctly operate the video recorder/player to locate, view, and critique their gymnastic routines.

Further Suggestions

Locate and let students view videotapes of gymnasts, including videotapes of gymnastic performances at the Olympics.

LESSON SIX

Title
Classification Systems—Scientific Know-How

Overview
The purpose of this lesson is to help students learn the basis for classification by observing order, relationship, and patterns in objects found in the outdoor environment. The students will collect objects such as rocks, leaves, or seeds and devise a classification system to arrange the objects into related groups. This lesson should be taught by the library media specialist at an outdoor education program or on a field trip.

Library Media Skills Objectives
Identify classification systems.

Select material based on specific criteria.

Arrange materials using a specific system.

Competency Goals and Objectives
The student will demonstrate the ability to classify objects according to their properties using similarities and differences.

Subject Area
Science or Outdoor Education Program.

Learning Strategy
Discussion, field trip, and demonstration.

Resources
Several sample collections of nuts, rocks, or leaves

Bags or boxes for collections

Cards and pencils

Guidelines for collections and classifying

Print
Coombes, Allen J. 1992. *Trees.*
Kneidel, Sally Stenhouse. 1993. *Creepy Crawlies and the Scientific Method: Over 100 Science Experiments for Children.*
McManners, Hugh. 1996. *Outdoor Adventure Handbook.*
Pellant, Chris. 1990. *Rocks and Minerals.*
Silverstein, Alvin, et al. 1996. *Plants.*

Nonprint and Courseware
Classification of living things. 1992. Understanding Science Series. Videocassette.
Flowers, plants, and trees. 1990. TMW Sales. Videocassette.
Rocks and minerals. 1977. Coronet. Videocassette.
STV: Plants. 1993. National Geographic Society. Videodisc.

Methods

The teacher will

1. Review discussion notes, guidelines, and objectives that were written by the library media specialist.
2. Make suggestions and/or comments.
3. Review and evaluate lesson after it is taught.

The library media specialist will

1. Lead students in a discussion of the needs for classification, which are: to establish order; and to find patterns and relationships.
2. Define classification:

   Classification is an act or method of arranging objects in groups:
   - Objects can be grouped by common properties using similarities and differences.
   - Objects can be grouped in categories that are meaningful, useful, and consistent.
   - There is no one correct way for grouping.
3. Show examples of nuts or leaves and let students tell how they could be classified.
4. Briefly discuss and review the Dewey decimal classification system emphasizing the 500s (Science Classification).
5. Ask students to explain how materials are organized in a music store. Give suggestions to add to student comments. Materials can be arranged by: format (audiocassettes, CDs, sheet music, etc.); or type of music: (classical, jazz, bluegrass, rock, country, etc., subgrouped by composer or performer).
6. Discuss the many ways that weather can be classified:
   - Seasons (properties of spring, summer, autumn, and winter)
   - Storms (tornadoes, hurricanes, floods, etc.)
   - Symbol (cloud cover, rain, snow, etc.)
   - Fronts (warm, cold, stationary, occluded, etc.)
   - Cloud forms (cirrus, stratus, cumulus, etc.)
7. Divide students into groups of two.
8. Give students guidelines for collecting and classifying objects.
9. Accompany students to an area for collection of objects.
10. Distribute materials to hold collections.
11. After students have collected objects, take them to an area where they can devise their classification systems.
12. Have all groups show their collection and tell how they classified it.
13. Remind every group that they were successful because there is no one right way for grouping.
14. If there is time, ask students about other ways that collections could be grouped or classified.

The students will

1. Discuss and define classification systems.
2. Read guidelines for collection and classification.
3. Work with a partner to collect related objects for classification.

    4.   Devise a classification system.

    5.   Show their collection and explain classification systems.

Time Table

Approximately 1 hour 30 minutes:

(30 minutes) Discussion; demonstration; explanation of guidelines

(30 minutes) Collecting

(15 minutes) Classifying

(15 minutes) Group time; sharing

Evaluative Criteria

The students will work with a partner to collect a group of objects and will successfully classify these objects.

Further Suggestions

As a follow-up to this lesson, the science teacher may want to teach a lesson on classifying living things using electronic and print encyclopedias. The *Dorling Kindersley Science Encyclopedia* has an excellent concise article titled "Classifying Living Things" (1993), 310-11, 420-21.

Guidelines for Collections and Classifying

Suggestions for objects to collect: soil, rocks, wildflowers, weeds, leaves, grass, pods, roots, seeds, bark, cones.

Guidelines for Collections

1.   Choose an object, such as a rock, and try to find at least five different types of rocks.

2.   Study the objects to see how they are related and how they differ.

3.   Collect objects that are small enough to carry easily.

4.   Be careful not to choose poisonous objects.

5.   Make brief notes on cards about your collection.

6.   Always stay within sight of your teacher.

Guidelines for Classifying

1.   Study the properties of the objects you have collected.

2.   Place objects in groups that have one or more characteristics in common (size, color, shape, texture, use, type, etc.)

3.   Write your classification system on a card.

4.   Tell how you grouped your objects.

5.   Show your objects and share your classification system with the entire group.

LESSON SEVEN

Title
Biography: Footprints

Overview
The purpose of this lesson is to have students locate, select, and read a biography about someone they would like to know or have known. They will present an oral character sketch of this person based on the point of view of the author. They will compile data about the biographee and make a bibliography of resources.

Library Media Skills Objectives
Locate print and nonprint materials using call numbers.

Locate information in electronic sources, including courseware and the Internet.

Select many different types of books according to reading level and interest.

Identify and describe the point of view.

Competency Goals and Objectives
1. The learner will use language for the acquisition, interpretation, and application of information.
2. The learner will use a variety of computer technologies to access, analyze, interpret, apply, and communicate information.

Subject Area
Reading, Language Arts, or Interdisciplinary Team.

Learning Strategy
Booktalk, reading, practice, and oral presentation.

Resources
Biography worksheet
Biography collection
Collective biographies and individual biographies. Include biographies of African Americans, Native Americans, Hispanic Americans, world leaders, women, scientists, sports superstars, historical figures, artists, and musicians.

Index to Collective Biography for Young Readers

Print
African-American Biography Series. 1996-1997.
Brownstone, David, and Irene Franck. 1997. *People in the News*.
Cary, Alice. 1996. *Jean Craighead George*.
Graham, Billy. 1997. *Just as I Am: The Autobiography of Billy Graham*.
Green, Rayna. 1992. *Native American Women*.
Kavanagh, Jack. 1992. *Sports Great Larry Bird*.
Leinwand, Gerald. 1996. *Heroism in America*.
Macnow, Glen. 1993. *Sports Great Cal Ripken, Jr*.
McKissack, Patricia, and Frederick McKissack. 1994. *African-American Scientists*.
Parker, Steve. 1992. *Marie Curie and Radium*.
Rodriguez, Consuelo. 1991. *Cesar Chavez*.

St. George, Judith. 1992. *Dear Dr. Bell . . . Your Friend, Helen Keller.*

Sullivan, Helen, and Linda Sernoff. 1996. *Research Reports: A Guide for Middle and High School Students.*

Webster's Biographical Dictionary.

World Book Encyclopedia.

The World Almanac and Book of Facts 1997.

Nonprint and Courseware

Animated hero classics series. Living History Productions, Inc. Videocassettes:

Benjamin Franklin, scientist and inventor. 1993.

Florence Nightingale. 1994.

Pocahontas. 1994.

Thomas Edison and the electric light. 1993.

The Wright Brothers. 1996.

U.X.L. biographies. 1996. U. X. L. CD-ROM.

Methods

The teacher will

1. Review plans with the library media specialist for the introductory lesson.
2. Schedule two class periods in the library media center.
3. Select and read a biography and give an oral presentation along with the students.
4. Evaluate student presentations.

The library media specialist will

1. Present an introductory lesson.
2. Give students the biography worksheet of interesting people, past and present, and ask them to match biographical data with names. Tell students to guess if they do not know the answers.
3. Before students arrive, arrange biographies on a display cart in numerical order of the entries on the biography worksheet. Include videocassettes that are available to match written biographies. Bring out the cart after the students have completed the worksheet.
4. Show each book and ask students to supply the biographical data from the worksheet about that person. Fill in additional data.
5. Explain that "point of view" is a literary term used to describe the way the author presents the actions of the story. Give several examples of the author's point of view.
6. Review the correct answers for the biography worksheet.
7. Discuss the call numbers for collective and individual biographies using the Dewey decimal classification of 920 and 921. Remind students that individual biographies are arranged by the last name of the person who is the subject of the book.
8. Tell students that there are a limited number of videocassettes that match written biographies. Remind them that they are required to read a biography, but they may also watch a videotape and use it to compare and contrast information in the written biography.
9. Give individual reading assistance to students to help them select and present an interesting biographical sketch.
10. Evaluate oral presentations.

The students will

1. Complete the biography worksheet.
2. Discuss answers with the library media specialist.
3. Locate and select a biography.
4. Read a biography.
5. Use reference books and electronic sources to gather information about the biographee.
6. Plan a character sketch based on the biography.
7. Use a word processor to compile data. Include title of biography, author's name, name of the biographee, birthdate, occupation, nationality, major accomplishments, obstacles overcome, and several interesting facts or happenings. Make a bibliography.
8. Present an oral character sketch based on the author's point of view. (Students may dress in costumes and include pictures or illustrations.)

Evaluative Criteria

The students will complete the biography worksheet: locate, select, and read a biography and compile a data sheet and bibliography. They will present an oral character sketch based on the author's point of view.

Further Suggestions

This suggested activity involves a longer period of time to complete. Students in the academically gifted classes in Moore County Schools, North Carolina, presented "A Night of the Notables" to the community. Each student chose a biography of a person whom they could emulate. They did research to become familiar with many aspects of that person's life. They dressed in appropriate costume and at the reception met with guests who tried to guess the name of the person they were portraying by asking questions. The students could only answer "yes" or "no" to the questions. After this period, guests were invited to an area where each student had prepared a display of relevant information, charts, and pictures. Students continued to portray their character and presented many interesting facts about the life and times of this person.

Answer Key for Biography Worksheet: 1 c, 2 d, 3 f, 4 g, 5 a, 6 i, 7 e, 8 o, 9 w, 10 b, 11 s, 12 x, 13 r, 14 h, 15 q, 16 m, 17 p, 18 u, 19 t, 20 k, 21 l, 22 v, 23 n, 24 j.

Biography Worksheet

Match the following names with the biographical data.

____ 1. Louisa May Alcott

____ 2. P. T. Barnum

____ 3. Amelia Earhart

____ 4. Nathaniel Bowditch

____ 5. Elizabeth Blackwell

____ 6. Aaron Burr

____ 7. Arthur Ashe

____ 8. Winston Churchill

____ 9. Mother Teresa

____ 10. James Bowie

____ 11. Father Junipero Serra

____ 12. Sacagawea

____ 13. Madame Curie

____ 14. Louis Braille

____ 15. Confucius

____ 16. Martin Luther

____ 17. Albert Schweitzer

____ 18. Maria Tallchief

____ 19. Cleopatra

____ 20. Hannibal

____ 21. Eleanor Roosevelt

____ 22. Laura Ingalls Wilder

____ 23. Frank Lloyd Wright

____ 24. Rachel Carson

a. First woman doctor

b. Inventor of the famous bowie knife

c. Author of *Little Women*

d. A great showman, producer of the "Greatest Show on Earth"

e. African American tennis star

f. Woman aviation pioneer

g. Author of the *American Practical Navigator* known as the Sailor's Bible

h. Developed a system of dots for use in books for the blind

i. Traitor, vice president, who killed his rival in a duel

j. American woman scientist and writer

k. Carthaginian general

l. Wife of a U.S. President, crusader

m. Leader of the Reformation

n. American architect

o. Prime Minister of Great Britain 1940-45 and 1951-55

p. Missionary doctor in Africa, theologian, musician

q. Great teacher in China

r. Woman scientist, discoverer of radium

s. Founder of California missions

t. Queen of Egypt

u. A prima ballerina

v. Author of *Little House on the Prairie*

w. Great humanitarian, "Saint of India"

x. Native American interpreter to Lewis and Clark

LESSON EIGHT

Title
Celebrating European Cultures

Overview
As a culminating activity to the study of Europe, students will work in groups of five or six, locating information using print and electronic resources to prepare a group report on a European country. The report will be given during a large group presentation celebrating European cultures. The report may be a multimedia production.

Library Media Skills Objectives
Use library catalogs to locate information and materials.

Use general reference works.

Use electronic resources and courseware.

Use vertical file/information file.

Compare figures in maps and graphs.

Use bibliographies as an aid in locating information.

Utilize organizational skills.

Use appropriate audiovisual equipment for selected presentations.

Competency Goals and Objectives
1. The learner will investigate the characteristics of the people of Europe and analyze cultural, political, and economic institutions.
2. The learner will work collaboratively with other students to complete a task.

Learning Strategy
Lecture, practice, complete project, and give large group presentation.

Resources
E-mail

Maps

Public library

Telephone directory

Vertical file/information file

Web sites

Worksheet instructions

Print

Burckhardt, Ann L. 1996. *The People of Russia and Their Food*.

Festivals of the World: Germany. 1997.

Ganeri, Anita. 1992. *Germany and the Germans*.

Ganeri, Anita. 1992. *France and the French*.

Lents, P. J. 1992. *Our Global Village: Germany*.

Lipson, Michelle, and friends. 1994. *The Fantastic Costume Book*.

National Geographic Index

Needler, Toby, and Bonnie Goodman. 1991. *Exploring Global Art*.

Readers' Guide to Periodical Literature.
Robinson, Dindy. 1996. World Cultures Through Art Activities.
Symynkywicz, Jeffrey B. 1996. Germany: United Again.
World Almanac and Book of Facts. 1997.

Nonprint and Courseware

Eyewitness history of the world. 1995. Dorling Kindersley Multimedia. CD-ROM.
Grolier multimedia encyclopedia. 1997. Mindscape. CD-ROM.
HyperStudio. 1995. Roger Wagner. CD-ROM.
Mayer, Alois. 1994. Everyday situations in French to develop vocabulary and oral proficiency. National Textbook. Transparency set.
Microsoft Encarta 97 encyclopedia: Deluxe edition 1997. Microsoft. CD-ROM.
NGS picturepack: Geography of Europe. 1995. National Geographic Society. Transparency set.
Picture atlas of the world. 1995. National Geographic Society. CD-ROM.
STV: World geography: Africa and Europe. 1994. National Geographic Society. Videodisc.

Professional Resources

Dornberg, John. 1995. Central and Eastern Europe.
Dornberg, John. 1996. Western Europe.
Winpenny, Patricia G., and Katherine W. Cadwell, with Louise Cadwell. 1995. Teaching Russian studies: History, language, culture, and art.

Methods

The teacher will

1. Make a list of European countries using an electronic encyclopedia or almanac.
2. Tell students that they will present a group report in a large group meeting celebrating European cultures. Posters, maps, flags, charts, costumes, music, language tapes, and artifacts may be used with the presentation. The report may be a multimedia production.
3. Let students select one country for a report.
4. Hand out copies of the guidelines.

The library media specialist will

1. Display a map of the world with the location of European nations.
2. Play a selection of music from a European composer during the introduction of the lesson.
3. Review and demonstrate use of reference sources: Readers' Guide to Periodical Literature, National Geographic Index, Statesman's Yearbook, etc.
4. Demonstrate use of HyperStudio [CD-ROM] program and how to creatively interface music, sound, graphics, and print materials.
5. Prepare a bibliography of print, nonprint, and courseware resources for student use.
6. Remind students to visit public libraries and to contact travel agencies.
7. Assist students in locating telephone numbers, addresses, and Web sites of embassies.
8. Work with each group to assist them with research and preparation of presentation.
9. Guide students in use of audiovisual equipment and the HyperStudio program.

10. If student productions are live, videotape presentations of each group and have them available for parents to view.
11. Schedule replays of multimedia productions for parents to view.

The students will
1. Work in groups to gather information, take notes, make an outline, write a report, and prepare a group presentation.
2. Prepare audiovisual aids such as a map, poster, or flag.
3. Rehearse group presentation.
4. Record multimedia productions.
5. Present group reports.

Evaluative Criteria

Selecting the name of a European country and given a worksheet with instructions, students will work in groups to locate and use specific resources. They will complete an outline and bibliography and prepare a group report for presentation at a large group session.

Further Suggestions

Use e-mail: Participate in an exchange of electronic mail with students in European countries.

Contact people who have lived in European countries and invite them to share information and artifacts.

Utilize Web sites: Locate directory for European embassies in the U.S.

Use National Geographic Online for additional information on European countries.

Guidelines for Group Presentation: Celebrating European Cultures

Step 1. Gather information.
   a. Go to the library media center and find as many resources as you can about a designated European country. Use at least three resources, including one periodical.
   b. Contact a foreign embassy located in the U.S.
   c. Contact a travel agency.

Step 2. Locate the following information about a designated country:
   a. population
   b. geography
   c. major cities
   d. sites to visit
   e. languages spoken
   f. currency (compare to U.S. dollar)
   g. arts, crafts, and music
   h. products
   i. sports and recreation
   j. foods

Step 3. Record information.
   a. Take notes in your own words.
   b. Prepare a bibliography of resources used.
   c. Make an outline.
   d. Write a brief report.
   e. Prepare visual aids.
   f. Rehearse group presentation.
   g. Use time limit of 15 minutes for group presentations.

Step 4. If making a group oral presentation:
   a. use your note cards and talk to the audience;
   b. present visual aids;
   c. use background music;
   d. dress in native costume, if available; or
   e. serve a sample of food eaten in the country you studied (optional).

Step 5. If making a group multimedia production:
   a. follow directions provided by the library media specialists for production procedures;
   b. orally introduce the multimedia production; and
   c. show the multimedia production at a large group session.

Schedule
   Week 1. Your notes and rough copy of outline will be checked.
   Week 2. Written outline and bibliography due.
   Week 3. Oral and multimedia presentations begin.

LESSON NINE

Title

You're Invited: Micro Demo

Overview

The purpose of this unit is to extend students' knowledge of the history and development of computers, computer-related terminology, and the capabilities and limitations of computers. Students will keep a computer literacy notebook listing these facts.

Library Media Skills Objectives:

Identify history and development of computers.

Identify computer hardware and software.

Use computer hardware and software.

Competency Goal and Objectives

The learner will demonstrate knowledge and skills in using computer technology.

Subject Area

Interdisciplinary Team or Language Arts.

Learning Strategy

Computer instruction, discussion, and complete project.

Resources

Computer manuals

Print

Atelsek, Jean. 1993. *All About Computers.*

Berger, Sandy. 1997. *How to Have a Meaningful Relationship with Your Computer.*

Freedman, Alan. 1995. *The Computer Glossary: The Complete Illustrated Dictionary.* 7th ed.

O'Hara, Shelley, Jennifer Fulton, and Ed Guilford. 1995. *The Big Basics Book of Windows 95.*

Schnyder, Sandy Eddy, David Haskin, and Ed Guilford. 1995. *The Big Basics Book of Word for Windows 95.*

White, Ron. 1995. *How Computers Work.* 2d ed.

Nonprint and Courseware

How multimedia computers work. 1994. Mindscape. CD-ROM.

Internet coach for kids: Mission to Planet X. 1996. APTE. CD-ROM.

Internet revealed video series. 1997. Classroom Connect. Videocassettes.

Mavis Beacon teaches typing for kids. 1994-95. Mindscape. CD-ROM.

Web workshop. 1996. Sunburst. CD-ROM.

Professional Resources

Ames, Sandra, ed. 1995. *Teaching electronic information skills: A resource guide, grades 6-8.*

Classroom connect newsletter. Classroom Connect.

Classroom Internet yellow pages—K-6. 1997. Classroom Connect. CD-ROM.

Educator's World Wide Web tour guide. 1996. Classroom Connect. CD-ROM.

Teaching grades K-12 with the Internet. 1996. Classroom Connect. CD-ROM.

Methods

The teacher will

1. Plan the unit with the library media specialist.
2. Ask the library media specialist to set up a computer resource center in the library media center.
3. Introduce the unit and explain the objectives to the students.
4. Show a portion of the CD-ROM *How Multimedia Computers Work* by displaying the computer screen onto an LCD panel or a television monitor. Lead a discussion on the history and development of computers.
5. Ask students to take notes and list pertinent facts in a computer literacy notebook.
6. Allow students to divide their notebooks into four parts: (1) history and development of computers; (2) computer-related terminology; (3) capabilities of computers; and (4) limitations of computers.
7. Collect and grade the notebooks.
8. Analyze data and discuss with class.

The library media specialist will

1. Set up a computer resource center adjacent to the computer lab. Include a glossary of computer terms.
2. Ask teachers and students to add magazine and newspaper articles to the resource center.
3. Assist groups of students in using the center.
4. Let students use the computer lab to locate information on computers using electronic encyclopedias and magazine indexes. Remind students to use cross-references.
5. Caution students to check for accuracy any data received from the Internet or through e-mail.
6. Remind students that working with computers can be fun by using Sandy Berger's book, *How to Have a Meaningful Relationship with Your Computer.*

Having Fun with Your Computer

Radio and television are primarily for entertainment. You can, of course, also use both the radio and television to gather information and learn. However, the computer is truly a multifunctional machine in this respect. It is equally valuable for both serious and playful endeavors. Without a doubt, the computer can help all of us to be more productive and have more fun by providing:

- Games
- Sports-Related Programs
- Travel
- Genealogy
- Cooking
- Drawing and Painting
- Desktop Publishing
- Photo Programs
- Music

The students will

1. View and discuss the CD-ROM *How Multimedia Computers Work.*
2. Use the computer resource center in the library media center.
3. Compile data on the history and development of computers, computer-related terminology, capabilities of computers, and limitations of computers.
4. Use the public library; talk with people who work with computers (optional).
5. Make a computer literacy notebook.
6. Turn in notebook to teacher.
7. Discuss data with class.

Evaluative Criteria

Students will make a computer literacy notebook listing facts about the history and development of computers, computer-related terminology, and the capabilities and limitations of computers.

Further Suggestions

Invite a computer specialist to talk to students. Ask a local computer hardware/software vendor to talk about computer products. Identify computer career opportunities. Plan a lesson on contemporary sports and sports heroes in which students use their knowledge of word processing, databases, and spreadsheets.

If your school has a computer/technology specialist, this lesson may be taught jointly with the classroom teacher. The library media specialist may be used as a resource person. Some middle schools have computer labs adjoining their classroom areas. The library media specialist serves these areas by providing resource materials, maintenance, and instruction as needed.

LESSON TEN

Title
Books: Page After Page

Overview
The purpose of this lesson is to extend the students' knowledge of the parts of books to enable them to more fully utilize all parts of books. The students will apply this information when preparing a list of resource materials.

Library Media Skills Objectives
Identify and use all parts of a book.

Competency Goals and Objectives
1. The learner will anticipate content and organization to apply strategies to comprehend information.
2. The learner will determine usefulness of information.

Subject Area
Language Arts or Reading.

Learning Strategy
Learning center.

Resources
Learning center with illustrations of parts of book
Cover, spine, call number, title page, copyright page, dedication, preface, foreword or introduction, table of contents, list of illustrations or maps, body or text, appendix, glossary, bibliography, and index.
Worksheet

Methods
The teacher will
1. Introduce the objectives.
2. Schedule students on a rotating basis to complete the learning center in the library media center.
3. Use follow-up activities in future assignments using the parts of books.

The library media specialist will
1. Make an attractive, colorful learning center with illustrations of the parts of books. Include the book used in the display.
2. Prepare the worksheet for students' use at the learning center.
3. Check and grade the worksheets with the nonfiction books used by the students.
4. Review incorrect answers with students.
5. Evaluate the learning center activity with the teacher.

Text continues on page 80.

Fig. 6-10-1. Illustration of Parts of a Book.

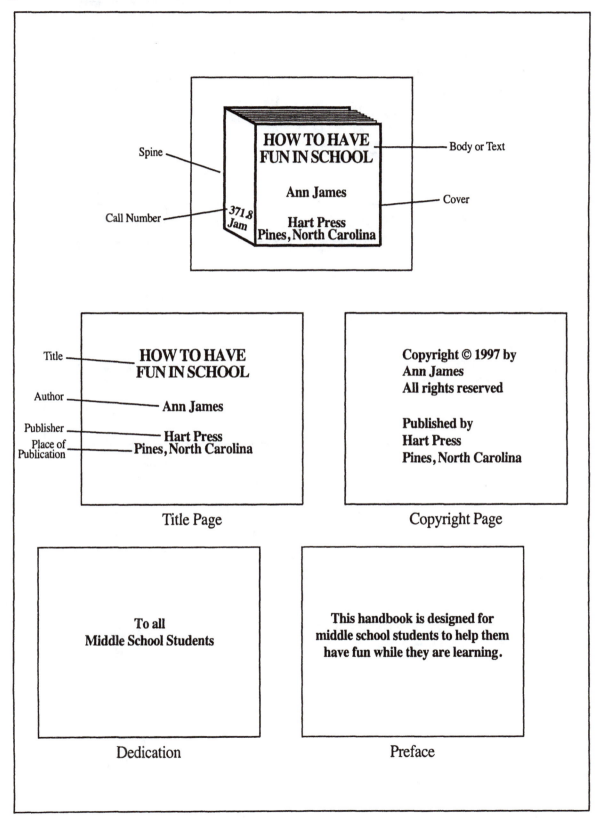

From *Media Skills for Middle Schools*. © 1999 Lucille W. Van Vliet. Libraries Unlimited. (800) 237-6124.

Table of Contents

List of Illustrations

Extracurricular Activities:
Bowling
Cooking Club
Dancing
Field Hockey
Gymnastics
Photography Club
Skating

Appendix

Index

From *Media Skills for Middle Schools.* © 1999 Lucille W. Van Vliet. Libraries Unlimited. (800) 237-6124.

Worksheet for Parts of a Book

Select a nonfiction book from the library media center. Use your own paper to respond to the following questions or directions about the book you have chosen:

1. What is the title? _____

    _____

2. Who is the author? _____

3. What is the call number? _____

4. Who is the publisher? _____

5. What is the copyright date? _____

6. Find the table of contents and list the first two entries

    _____

    _____

7. List the page number where the main body or text begins _____

8. List the page numbers of the following items if they are found in the book you have chosen: preface, foreword, introduction, dedication, glossary, bibliography, and index.

    _____

    _____

9. Give the nonfiction book and the completed worksheet to the library media specialist.

The students will

1. Read the background information at the learning center.
2. Select a nonfiction book from the media center collection.
3. Complete the worksheet.
4. Refer any questions about parts of books to the library media specialist.

Evaluative Criteria

The students will correctly answer all questions on the worksheet on page 79 using all parts of a book.

Further Suggestions

Use a children's book like *How a Book Is Made* (Aliki 1986) or the more advanced "The Parts of a Book" in *The Chicago Manual of Style* (1993) to explain the stages in making a book and explaining the technical processes. Students may enjoy writing and illustrating their own book, complete with cover and parts of the book.

LESSON ELEVEN

Title
Wheels

Overview
The purpose of this lesson is to provide students with a directed reading activity using a selected topic in magazines. They will complete a project related to their reading.

Library Media Skills Objectives
Identify and locate magazines.

Locate topics using table of contents.

Skim to find relevant ideas.

Prepare a summary.

Use word processing skills.

Competency Goals and Objectives
1. The learner will experience a wide variety of reading resources to interact with ideas and use reading skills that are appropriate for a specific format and purpose.
2. The learner will demonstrate knowledge and skills in using computer technology to complete a report.

Subject Area
Reading or Language Arts.

Learning Strategy
Discussion, reading, word processing, and complete project.

Resources
Print
Magazines
American Motorcyclist, Bicycling, Car and Driver, Car Craft, Cycle Track, Cycle World, Dirt Rider Magazine, Hot Rod, Motor Trend, Petersen's 4 Wheel and Off-Road Truckin', Safe Cycling, Skating, Snowmobile, Sports 'n Spokes, Zillions, etc.

Books
Keller, Charles. 1989. *Driving Me Crazy: Fun on Wheels Jokes.*
Martin, John. 1994. *In-Line Skating.*

Methods
The teacher will
1. Introduce the lesson and objective.
2. Define purpose for reading.
3. Ask students to name vehicles that have wheels.
4. Discuss student responses.

5. State that many of the vehicles they have named are listed on cards as topics for reports. Such wheeled items as wheelbarrows, rickshaws, carts, and wheelchairs are not included in the list because they are more difficult topics to locate in the magazines that are available in the school's library media center.

6. Let students select one of many cards contained in a box with such topics as: motorcycles, automobiles, trucks, bicycles, mountain bikes, motorbikes, mopeds, motor scooters, go-carts, in-line skates, off-road vehicles, trucks, skateboards, ice skates, and racing cars, etc.

7. Schedule students for an introduction to magazines in the library media center and to work on their reports in the computer lab.

8. Work with individual students to develop vocabulary.

9. Reinforce skills for skimming, determining main idea, sequence of events, and summarizing.

10. Reinforce skills of word processing: spell checker, grammar checker, electronic thesaurus, and clip art.

11. Guide students in preparing a booklet.

12. Evaluate booklet.

The library media specialist will

1. Locate magazines with articles on wheeled vehicles, making certain to have magazines for each topic listed on the cards distributed by the teacher. It may be necessary to purchase or borrow additional magazines for this lesson.

2. Reserve magazines on a display rack in the magazine section of the library media center.

3. Show the students the special rack of reserved magazines and allow them to select a magazine that might have information on their topic.

4. Demonstrate the use of the table of contents to locate a topic in a magazine.

5. Assist students in locating a magazine article on their topic.

6. Allow students to check out the magazines.

7. Assist the students in using the information they collect on their topic.

8. Accompany the students to the computer lab and provide assistance in using the word processing tools.

9. Provide back copies of magazines that students may use to cut out pictures for their reports.

10. As a culminating activity, read jokes from Keller's (1989) *Driving Me Crazy: Fun on Wheels Jokes*. These are flip, wacky, and contagious jokes about cars, buses, trucks, bicycles, and other vehicles on wheels. Let students show their reactions to each joke by giving a thumbs up or thumbs down.

The students will

1. Select one of the cards from the box with topics about wheeled vehicles.

2. Select a magazine from the reserved collection in the library media center.

3. Use the table of contents to locate an article on assigned topic.

4. Check out the magazine from the library media center.

5. Read the magazine article during class periods and for homework assignment.

6. Make a list of vocabulary words.

7. Skim the article to find relevant ideas.

8. Determine the main idea.

9. List the sequence of events.
10. Using a word processor, write a summary of the article and make a list of vocabulary words; check spelling and definitions.
11. Prepare a booklet using the objectives as stated by the teacher.

Evaluative Criteria

The student will successfully complete a booklet that contains illustrations of a wheeled vehicle, the titles of magazine sources, titles of articles used, a summary of the article, and a list of vocabulary words.

LESSON TWELVE

Title
Discover the Discoverer

Overview
The purpose of this lesson is to encourage students to discover the fascinating facts about the European explorers. They will locate information about an explorer, trace the route of a specific explorer on a map, provide data about discoveries, assess the influence of exploration and discoveries on life in Europe, and prepare a concise written report.

Library Media Skills Objectives
Use atlases, almanacs, biographical dictionaries.

Use subject headings in library catalogs.

Use *Dewey decimal classification and relative index.*

Use print, nonprint, and courseware materials.

Competency Goals and Objectives
1. The learner will identify and apply strategies to access, evaluate, use, and communicate information.
2. The learner will demonstrate knowledge and skills in writing and use of computer technology.

Subject Area
Social Studies or Interdisciplinary Team.

Learning Strategy
Research, lecture, practice, and use of computer technologies.

Resources
Print
Arnold, Nick. 1995. *Voyages of Exploration.*

Brantley, C. L. 1995. *The Princeton Review Writing Smart Junior: The Art and Craft of Writing.*

Children's Atlas of World History. 1988.

Cooper, Kay. 1990. *Where in the World Are You? A Guide to Looking at the World.*

Fritz, Jean. 1994. *Around the World in a Hundred Years: From Henry the Navigator to Magellan.*

Grant, Neil. 1992. *The Great Atlas of Discovery.*

Langley, Andrew. 1990. *Twenty Explorers.*

Lomask, Milton. 1984. *Exploration: Great Lives.*

National Geographic Index.

Saari, Peggy, and Daniel B. Baker. 1995. *Explorers and Discoverers: From Alexander the Great to Sally Ride.*

West, Delno C., and Jean M. West. 1996. *Braving the North Atlantic: The Vikings, the Cabots, and Jacques Cartier Voyage to America.*

Nonprint and Courseware

Explorers of the new world. 1995. Future Vision Multimedia. CD-ROM.

NGS picturepack: *The age of exploration.* 1995. National Geographic Society. Transparency Sets.

NGS pictureshow: The age of exploration 1. 1996. National Geographic Society. CD-ROM.

NGS pictureshow: The age of exploration 2. 1996. National Geographic Society. CD-ROM.

Methods

The teacher will

1. Introduce the lesson by showing a videotape or CD-ROM such as *Explorers of the New World.*
2. Review map-making skills.
3. Discuss the objectives and research topics with the library media specialist.
4. Schedule the classes in the library media center and the computer lab.
5. Provide outline maps for students.
6. Make a list of European explorers. Cut the list into strips. Let students pick a name from a small chest or bowl.
7. Accompany students to the library media center and computer lab.
8. Evaluate written reports.

The library media specialist will

1. Give a brief review of reference and research skills:
   - search strategies, library catalogs
   - subject headings: EXPLORERS, DISCOVERIES IN GEOGRAPHY
   - Dewey decimal classification: 910, 920, 921
   - indexes
   - bibliography notation
2. Assist students with print and electronic research questions.
3. Evaluate lesson with teacher.

The students will

1. Pick a name of a European explorer.
2. Take notes on lecture given by library media specialist.
3. Use research skills to locate print, nonprint, and courseware resources for information on specific explorer.
4. Trace the route of explorer on the blank map. Label the map and make a legend.
5. Use a word processor to prepare a report on a specific explorer including nationality and accomplishments.

Evaluative Criteria

The students will prepare a concise written report on a European explorer, assess the influence of exploration and discoveries on life in Europe, and include a map showing the route of the explorer.

Further Suggestions

An interesting follow-up would be to continue the discussion and study on explorers and discoverers with the topic of modern exploration in the world. This could include the exploration by: The Hubble Space Telescope, Sputnik, Viking, Voyager 1 and 2, *U.S.S. Nautilus*, *H.M.S. Challenger*, and *Explorer I*. Modern explorers could include Jacques Cousteau, Amelia Earhart, Yury Gagarin, Chuck Yeager, John Glenn, and Sally Ride.

Explorers

List of Explorers

Francisco Pizarro	Vasco de Balboa
Juan Ponce de León	Sir Francis Drake
Bartholomeu Dias	Leif Eriksson
John Cabot	Ferdinand Magellan
Pedro Cabral	Jacques Marquette
Juan Cabrillo	Giovanni da Verrazano
Jacques Cartier	Amerigo Vespucci
Christopher Columbus	Henry Hudson
Francisco de Coronado	James Cook
Hernando Cortés	Roald Amundsen
Vasco da Gama	Hernando de Soto

LESSON THIRTEEN

Title
It Pays to Listen

Overview
The purpose of this lesson is to instruct students in the art of listening. They will use telecommunication processes to locate and collect data to share orally with other class members. Students will diagram a communications and a telecommunications model and explain the meaning of the terms to help them better understand the communication process. After a listening exercise, students will identify the sequence of events.

Library Media Skills Objectives
Identify an audio sequence of events.

Interpret a communications model.

Identify telecommunication terms relative to computers: bulletin board, modem, e-mail, online, news groups, and World Wide Web.

Competency Goals and Objectives
1. The learner will experience a wide variety of listening resources that interact with ideas in an information-rich environment.
2. The learner will explore listening sources and formats.

Subject Area
Language Arts or Interdisciplinary Team.

Learning Strategy
Lecture, audiovisual instruction, and telecommunications.

Resources
Print
Diagram of sample communications model.

Hawkes, Nigel. 1994. *New Technology: Communications.*

Van Vliet, Lucille W. 1992. Focus on Critical Thinking and Communication Skills: Listening Skills. In *Approaches to Literature Through Genre.*

Nonprint and Courseware
Avi. 1995. *The man who was Poe.* Audio Bookshelf. Audiocassette.

Learn to speak English for speakers of Spanish 6.0. 1995. HyperGlot Software. CD-ROM

Personal communications. 1991. STV. Videocassette.

Rawls, Woodrow Wilson. 1991. *Where the red fern grows.* Listening Library. Audiocassette.

Professional
Martin, Judith. 1997. *Miss Manners' basic training: Communication.*

Tanner, Fran A. 1996. *Creative communication: Projects in acting, speaking, and oral reading.* 5th ed.

Fig. 6-13-1. Sample Communications Model.

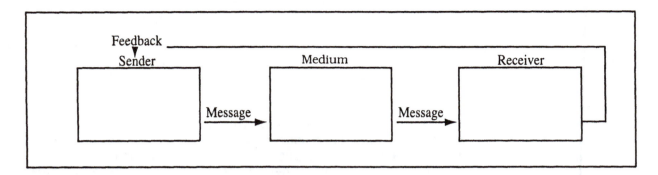

Methods

The teacher will

1. Discuss with the students the importance of listening skills.
2. Ask the students to define communication.
3. Explain that communication is a broad subject and that communications skills are interrelated throughout the curriculum. Clarify that this lesson is only one aspect of the dynamic communication process.
4. Invite the library media specialist to come to the classroom to diagram and explain a simple communication model and a model of telecommunications.
5. Schedule a class in the computer lab for a computer telecommunications exercise using e-mail and the bulletin board.
6. Tell students to send an e-mail message requesting short, humorous poetry that would be appropriate to share with a sixth-grade class.
7. Ask students to listen to a portion of an audiocassette such as *Where the Red Fern Grows* and list a sequence of events.
8. Share some humorous comments by Judith Martin in *Miss Manners' Basic Training: Communication*.

The library media specialist will

1. Diagram a simple communications model.
2. Show the videotape *Personal Communications*. Interact with students by discussing the ideas presented.
3. Give the teacher several audiocassettes to choose from for the class.
4. Collect and distribute the bulletin board and e-mail messages to students.
5. Evaluate the lesson with the teacher.

The students will

1. Label the parts of a communication model.
2. Orally explain the meaning of each part.
3. View a videotape program on communications. Discuss ideas.
4. Listen to an audiocassette recording and make a list of the sequence of events.

Evaluative Criteria

The students will locate and collect data to share orally with other class members. Students will diagram a communications and a telecommunications model and explain the meaning of the terms. After a listening exercise, students will identify the sequence of events.

Further Suggestions

Use the CD-ROM *Learn to Speak English* by HyperGlot Software to help speakers of Spanish with speaking and listening comprehension skills.

LESSON FOURTEEN

Title
Fiesta Español!

Overview
The purpose of this lesson is to introduce students to Spanish culture and customs through the study of Spanish holidays and holy days. Students will choose a topic from a prepared list of holidays and holy days observed in Spain. They will complete a written report, prepare visuals, and present an oral report.

Library Media Skills Objectives
Select a reference source.

Organize information around a topic.

Infer facts from maps, charts, and graphs.

Use a wide variety of resources.

Use a word processor.

Use clip art.

Competency Goals and Objectives
1. The learner will engage in a research process to meet information needs.
2. The learner will create a product.
3. The learner will exchange e-mail with students in a foreign country via a telecommunications project.

Subject Area
Spanish or Social Studies.

Learning Strategy
Research, discussion, and practice.

Resources
Worksheet

Electronic encyclopedias

E-mail

Print
Christmas in Spain: Christmas Around the World from World Book. 1983.
Facaros, Dana, and Michael Parks. 1992. *Spain.* 3d ed.
Fodor's Exploring Spain. 1995.
Kohen, Elizabeth. 1992. *Spain.*
NTC's Beginner's Spanish and English Dictionary. 1992.
Selby, Anna. 1994. *Spain.*
Webb, Lois Sinaiko. 1996. *Holidays of the World Cookbook for Students.*

Nonprint and Courseware
Folb, Kate Langrall. 1996. *Spanish for Natalie: A new friend.* Performed by Linda Ronstadt. Dove Audio. Audiocassette.
Language discovery 1993. Applied Optical Media. CD-ROM.

Professional

Kattán-Ibarra, Juan. 1995. *Panorama de La Prensa: Temas contemporàneos del mundo Hispano*. Kit with audiocassettes.

Methods

The teacher will

1. Introduce the lesson by telling the students that in Spain festivals and town celebrations are an important part of the culture. Somewhere in Spain, almost every day, there is a fiesta taking place. Every town celebrates a fiesta once a year. Two cities never want to have their fiestas simultaneously, therefore, one can travel from town to town to observe the many fiestas. In Madrid, Seville, and other large cities, the fiestas are called La Feria. People come from all over Spain and Europe to attend these special fiestas. Every town in the Hispanic world has at least one big religious festival celebration each year in honor of the patron saint. The fiesta begins with a religious ceremony and prayers said at the local church. In the evening, there are parties with dancing, eating, and sometimes fireworks. Other festivals celebrate the coming of spring and harvest and grape pressing. Everybody in the town participates in these celebrations.
2. Prepare a worksheet on Spanish holidays and holy days.
3. Discuss the objectives.
4. Schedule small groups of students to work in the library media center and computer lab to search the World Wide Web.
5. Allow students to exchange e-mail with students in Spain.
6. Appraise the oral and written reports.

The library media specialist will

1. Select and reserve resources.
2. Help students in locating information.
3. Assist students in exchanging e-mail using the World Wide Web.
4. Attend the oral presentations.

The students will

1. Select a Spanish holiday or holy day for their report.
2. Locate, select, and interpret appropriate resources.
3. Use maps and charts.
4. Prepare a written and an oral report.
5. Make a poster or other visuals to use when presenting the oral report.

Evaluative Criteria

The students will successfully complete the assignment. They will complete a written report, prepare visuals, and present an oral report on a Spanish holiday or holy day.

Further Suggestions

Teachers may want to discuss the following questions with their students:

1. What kinds of festivals take place where you live?
2. Where are they held?
3. What is the purpose behind them?
4. Does everyone in the town attend?
5. What can you find there?

Fiesta Español Worksheet: Holidays and Holy Days

Select one of the following topics and complete a written report, prepare an oral report, and construct visuals to accompany the report.

Some examples of important fiestas in Spain are:

La Feria de Abril, Seville

La Semana Santa, Seville

La Fiesta de San Isidro, Madrid

La Fiesta de Santiago, Santiago de Compostela

Las Fallas, Valencia

San Fermín Festival, Pamplona

El día del Año Nuevo

Día de los Reyes

Viernes Santo

El día de Navidad

Romeria del Rocío

San Isidro

Include the following in Spanish:

Greetings and salutations

Dates

Expressions

LESSON FIFTEEN

Title

Pick Your Own!

Overview

The purpose of this lesson is to allow students to select fiction books of their choice for use in the classroom. All books must be from the library media center or on the approved list. The students will create a product that effectively demonstrates a personal response to a selection.

Library Media Skills Objectives

Recognize different genres or types of fiction books.

Define and identify the following in fictional works: Plot, character, setting, and theme.

Select reading material relevant to interests and purposes.

Read for enjoyment.

Competency Goals and Objectives

1. The learner will use language for aesthetic and personal response.
2. The learner will use language for the acquisition, interpretation, and application of information.

Subject Area

Reading or Language Arts.

Learning Strategy

Reading, discussion, and creation of product.

Resources

Booktalks

Fiction collection in the library media center

Fiction self-selection guidelines

Examples of fiction classification labels

Suggested reading lists

Print

Reading Guidance

Bibliographies: Newbery Award Books.

Berman, Matt. 1996. *What Else Should I Read? Guiding Kids to Good Books*, Vol. 2.

Colborn, Candy. 1994. *What Do Children Read Next? A Reader's Guide to Fiction for Children.*

Donavin, Denise Perry, ed. 1992. *American Library Association Best of the Best for Children.*

Freeman, Judy. 1990. *Books Kids Will Sit Still For.* 2d ed.

Gillespie, John T., and Corinne J. Naden. 1996. *The Newbery Companion: Booktalk and Related Materials for Newbery Medal and Honor Books.*

Fig. 6-15-1. Examples of Fiction Classification Labels.

Used by permission of Highsmith, Inc.

Norton, Donna E. 1991. *Through the Eyes of a Child: An Introduction to Children's Literature*. 3d ed.

Odean, Kathleen. 1997. *Great Books for Girls: More Than 600 Books to Inspire Today's Girls and Tomorrow's Women*.

Fiction

Avi. 1996. *Beyond the Western Sea: The Escape from Home*.

Blos, Joan W. 1994. *Brooklyn Doesn't Rhyme*.

Burnford, Sheila. 1961. *The Incredible Journey*.

Cleary, Beverly. 1983. *Dear Mr. Henshaw*.

Hahn, Mary Downing. 1996. *The Gentleman Outlaw and Me—Eli: A Story of the Old West*.

Konigsburg, E. L. 1996. *The View from Saturday*.

Korman, Gordon. 1996. *The Chicken Doesn't Skate*.

Laird, Elizabeth. 1991. *Kiss the Dust*.

Skinner, David. 1992. *You Must Kiss a Whale*.

Sreenivasan, Jyotsna. 1997. *Aruna's Journeys*.

Trevor, William. 1991. *Juliet's Story*.

Van Leeuwen, Jean. 1996. *Blue Sky, Butterfly*.

Nonprint and Courseware

Paulsen, Gary. *Hatchet*. 1990. American School Publishers. Videocassette.

Methods

The teacher will

1. Plan with the library media specialist for students from reading or language arts classes to come to the library media center to select books.

2. Explain the objective.

3. Discuss the literary analysis skills that will be used during the reading period: setting, characters, plot, conflict, theme, and style.

4. Encourage students to read many different genres of fiction books: science fiction, fantasy, historical fiction, humor, mystery, and detective stories.

5. Discuss the types of products that students may use to report on the books they read: Puppetry, art interpretations such as collage or shadow boxes, oral discussion, creative dramatization, hand-drawn slides, booklets, or news stories written with a word processor.

6. Hold a large group discussion period to allow students to talk about the book they read and to discuss its literary elements.

The library media specialist will

1. Develop an up-to-date, comprehensive fiction collection.

2. Read as many fiction books as possible from the collection.

3. Make attractive displays of fiction books.

4. Make a fiction self-selection guidelines worksheet.
5. Make a chart displaying examples of fiction classification labels.
6. Use genre labels on spines of fiction books.
7. Give reading guidance as needed.
8. Give booktalks.
9. Make a display of reading guidance books.
10. Assist students with products.

The students will

1. Use self-selection guidelines.
2. Select and read books.
3. Plan and produce a project.
4. Review setting, characters, plot, conflict, theme, and style for the large group discussion.
5. Visit a public library and bookstores for additional selections (optional).

Evaluative Criteria

The students will select and read at least three fiction books each grading period and will produce a product to report on the books read.

Fiction Self-Selection Guidelines

All fiction books are arranged on the shelves alphabetically by the author's last name.

1. Look for books by your favorite author.

2. Look at the chart displaying examples of fiction classification labels. Many books have these labels on the spines.

3. Browse: Look at cover and blurb on book jacket.

4. Look at displays in the library media center.

5. Check author, title, and subject headings in library catalogs.

6. Use bibliographies in reading textbook.

7. Use reading guidance books.

8. Ask for suggestions from a friend, your reading or language arts teacher, and your library media specialist.

Skills Lessons for Grade Seven

LESSON ONE

Title
African Nations: Fascinating Facts

Overview
The purpose of this lesson is to help each student identify, locate, select, interpret, and utilize facts about a country in Africa by completing a booklet on an African nation. Students will investigate the characteristics of the African people. Many library media, information, and computer skills can be incorporated into this English/Language Arts, Social Studies, or Interdisciplinary Team lesson.

Library Media Skills Objectives
Identify and use library catalogs.

Identify and use the vertical file/information file.

Locate and use periodicals and newspapers.

Select general reference books.

Select nonprint and courseware resources.

Use a variety of resources to find information on a given subject.

Compare facts from different sources.

Interpret maps, graphs, and charts.

Use an index.

Summarize information.

Prepare a bibliography.

Competency Goals and Objectives
1. The learner will use language for the acquisition, interpretation, and application of information.
2. The learner will investigate the characteristics of the people of Africa.

Subject Area
English/Language Arts, Social Studies, or Interdisciplinary Team.

Learning Strategy
Lecture, demonstration, and completing project.

Resources

Bibliographic Form

Project Guidelines

Sample Booklet

Print

Reference Books

Dorling Kindersley World Reference Atlas.
Merriam-Webster's Intermediate Dictionary.
The World Almanac and Book of Facts.
World Book Encyclopedia.

Books

Bangura, Abdul Karim. 1994. *The Heritage Library of African Peoples: Kipsigis.*
Burckhardt, Ann L. 1996. *The People of Africa and Their Food.*
Iwago, Mitsuaki. 1986. *Serengeti: Natural Order of the African Plain.*
Klepper, Nancy. 1990. *Our Global Village: Africa.*
Murray, Jacelyn. 1993. *Africa.*
Silverman, Jerry, ed. 1994. *African Roots.*

Nonprint and Courseware

African wildlife. 1986. National Geographic Society. Videocassette.
Children of Ghana. 1991. Coronet. Videocassette.
Children of Morocco. 1991. Coronet. Videocassette.
Children of Rwanda. 1991. Coronet. Videocassette.
Children of Zimbabwe. 1991. Coronet. Videocassette.
John Coltrane Quartet. 1995. *The Complete Africa/Brass sessions.* MCA Records. Compact Disc.
Microsoft Encarta 97 encyclopedia. 1996. Microsoft. CD-ROM.
The music and dance of Africa. 1990. N. C. State University Humanities Extension. Videocassette.
NGS picturepack: Geography of Africa. 1995. National Geographic Society. Transparency Set.
Picture atlas of the world. 1995. National Geographic Society. CD-ROM.
Sirs discoverer. 1997. Sirs. CD-ROM.
STV world geography: Africa and Europe. 1994. Vol. 2. National Geographic Society. Videodisc.
ZipZapMap! World. 1994. National Geographic Society. Diskette.

Professional

Bever, Edward. 1996. *Africa.*
Byrnes, Ronald S., and Peter Downing, with Carol Vogler. 1995. *Teaching about Africa: A continent of complexities.*

Fig. 7-1-1. Sample Booklet: African Nations.

Methods

The teacher will

1. Assign a country of Africa as a topic.
2. Show transparency of map of Africa.
3. Play recording of African music.
4. Show sample booklet and explain procedures for completing booklet.
5. Distribute project guidelines.
6. Schedule class periods in the library media center and in the computer lab.
7. Assist with research.
8. Provide craft materials for booklet.
9. Grade projects.

The library media specialist will

1. Review location of library media center resources.
2. Instruct students in the use of print, nonprint, and courseware resources: almanacs, special encyclopedias, and atlases.
3. Give individual reference assistance as needed.
4. Explain the bibliographic format.
5. Evaluate projects.

The students will

1. View transparency of map of Africa and listen to recording of African music.
2. Observe demonstration.
3. Locate and use information.
4. Complete project booklet.

Evaluative Criteria

The students will complete a project booklet using correct facts.

Further Suggestions

If this lesson is used as an integrated English/Language Arts and Social Studies lesson or by an Interdisciplinary Team, it can be expanded to include additional computer and information skills, arts and crafts, home arts, and music.

Project Guidelines

Complete the following data using a word processor, if available. The completed pages will be inserted in the booklet.

Page 1:   Name of country

           Flag

           Student's name and section number

Page 2:   Map

Page 3:   Facts-in-brief

           Area in square miles

           Capital city

           Population

           Official language

Page 4:   Geography (Climate)

Page 5:   Geography (Topography)

Page 6:   Resources

Page 7:   Famous people

Page 8:   Historical events

Page 9:   Housing

Page 10:   Transportation

Page 11:   Government

Page 12:   Schools

Page 13:   Current events

Page 14:   Bibliography

LESSON TWO

Title

Computers: More Basics

Overview

The purpose of this unit is to build upon the students' knowledge of computers and the skills learned in previous grades. They will review the development of computers and computer-related terminology, discuss societal and ethical issues, and demonstrate knowledge and skills in using computer technology including the Internet. They will add pertinent information to their computer literacy notebook. They will use this knowledge by integrating computer and information skills into research projects in curricular areas.

Library Media Skills Objectives

Identify types of computers and peripherals.

Identify computer software and courseware.

Identify computer terms.

Identify societal and ethical issues.

Utilize computers to generate products.

Competency Goals and Objectives

1. The learner will understand the role of technology in society.
2. The learner will demonstrate knowledge and skills in using computer technology.

Subject Area

Interdisciplinary Team or Language Arts.

Learning Strategy

Computer instruction, discussion, project.

Resources

Manuals

Glossary

Print

Berger, Sandy. 1997. *How to Have a Meaningful Relationship with Your Computer. Classroom Connect Newsletter.*

McLain, Tim, and Gregory Giagnocavo. 1997. *The Internet Homework Helper.*

Oleksy, Walter. 1995. *Science and Medicine.*

Rathbone, Andy. 1994. *Multimedia and CD-ROMs for Dummies.*

Salzman, Marian, and Robert Pondisco. 1995. *Kids On-Line: 150 Ways for Kids to Surf the Net for Fun and Information.*

Nonprint and Courseware

Typing Tutor 7. 1996. Davidson. CD-ROM.

Professional

Print

Barron, Ann. 1997. *How to Create Great School Web Pages.*

Calishain, Tara. 1996. *Official Netscape Guide to Internet Research.*

Educator's Internet Companion: Classroom Connect's Complete Guide to Educational Resources on the Internet. 1995.
How to Create Successful Internet Projects. 1997.
Williams, Bard. 1995. *The Internet for Teachers.*

Nonprint and Courseware

How multimedia computers work. 1994. Mindscape. CD-ROM.
Internet coach for Netscape Navigator. 1996. *Release 3.* APTE. CD-ROM.
Thematic applications: General. 1995. Educational Activities, Inc. CD-ROM.

Methods

The teacher will

1. Plan the unit with the library media specialist.
2. Assist the library media specialist in setting up a computer resource center in the library media center containing diagrams of computers and peripherals and a glossary of computer skills.
3. Introduce the unit and explain the objectives to the students.
4. Show selections from *How Multimedia Computers Work* [CD-ROM] and lead a review of the history and development of computers.
5. Tell students that they will go in small groups to use the computer resource center to review the parts of the computer and peripherals and to learn the meaning of the computer terms as defined in the glossary. They will add these definitions and terms to their computer literacy notebook. They will use the computer lab to practice using the keyboard, word processing, and making a database. They will research a topic using the Internet.
6. Tell students that they will discuss societal and ethical uses of the computer in the classroom.

The library media specialist will

1. Set up a computer resource center adjacent to the computer lab. Include computer diagrams and a glossary of computer terms. Provide student-oriented manuals on typing, word processing, database, spreadsheet, tele-computing, and the Internet.
2. Ask teachers and students to add magazine and newspaper articles to the resource center.
3. Divide the students into groups according to their level of computer competency and assist students in using the resource center and computer lab.
4. Let students use the computer lab to locate information on computers using electronic encyclopedias and magazine indexes. Remind students to use cross references.
5. Customize the exercises in *Thematic Applications: General* [CD-ROM] for students to work on related subject matter such as a social studies assignment on nations of the world.
6. Caution students to check the accuracy of any data received from the Internet or through e-mail.
7. Assist students in integrating computer and information skills into research projects in curricular areas.

The students will

1. Review and discuss *How Multimedia Computers Work* [CD-ROM] with their classroom teacher.

2. Use the computer resource center and computer lab in the library media center to make a glossary of computer terms, to locate information on computers using electronic resources, to practice typing skills, and to become proficient users of databases, spreadsheets, word processing, and the Internet.
3. Add information to their computer literacy notebooks.
4. Turn in notebook to teacher.
5. Integrate computer and information skills into research projects in curricular areas.
6. Discuss societal and ethical uses of computers with the teacher.

Evaluative Criteria

Students will practice typing skills and using computers to become proficient users of databases, spreadsheets, word processing, and the Internet. They will add a glossary of computer terms to their computer literacy notebook. They will use this knowledge by integrating computer and information skills into research projects in curricular areas.

Further Suggestions

Plan a lesson on contemporary sports and sports heroes for students to use their knowledge of word processing, databases, and spreadsheets.

LESSON THREE

Title
Who Reads the Classics?

Overview
The purpose of this lesson is to have students select and read a novel from a selected list of the classics. They will read for enjoyment, as well as to strengthen critical thinking skills. Three to five students may select the same novel. After students complete the reading of the novel, they will form a discussion group, complete an activity, and plan and produce a videotape based on a scene from the novel.

Library Media Skills Objectives
Select and read a novel from the classics list.

Identify the literary elements of a novel: setting, characterization, plot, tone, style, and point of view.

Plan and produce a videotape.

Competency Goals and Objectives
1. The learner will experience a wide variety of reading resources that interact with ideas appropriate for a specific purpose.
2. The learner will demonstrate knowledge and skills in using computer technology.
3. The learner will create, produce, and present a final product.

Subject Area
Language Arts, Reading, Art, or Interdisciplinary Team.

Learning Strategy
Lecture, discussion, booktalk, demonstration, audiovisual project.

Resources
Book analysis worksheets

Guidelines for group discussions

Sample storyboard

Print

The Classics

Three to five copies of each title. Suggested titles appear below.

Alcott, Louisa M. *Little Women.*
Baum, Frank. *The Wizard of Oz.*
Collodi, Carlo. *Adventures of Pinocchio.*
Carroll, Lewis. *Alice in Wonderland.*
Defoe, Daniel. *Robinson Crusoe.*
Dickens, Charles. *David Copperfield.*
London, Jack. *Call of the Wild.*
Rawlings, Marjorie. *The Yearling.*
Richter, Conrad. *The Light in the Forest.*
Sewell, Anna. *Black Beauty.*

Fig. 7-3-1. Sample Storyboard.

MUSIC
(Cassette recording of a student playing a medley of classical tunes on the Piano)

NARRATOR: "Jim Hawkins drew near the foot of a little hill and saw a figure leap behind a tree."

MUSIC

NARRATOR: "The strange man threw himself on his knees and held out his clasped hands."

By
Robert Louis
Stevenson

MUSIC

JIM: "Who are you?"

Spyri, Johanna. *Heidi.*
Steinbeck, John. *The Red Pony.*
Stevenson, Robert Louis. *Treasure Island.*
Swift, Jonathan. *Gulliver's Travels.*
Twain, Mark. *The Adventures of Tom Sawyer.*
Verne, Jules. *20,000 Leagues Under the Sea.*

Nonprint and Courseware

Multimedia workshop. 1996. Davidson. CD-ROM.
Twain, Mark. 1996. *The adventures of Tom Sawyer.* Southern Star Interactive. CD-ROM.
Videotapes of novels read by the students.

Professional

Herz, Sarah K., with Donald R. Gallo. 1996. *From Hinton to Hamlet: Building bridges between young adult literature and the classics.*

Methods

The teacher will

1. Introduce the lesson and discuss the objectives and evaluation criteria.
2. Review the literary elements of a novel: setting, characterization, plot, tone, style, and point of view.
3. Use selections from the CD-ROM *The Adventures of Tom Sawyer* to show to the class or to supplement a class reading.
4. Discuss the guidelines for group discussions and the book analysis worksheets.
5. Schedule activities in the library media center and the production area.
6. Confer with groups.
7. Grade book analysis worksheets.

The library media specialist will

1. Select and reserve classic novels.
2. Prepare a list of the novels.
3. Give a booktalk on the classics.
4. Assist students with worksheets: Guidelines for group discussions and the book analysis worksheets.
5. After students have completed the worksheets, show a videotape of the book they read, if one is available in the library media center.
6. Use *Multimedia Workshop,* if available. It includes a word processor, scene maker, and storyboard grid to produce multimedia videos.
7. Demonstrate storyboard techniques.
8. Show a sample videotape made by students.
9. Ask the art teacher to assist with preparation of graphics and backdrops.
10. Direct rehearsals.
11. Assist student crew with videotape productions.
12. View and evaluate productions.
13. Grade group worksheets from Discussion Period III.

The students will

1. Take notes on objectives and work schedules.
2. Listen to booktalk.
3. Read novels.

4. Work with group using group guidelines.
5. Complete worksheets.
6. View sample videotape.
7. Plot storyboard.
8. Select background music.
9. Prepare graphics and backdrops.
10. Assemble costumes and properties.
11. Videotape production.
12. View class productions and evaluate them on a closed ballot with a rating scale of 1 to 4 (poor to excellent).

Evaluative Criteria

Given specific information about the elements of a novel, a list of the classics, student activity sheets, a sample storyboard, and directions, students will select and read a novel from the classics, participate in small group discussions, and discuss the elements of style. They will make a videotape production.

Further Suggestions

This lesson can be shortened by omitting the videotape production. Students who need extra help in reading may enjoy using the Wishbone Classics, retold classics in a simplified version, such as:

Shelly, Mary Wollstonecraft. 1996. *Frankenstein.*
Shakespeare, William. 1996. *Romeo and Juliet.*

Another suggestion is to use the Audio Language Studies from Durkin Hayes audiocassettes (PermaBound Read-Along with Perma-Bound Book, abridged version):

Adventures of Huckleberry Finn

Black Beauty

Little Women

Moby Dick

Red Badge of Courage

Tom Sawyer

The Secret Garden

Treasure Island

Students who are more advanced readers will benefit from the suggestions in the professional resource for teachers *From Hinton to Hamlet: Building Bridges Between Young Adult Literature and the Classics* by Sarah Herz, with Donald Gallo (1996).

Guidelines for Group Discussions

Name: _____

Group Number: _____

Date: _____

Directions: After reading the novel, select a group leader to guide the discussion periods and a recorder to list the major ideas discussed. Students may take the completed notes and use a word processor to record Discussion Period conclusions.

Discussion Period I:

Overview of the novel: Briefly summarize the novel by stating the beginning, middle, and end of the novel. Each person should contribute ideas.

Discussion Period II:

Discuss each part of the Book Analysis Worksheet. Students may use their books to verify answers. Choose the best answers for the recorder to write on the worksheet.

Turn in group worksheet to the teacher for a letter grade.

Discussion Period III:

Review and recall comments, ideas, and the booktalks on the classics. Define what is meant by the classics. Dictionaries and literary reference books and materials in the library media center may be used. Answer the following question: Why do you think that the novel your group read is considered a classic? Record the group's answer and turn it in to the library media specialist for a letter grade.

Discussion Period IV:

Brainstorm with group to choose a scene from the novel to dramatize for the videotape production. You may want to read some selections aloud and to do some role-playing. Remember to use imagination!

Book Analysis Worksheet

Name: _____

Group Number: _____

Date: _____

Author: _____   Title: _____

Publisher: _____   Copyright: _____

Directions: As a group, complete the following outline. Books may be used.

Setting: Time _____

Place _____

Identify the main characters:

_____

_____

Briefly describe the plot:

_____

_____

Describe the tone:

_____

_____

Briefly characterize the author's style of writing:

_____

_____

Specify the point of view:

_____

_____

_____

LESSON FOUR

Title
"R. G. T. P. L.—Over!"

Overview
The purpose of this lesson is to instruct students in the use of the *Readers' Guide to Periodical Literature* and electronic indexes to locate information in magazines and newspapers on catastrophes or disasters that have happened in the last five years. Students will complete a chart on worldwide catastrophes. They will use print, nonprint, and courseware materials to locate additional background information on at least three disasters.

Library Media Skills Objectives
Use *Readers' Guide to Periodical Literature.*

Use electronic periodical databases.

Locate and use microfiche.

Competency Goals and Objectives
The learner will have an understanding of the relevant historical and current topics in science or social studies.

Subject Area
Science, Social Studies, or Interdisciplinary Team.

Learning Strategy
Discussion, demonstration, research, and practice.

Resources
Readers' Guide to Periodical Literature
Bibliographic databases: *Wilsonline, NewsBank CD Jr., and Tom Jr. (Infotrac)* magazine database with full text articles

Dictionaries

Magazines

Microfiche

Worldwide Catastrophes Chart

Transparencies for teaching use of *Readers' Guide to Periodical Literature*

Print
Branley, Franklyn. 1987. *Raining Cats and Dogs*: *All Kinds of Weather and Why We Have It.*
Lauber, Patricia. 1996. *Flood*: *Wrestling with the Mississippi.*
Lauber, Patricia. 1996. *Hurricanes: Earth's Mightiest Storms.*
McMillan, Bruce. 1991. *The Weather Sky.*
McVey, Vicki. 1991. *The Sierra Club Book of Weather Wisdom.*
The World Almanac and Book of Facts. 1997.

Nonprint and Courseware
Earthquakes: Be prepared! 1994. Cambrix. CD-ROM.
Eyewitness virtual reality earth quest. 1997. Dorling Kindersley Multimedia. CD-ROM.
Geomedia. 1996. InterNetwork Media. CD-ROM.
Violent storms. 1986. Coronet. Videocassette.

Professional
Munsart, Craig A. 1997. *American history through earth science.*

Methods

The teacher will

1. Plan the unit with the library media specialist and decide on areas of responsibility for teaching.

2. Introduce the unit by using a multimedia projection panel to show either a videocassette or CD-ROM on the violence of earthquakes or volcanoes. An excellent choice would be the Dorling Kindersley Violent Earth section in *Eyewitness Virtual Reality Earth Quest.*

3. Ask the students to define: Catastrophes, drought, disasters, hurricane, volcano eruption, tornado, flood, typhoon, monsoon, earthquake, tidal wave, and avalanche. Give out dictionaries or ask students to find the best meanings in electronic encyclopedias and dictionaries.

4. Discuss historic catastrophes: San Francisco Earthquake of 1906, tornadoes in Mississippi and Georgia in 1936, flood in Hunan Province in China in 1995, cyclone in Bangladesh in 1970, hurricane in the Caribbean and southeast United States in 1989, and typhoon in Hong Kong in 1906. Give statistics about the loss of lives during these disasters.

5. Give out chart on worldwide catastrophes. Tell the students that they will complete the charts by using magazines or databases from the last five years. The library media specialist will instruct them in using an index to locate magazines, microfiche, or databases.

6. Schedule classes in the library media center and computer lab for instruction and research.

7. Divide students into five groups for orientation purposes.

8. Check and grade completed charts.

9. Evaluate unit with library media specialist.

10. Use Craig A. Munsart's *American History Through Earth Science* for additional suggestions regarding hands-on activities, references, and resources.

The library media specialist will

1. Prepare transparencies for teaching the use of *Readers Guide to Periodical Literature.*

2. For each group, arrange cumulative copies (semimonthly, quarterly, and annually) of the *Readers' Guide to Periodical Literature* for the last five years.

3. Use transparencies and copies of the *Readers' Guide to Periodical Literature* for discussion with class involvement, flashing the transparencies on the screen to focus student attention during the discussion. Tell students that even though they will often be using electronic resources, it will be helpful for them to know how to use cumulative indexes.

4. Tell students that to locate magazine articles, they will need the following information:
   - title of magazine

- date of magazine
- title of article
- volume and pages

5. Instruct students in the use of the entries in the *Readers' Guide to Periodical Literature*.
6. Instruct students in the use of available electronic magazine databases.
7. Assess students' ability to successfully locate information on catastrophes and disasters in magazines and newspapers.

The students will

1. View the introductory program.
2. Use dictionaries to define terms.
3. Discuss historical catastrophes.
4. Follow directions given by the library media specialist in using the *Readers' Guide to Periodical Literature* and electronic databases.
5. Use information in magazines and other resources to complete the worldwide catastrophes chart.

Evaluative Criteria

The students will correctly use the *Readers' Guide to Periodical Literature* and electronic databases to locate information in magazines and newspapers and use additional resources to complete the worldwide catastrophes chart.

Further Suggestions

The lesson may be expanded to include other catastrophes such as shipwrecks, aircraft disasters, railroad disasters, explosions, drought, famine, fires, oil spills, kidnappings, assassinations, and nuclear accidents.

Worldwide Catastrophes Chart

Name of Catastrophe	Cause (Man or Nature)	Country	Year	Description of Event

Readers' Guide to Periodical Literature

Suggestions for Transparencies

Readers' Guide to Periodical Literature
- a subject index to magazine articles
- authors of articles are provided, if available
- lists of magazines indexed and abbreviations used in citations are included
- published semimonthly; cumulative issues published quarterly and annually (in hard-bound issue)

A. Sample Entry

   FLOODS-subject entry

   title of article

   title of magazine

   volume and page

   date of magazine

B. Important terms
   - subject entry
   - author entry
   - see reference
   - see also reference

LESSON FIVE

Title
Kaleidoscope of Inventions

Overview
The purpose of this lesson is to allow students to use critical and creative thinking skills by gathering, processing, and using information. They will learn about the history of inventions and the inventors themselves. Students will work in groups and will be encouraged to discover some of the ingredients of the creative process as they learn by inventing their own solutions to everyday problems. The best products will be entered in the science fair. Parents will be invited to participate in a workshop on how to assist the students in displaying and explaining their experiments.

Library Media Skills Objectives
Use systematic processes to seek and use information.

Judge quality and usefulness of resources for specific tasks.

Communicate information and ideas through products and presentation.

Locate illustrations.

Use books and electronic media to obtain information.

Prepare a bibliography.

Competency Goals and Objectives
1. The learner will explore research processes and use information to create, produce, and present the final product.
2. The learner will work collaboratively with other students to communicate information and complete a task.

Subject Area
Science, Language Arts, Industrial Arts, or Art.

Learning Strategy
Lecture, demonstration, group projects, and displays.

Resources
List of inventors

Bibliographic cards on 4" x 6" index cards

Transparency of a sample bibliographic card

Print
Aaseng, Nathan. 1988. *The Inventors: Nobel Prizes in Chemistry, Physics, and Medicine.*
Bender, Lionel. 1991. *Invention.*
Caney, Steven. 1985. *Invention Book.*
Clements, Gillian. 1993. *The Picture History of Great Inventors.*
Eureka! Scientific Discoveries and Inventions That Shaped the World. 6 volumes. 1995.
Jeffrey, Laura S. 1996. *American Inventors of the 20th Century.*

Karnes, Frances A., and Suzanne M. Bean. 1995. *Girls and Young Women Inventing: Twenty True Stories About Inventors Plus How You Can Be One Yourself.*

Lomask, Milton. 1991. *Great Lives: Invention and Technology.*

Mitchell, Barbara. 1986. *A Pocketful of Goobers: A Story About George Washington Carver.*

Mitchell, Barbara. 1986. *Shoes for Everyone: A Story About Jan Matzeliger.*

Science and Technology: Inventions. 1997. In *The World Almanac and Book of Facts.*

Tucker, Tom. 1995. *Brainstorm! The Stories of Twenty American Kid Inventors.*

Vecchione, Glen. 1995. *100 Amazing Make-It-Yourself Science Fair Projects.*

Williams, Trevor I. 1987. *The History of Invention.*

Nonprint and Courseware

Invention studio. 1996. Discovery Channel. CD-ROM.

Macaulay, David. 1994. *The way things work.* Dorling Kindersley Multimedia. CD-ROM.

Methods

The teacher will

1. Explain the purpose of the activity.

2. Explain the process of using the scientific method, which is necessary for investigation involving the observation of phenomena, the formulation of a hypothesis, experimentation to demonstrate the truth or falseness of the hypothesis, and arriving at a conclusion that validates or modifies the hypothesis.

3. Distribute a list of inventors to each student group.

4. Tell the students that each group must choose three individuals from their list of inventors. They must locate information about the inventors and their inventions and complete a bibliographic card that includes a summary of their work. They should brainstorm ideas for a group project and use scientific procedures to invent their own solutions to an everyday problem. The best products will be entered in the science fair.

5. Schedule classes to use the library media center and computer lab.

The library media specialist will

1. Reserve books on inventors and inventions.

2. Review use of an index in books and encyclopedias.

3. Review search strategies for electronic media.

4. Make bibliographic cards for students' use.

5. Demonstrate how to locate bibliographic information and transfer it to cards.

6. As an example show Jeffrey's book, *American Inventors of the 20th Century.* Demonstrate how to locate information on Lonnie Johnson and his unusual invention.

7. Show a transparency sample of the completed bibliographic data card.

8. Assist students in locating and compiling bibliographic information.

9. Use the CD-ROM *Invention Studio,* if available, to show a sample of a student-designed invention that will heighten students' interest in creating inventions.

The students will

1. Work in groups to select three inventors for research.
2. Locate information and discuss data with each other.
3. Compile information on bibliographic cards.
4. Discuss ideas for experiments and focus on the process of making connections of common objects in ways to make whimsical inventions.
5. Work as a group to construct a model of their invention.
6. Prepare a display for their invention. Parents may assist with the display.

Evaluative Criteria

The students will successfully locate information about inventors and inventions and will compile bibliographic data on cards. They will produce a group project.

List of Inventors

List of Inventors for Group 1: Archimedes, Johann Gutenberg, Robert Fulton, Thomas Edison, Jan Matzeliger

List of Inventors for Group 2: Leonardo da Vinci, Gerhardus Mercator, Wilbur and Orville Wright, Enrico Fermi, Philo Farnsworth

List of Inventors for Group 3: Isaac Merritt Singer, Galileo Galilei, Alexander Graham Bell, Auguste Lumière, George Washington Carver

List of Inventors for Group 4: Blaise Pascal, Isaac Newton, Joseph Lister, Eli Whitney, Louis Braille

List of Inventors for Group 5: Wernher von Braun, Antoni van Leeuwenhoek, Alfred Nobel, Albert Einstein, John Dunlop

List of Inventors for Group 6: Benjamin Franklin, Richard Arkwright, Elisha Otis, Samuel Colt, Guglielmo Marconi

List of Inventors for Group 7: James Watt, Antoine Lavoisier, Samuel Morse, Michael Faraday, George Eastman

List of Inventors for Group 8: Edward Jenner, Alessandro Volta, Karl Benz and Gottlieb Daimler, Carl Zeiss, Rosalind Franklin

Bibliography Card

Group number: _____

Subject: _____

Author: _____

Copyright: _____

Title: _____

Place of publication: _____

Publisher: _____

Type of medium: _____

Illustrations: _____

Include a brief summary of the collected data on the back of this card.

Sample Bibliography Card 1

Group number: 1 _____

Subject: Lonnie Johnson and the Super Soakers Toy Water Gun _____

Author: Jeffrey, Laura S. _____

Copyright: 1996 _____

Title: *American Inventors of the 20th Century.* _____

Place of publication: Springfield, N.J.; Publisher: Enslow _____

Type of medium: Book _____

Pages: 94-104 _____

Illustrations: p. 94 _____

Include a brief summary of the collected data on the back of this card.

Sample Bibliography Card 2

Lonnie Johnson invented a water gun called Super Soakers. When he was young, he took his toys apart to see how they were made. When he was a senior in high school, he built a four-and-a-half-foot robot. He received a college scholarship to Tuskegee University. He joined the Air Force and became a spacecraft engineer. Later he tried to start his own business, but it failed.

In 1989, he took his water gun to the Toy Fair in New York City. He met an executive from the Larami Toy Company who wanted to manufacture the water guns. The Super Soakers were an instant success on the market. More than $47 million worth of Super Soakers have been sold.

LESSON SIX

Title

The Past Is Prologue

Overview

The purpose of this lesson is to encourage students to read a historical fiction book of their choice for their enjoyment.

Library Media Skills Objectives

Recognize different types of fiction.

Select reading as a leisure time activity.

Use library catalogs.

Competency Goals and Objectives

The learner will experience a wide variety of reading, listening, and viewing experiences; participate in booktalk experiences; and identify characteristics of different genres.

Subject Area

Reading, Language Arts, Social Studies, or Interdisciplinary Team.

Learning Strategy

Discussion, booktalk, practice, and using learning center.

Resources

Information card

Print

Blos, Joan W. 1994. *A Gathering of Days: A New England Girl's Journal, 1830-32.*

Clapp, Patricia. 1968. *Constance: A Story of Early Plymouth.*

Denenberg, Barry. 1996. *When Will This Cruel War Be Over? The Civil War Diary of Emma Simpson, Gordonville, Virginia.*

Fleischman, Paul. 1991. *The Borning Room.*

Forbes, Esther. 1943. *Johnny Tremain.*

Fox, Paula. 1973. *The Slave Dancer.*

Fritz, Jean. 1967. *Early Thunder.*

Gregory, Kristiana. 1997. *The Winter of the Red Snow: The Revolutionary Diary of Abigail Jane Stewart.*

Heneghan, James. 1997. *Wish Me Luck.*

Hunt, Irene. 1964. *Across Five Aprils.*

Keith, Harold. 1957. *Rifles for Watie.*

Lasky, Kathryn. 1996. *A Journey to the New World: The Diary of Remember Patience Whipple, Mayflower, 1620.*

MacLachlan, Patricia. 1985. *Sarah, Plain and Tall.*

Nixon, Joan Lowery. 1992. *Land of Hope.*

Paterson, Katherine. 1974. *Of Nightingales That Weep.*

Reiss, Johanna. 1972. *The Upstairs Room.*

Speare, Elizabeth George. 1958. *The Witch of Blackbird Pond.*

Sutcliff, Rosemary. 1976. *Blood Feud.*

Taylor, Mildred. 1976. *Roll of Thunder, Hear My Cry.*

Turner, Megan Whalen. 1996. *The Thief.*
Wilder, Laura Ingalls. 1953. *Little House on the Prairie.*
Wood, Frances M. 1996. *Becoming Rosemary.*

Professional

Hartman, Donald K., and Greg Sapp. 1994. *Historical figures in fiction.*
Norton, Donna E. 1991. *Through the eyes of a child: An introduction to children's literature.* 3d ed.
Spencer, Pam. 1994. *What do young adults read next? A reader's guide to fiction for young adults.*

Methods

The teacher will

1. Discuss the characteristics of historical fiction.
2. Explain the objectives of reading for enjoyment.
3. Schedule one class period for booktalks and one for learning center activities.

The library media specialist will

1. Dress in costumes to present booktalks on historical fiction.
2. Review historical fiction books that have won the Newbery Award.
3. Use transparencies to show examples of subject headings of historical fiction books.
4. Utilize videotapes for learning centers.

The students will

1. Listen to booktalks.
2. View videotapes in learning centers.
3. Locate titles and authors of historical fiction in the library catalogs.
4. Select and read a historical fiction book of their choice for their enjoyment.
5. Complete the information card for the teacher.

Evaluative Criteria

The students will locate, select, and read a historical fiction book of their choice for their enjoyment. They will not be required to make a report or project.

Further Suggestions

- Many videotapes are available on the books listed in the resource list. Also, many of these books are available in paperback editions with later copyright dates.

- This lesson can also be used with Social Studies units by using the book *Historical Figures in Fiction.* 1994. It has an index to characters in historical fiction featuring 1,300 famous people.

- Students could make a time line using the *Timeliner* computer program that shows the chronological and historical aspects of the historical novels.

- At Hammond Middle School in Howard County, Maryland, students made a videotape entitled "Historical Hat Parade!" Students wore hats or headdress as they portrayed characters from historical fiction books. For more information on this production, see the article "Historical Hat Parade! A Single-Camera Video Production" (1985, 38-39, 42, 45).

Sample Information Card

Name: _____

Date: _____

I have read the following historical fiction book:

Author: _____

Title: _____

Publisher: _____

Copyright date: _____

Place and historical period: _____

_____

LESSON SEVEN

Title
Here's to Health

Overview
The purpose of this lesson is to provide students with the necessary skills to effectively research and prepare a written report on a disease.

Library Media Skills Objectives
Locate material using library catalogs.

Use print and electronic encyclopedias.

Use the vertical file/information file.

Use the *Readers' Guide to Periodical Literature.*

Select material based on usefulness, appropriateness, and accuracy.

Interpret information.

Identify the main idea.

Prepare notes, an outline, and a bibliography.

Competency Goals and Objectives
1. The learner will identify elements of composition and assess reliability, relevance, and integrity of resources.
2. The learner will create a report using a word processor.

Subject Area
Health or Social Studies.

Learning Strategy
Lecture, demonstration, and individual project.

Resources
Sample note card

Transparencies of a sample report (including notes, outline, and bibliography)

Report guidelines

General encyclopedias

Science encyclopedias

Health textbook

Dictionaries

Print
Aaseng, Nathan. 1995. *Autoimmune Diseases.*
American Medical Association Family Medical Guide. 1994. rev. ed.
Burnett, Gail Lemley. 1996. *Muscular Dystrophy.*
Gold, John Coopersmith 1996. *Heart Disease.*
Gold, Susan Dudley. 1996. *Alzheimer's Disease.*
Harris, Jacqueline L. 1993. *Communicable Diseases.*
Kehret, Peg. 1996. *Small Steps: The Year I Got Polio.*

McKeever, Susan, ed. 1993. *The Dorling Kindersley Science Encyclopedia.*
Semple, Carol McCormick. 1996. *Diabetes.*
Sullivan, Helen, and Linda Sernoff. 1996. *Research Reports: A Guide for Middle and High School Students.*
Thomas, Peggy. 1997. *Medicines from Nature.*

Nonprint and Courseware

Expression. 1995. Sunburst Communications. Diskette.
Researcher. 1995. Learning in Motion. Diskette.

Methods

The teacher will

1. Suggest topics for disease reports.
2. Suggest subtopics: Description, symptoms, causes, prevention, and treatment.
3. Remind students to include the sources of information in notes.
4. Schedule classes in the library media center and in the computer lab.
5. Assist students with research.
6. Grade disease reports.

The library media specialist will

1. Review location and use of print, nonprint, and courseware resources including software programs such as *Expression* and *Researcher.*
2. Discuss note taking, outlining, and summarizing.
3. Demonstrate study skill procedures by showing transparencies of a completed disease report with notes, outline, and bibliography. As an alternative, show excerpts from a software program.
4. Read a sample report to the class, such as one included in the book *Research Reports: A Guide for Middle and High School Students* by Sullivan and Sernoff.
5. Assist individual students as necessary.
6. Read and evaluate completed reports.

The students will

1. Attend lecture.
2. Review note taking, outlining, and summarizing using a software program.
3. Observe demonstration of sample reports.
4. Locate source material, prepare notes and outline, write a report using a word processor, and compile a bibliography.

Evaluative Criteria

The students will follow all directions correctly and will submit a research report on a disease.

Sample Note Card: Disease Reports

Chicken pox

Description: Acute infectious disease. Itchy rash of blister-like lesions.

Symptoms: Rash, crusty sores, low-grade fever. Adults, after years of dormancy, may develop shingles with flu-like symptoms before the rash appears.

Causes: Herpes zoster virus.

Prevention: There is no general vaccine. It is highly contagious. It is usually a child-hood disease that results in a life-long immunity. Adults are susceptible to the disease and may develop complications.

Treatment: Topical medication, such as a soothing cream or lotion applied to relieve the itching. An antihistamine may be prescribed in severe cases. An antibiotic ointment may be necessary if spots become infected.

Source of information:
The Concise Columbia Encyclopedia. 1995. Columbia University Press. Online.
American Medical Association Family Medical Guide. 1994. rev. ed.

Report Guidelines

Writing a Research Paper on Diseases

Objective: The student will write a well-organized, concise report on a disease and include a bibliography showing the sources of information. The student will use the following steps in preparing the report:

1. Determine the topic.
2. Locate information.
3. Skim information.
4. Make an outline of subtopics.
5. Take notes on cards or use printed notes from a software program. Include bibliographic information.
6. Write report using a word processor.
7. Make bibliography.
8. Turn in notes with the report.

LESSON EIGHT

Title
Big Time Productions

Overview
The effects of advertising are keenly felt by middle school students. As they view television, listen to the radio, read magazines and newspapers, and spend hours in shopping malls, they are bombarded with advertisements. To help them identify propaganda, fact, and opinion, students will complete assignments concerning advertising techniques and use these techniques to create their own commercials on videotape or as live presentations to the class. Students will complete a written group assignment.

Library Media Skills Objectives
Locate and use all necessary sources to gather information for a specified subject.

Distinguish between fact and opinion.

Use organizational skills to produce a videotape recording or a live production.

Competency Goals and Objectives
The learner will critique information sources and formats, assess reliability, relevance, and integrity of resources, and recognize the power of media to influence.

Subject Area
Reading, Language Arts, or Interdisciplinary Team.

Learning Strategy
Reading, practice, viewing, discussion, and completing audiovisual project.

Resources
Group guidelines
Group report forms
Print
Bielak, Mark. 1995. *Television Production Today*. 3d ed.

Lipson, Michelle, and friends. 1994. *The Fantastic Costume Book: 40 Complete Patterns to Amaze and Amuse*.

Miles, Betty. 1981. *The Secret Life of the Underwear Champ*.

Journal Articles
McDonnell, Sharon. 1995. In from the cold. *American Journalism Review* 17 (June): 16-17. Available: WilsonDisc. CD-ROM.

Munk, Nina. 1997. Give me more commercials. *Forbes* 159 (June): 39-40. Available: WilsonDisc. CD-ROM.

Nonprint and Courseware
Holzman, Keith. 1987. *Authentic sound effects*. Elektra/Asylum Records. Compact disc.

Kid pix studio. 1995. Broderbund. CD-ROM.

Propaganda. 1993-95. Microsoft Encarta 96 Encyclopedia. Funk and Wagnalls Corporation. CD-ROM.

3D movie maker. 1995. Microsoft. 1995.

World War II: The propaganda battle. 1988. PBS. Videocassette.

Professional

Palmer, Edward. 1988. *Television and America's children: A crisis of neglect.*

Spero, Robert. 1980. *The duping of the American voter: Dishonesty and deception in presidential television advertising.*

Winn, Marie. 1987. *Unplugging the plug-in drug.*

Methods

The teacher will

1. Lead a discussion on propaganda, fact, and opinion by giving examples of each. Help students to understand that propaganda attempts to persuade by the use of rational or emotional appeal. It is not only used to distort fact but also is often used in organizations to promote good causes. Inform students that in this lesson they will focus on the techniques used in advertising.

2. Analyze techniques used in television advertising. Use excerpts from current journal articles.

3. Provide directions for completing propaganda/advertisement booklets.

4. Schedule library media center activities and reserve the computer lab with library media specialist.

5. Divide class into groups. Appoint chairpersons.

6. Explain group guidelines and group report forms.

7. Provide daily copies of group report forms.

The library media specialist will

1. Conduct a discussion about the purposes of commercials and their impact on the consumer.

2. Read selections from *The Secret Life of the Underwear Champ*, which is about a boy who makes underwear commercials.

3. Present information on making television commercials from *Television Production Today: Teachers' Resource Book*.

4. Show video demonstration of student-made commercials.

5. Assist students with planning and producing a commercial on videotape or a live commercial presentation.

6. View and evaluate student productions.

The students will

1. Identify propaganda, fact, and opinion used in advertisements.

2. Illustrate advertisement/propaganda techniques in booklet form.

3. View and analyze television commercials.

4. Work with an assigned group of students to plan, create, and produce a videotaped commercial or a live production.

Evaluative Criteria

The students will correctly illustrate propaganda/advertisement techniques in booklet form. They will work with their assigned group to successfully plan and produce a commercial on videotape or as a live production. Each group will be graded daily on accomplishments and work habits. The chairman is responsible for turning in a group report each day. These reports will be returned to the chairman with comments from the teacher and/or the library media specialist.

Further Suggestions

The lesson may be expanded to include information on television and the role it plays in the lives of children, the television habits of children, and suggestions for a "No TV Week."

Group Guidelines

Project: Plan and produce a commercial on videotape or as a live production.

1. Brainstorm ideas.
2. Determine objective.
3. Select product.
4. Write script.
5. Assign duties.
   a. Write storyboard or script.
   b. Prepare graphics and scenery.
   c. Select actors.
6. Rehearse scenes.
7. Produce videotape or live presentation.
8. Evaluate.

Group Report Form

Date: _____

Chairperson: _____

Group members: _____

_____

Group report: _____

_____

_____

_____

Goal accomplished today: _____

_____

_____

Goals for tomorrow: _____

_____

_____

LESSON NINE

Title

Unaccustomed As I Am to Public Speaking

Overview

The purpose of this unit is to provide students with the opportunity to develop their public speaking ability by planning, presenting, recording, viewing, and evaluating a speech.

Library Media Skills Objectives

Select resources using the library catalogs.

Select reference sources to find information on a given subject.

Select periodicals and newspapers for current information.

Summarize information found in resources.

Use note-taking skills.

Organize information.

Prepare a videotape or audiotape.

Competency Goals and Objectives

The learner will communicate reading, listening, and viewing experiences and produce media in various formats based on these experiences.

Subject Area

Reading or Language Arts.

Learning Strategy

Lecture, demonstration, practice, and creation of audiovisual project.

Resources

Bibliographic guidelines

Guidelines for making a storyboard or script

Videotape or audiotape of student speeches from previous year

Print

Dietz, Joan. 1986. *You Mean I Have to Stand Up and Say Something?*

Kaplan, Justin, ed. 1992. *Bartlett's Familiar Quotations*. 16th ed.

Lass, Abraham, David Kiremidjian, and Ruth M. Goldstein. 1987. *Dictionary of Classical, Biblical, and Literary Allusions.*

Nonprint and Courseware

Famous American speeches: A multimedia history. 1995. Oryx Press. CD-ROM.

Writer's solution: Bronze level. 1995. Prentice Hall. CD-ROM, videodisc, videotape.

Methods

The teacher will

1. Present information on effective public speaking techniques.
2. Suggest topics for speeches.
3. Define objectives and evaluative criteria.

4. Schedule reference and videotape or audiotape sessions with the library media specialist.
5. Grade written report and videotape or audiotape presentations.

The library media specialist will

1. Demonstrate use of reference sources.
2. Provide examples of videotapes or audiotapes of students' speeches from previous year.
3. Explain use of inter-library loan of material.
4. Obtain resources from other libraries.
5. Assist with research.
6. Review skills of making a bibliography.
7. Review and demonstrate storyboard and script-writing techniques.
8. Assist with videotape or audiotape productions.
9. Evaluate unit.

The students will

1. Select a topic.
2. Locate and use resources.
3. Take notes, summarize information, prepare written report, and prepare bibliography.
4. Plan and present videotaped or audiotaped speech using at least one visual aid.
5. Evaluate speeches.

Evaluative Criteria

Students will follow directions to successfully prepare a written report and an oral presentation recorded on videotape or audiotape on a topic of their choice.

LESSON TEN

Title

To Buy or Not to Buy

Overview

The purpose of this lesson is to introduce the magazines *Consumer Reports* and *Zillions* to provide students with sources of information on comparative shopping.

Library Media Skills Objectives

Use table of contents of magazines to locate articles.

Draw appropriate conclusions based on information presented.

Distinguish between fact and opinion.

Competency Goals and Objectives

The learner will critique information sources and formats and assess reliability, relevance, and integrity of resources.

Subject Area

Social Studies or Interdisciplinary Team.

Learning Strategy

Large group presentation, practice.

Resources

Classroom sets of *Consumer Reports* and *Zillions* magazines

Worksheet

Newspaper and magazine ads

Television ads

Products for taste test (cola, peanut butter, potato chips, etc.)

Transparencies ("Think Before You Spend")

Ballots

Print

Consumer Reports and *Zillions* magazines.

Schmitt, Lois. 1989. *A Young Consumer's Guide: Smart Spending*.

Webb, Farren, et al. 1995. *The World Wise Consumer: Consumer Strategies in an Age of Scarcity*.

Methods

The teacher will

1. Jointly plan the unit with the library media specialist and designate responsibilities.
2. Purchase products for taste test.
3. Schedule large group meeting of class.
4. Participate in discussion led by the library media specialist.
5. Tabulate scores from taste test.

6. Present follow-up lesson in class by distributing worksheets and copies of *Consumer Reports* and *Zillions* magazines.

The library media specialist will

1. Prepare a large group presentation.
2. Have transparency, "Think Before You Spend," on overhead projector and play a lively recording while students are being seated.
3. Ask the question, "If you want to purchase a product, where do you get information that helps you to make a wise choice?"
4. Show sample newspaper ads, magazine ads, and a television commercial. Use commercial made by students or made by teachers, if possible. Examples could be a "Fizzle Cola" or "Bubblemania" commercial.
5. Show a transparency of pages from *Zillions* (July/August 1996) on purchasing in-line skates. Tell the students that the Consumers Union provides shoppers with information on comparative shopping in *Consumer Reports* and *Zillions* magazines.
6. Give background information on the Consumers Union, laboratory tests, and ratings.
7. Present current information from the two magazines on topics of interest to middle school students such as fast foods, athletic shoes, and electronic games.
8. Ask students to participate in a taste test in which they will rate the appearance, smell, texture, and taste of several products labeled "A," "B," or "C."
9. Hand out ballots. Ask students to circle the brand that they like best.
10. Tabulate scores on chalkboard.
11. Reveal brand names for each product, which may be colas, peanut butter, potato chips, etc.
12. Evaluate lesson with teacher after students complete worksheet in class.

The students will

1. Participate in large group instruction.
2. Take taste test.
3. Complete worksheet in classroom.

Evaluative Criteria

The students will use *Consumer Reports* and *Zillions* magazines to successfully complete the worksheet.

Worksheet: To Buy or Not to Buy

1. The title of the magazine that is a special consumer magazine for young people is:

_____

2. Read an article in the consumer magazine for young people. List title of article:

_____

3. The purpose of the magazine produced by the Consumers Union is:

_____

4. How are products obtained for testing?

_____

5. Use the table of contents in one of the magazines produced by the Consumers Union to locate an article of interest to you. List the name of the magazine:

_____

Fill in the following information:

Date of issue of magazine: _____

Title of article: _____

Name of product: _____

Skim and summarize background information about the product:

_____

_____

List of terms used in ratings:

_____

_____

Is a "best buy" designated?

_____

_____

State your conclusions about the products being evaluated. Are they based on fact or opinion?

_____

_____

LESSON ELEVEN

Title
Dinosaurs Revisited

Overview
The purpose of this lesson is to use print, nonprint, and courseware to provide information on dinosaurs for students with special needs.

Library Media Skills Objectives
Find out specific information using a variety of resources.

Use an electronic resource.

Utilize collected information.

Competency Goals and Objectives
The learner will experience a wide variety of reading, listening, and viewing resources to interact with ideas.

Subject Area
Reading or Science.

Learning Strategy
Reading, viewing, listening, and discussion.

Resources
Print
Cohen, Daniel. 1987. *Dinosaurs.*
Lessem, Don. 1996. *Dinosaur Worlds: New Dinosaurs, New Discoveries.*
Norman, David. 1996. *Dinosaurs.*
Wallace, Joseph. 1994. *The American Museum of Natural History's Book of Dinosaurs and Other Ancient Creatures.*

Professional
Charlesworth, Liza, and Bonnie Sachatello-Sawyer. 1995. *Dinosaurs.*

Nonprint and Courseware
Dinosaur discovery. 1993. Applied Optical Media. CD-ROM.
Dinosaurs on Earth: Then . . . and now. 1995. National Geographic Society. Videocassette.
Eyewitness virtual reality dinosaur hunter. 1996. Dorling Kindersley Multimedia. CD-ROM.
Prehistoria. 1994. Grolier Electronic. CD-ROM.

Methods
The teacher will
1. Introduce the lesson by writing these vocabulary words on the chalkboard or on a transparency: dinosaurs, fossils, paleontologist, virtual reality, and extinct.
2. Tell the students that they are going to the library media center and the computer lab to learn about dinosaurs.
3. Schedule class with library media specialist.

4. Discuss lesson with students after they return to class.
5. Plan a field trip to a museum to view exhibits of fossils or use the CD-ROM *Eyewitness Virtual Reality Dinosaur Hunter*.

The library media specialist will

1. Show portions of the CD-ROM *Prehistoria*.
2. Discuss the information presented.
3. Display books of dinosaurs and prehistoric mammals and birds.

The students will

1. Learn vocabulary words.
2. View multimedia presentations.
3. Discuss the world in which dinosaurs lived.
4. Do such optional activities as
   - make a booklet to record scientific names and descriptions of dinosaurs;
   - check out and read a book on dinosaurs;
   - draw pictures of dinosaurs;
   - make clay models of dinosaurs;
   - record a story about dinosaurs;
   - follow suggestions of the teacher for additional activities.

Evaluative Criteria

The students will correctly identify scientific names and descriptions of at least five dinosaurs.

Further Suggestions

Use the book *Dinosaurs* by Charlesworth and Sachatello-Sawyer for suggested activities on a thematic unit of study. The material can be adapted to the ability and interest levels of the students.

LESSON TWELVE

Title

What's Cooking?

Overview

The purpose of this lesson is for students to locate information on foods, nutrition, health, and fitness using a variety of print, nonprint, and courseware resources. Students will prepare a project using the information from the resources.

Library Media Skills Objectives

Use subject headings to locate resources.

Use the Dewey decimal classification system to locate resources.

Competency Goals and Objectives

The learner will collect information and ideas, synthesize and organize information, and follow or produce directions to create a product.

Subject Area

Home Economics, Health, or Interdisciplinary Team.

Learning Strategy

Lecture, discussion, research, and creating project.

Resources

Transparencies (subject headings)

Dewey decimal classification system

The Internet

E-mail

Print

Albyn, Carole Lisa, and Lois Sinaiko Webb. 1993. *The Multicultural Cookbook for Students.*

Cleary, Frances. 1995. *American Home Cooking.*

Diamond, Wendy, comp. 1995. *A Musical Feast: Recipes from over 100 of the World's Most Famous Musical Artists.*

Fraser, Linda, consultant ed. 1996. *Best-Ever Chicken: 200 Step-by-Step Chicken Recipes.*

Galperin, Ann. 1990. *Nutrition.*

Parker, Steve. 1994. *How the Body Works.*

Patent, Dorothy Hinshaw. 1992. *Nutrition: What's in the Food We Eat.*

Nonprint and Courseware

Better Homes and Gardens healthy cooking deluxe. 1996. Multicom. CD-ROM.

Mayo Clinic sports health and fitness. 1994. IVI. CD-ROM.

The magic school bus explores the human body. 1996. Scholastic. CD-ROM.

The teacher will

1. Plan the objectives and activities with the library media specialist.

2. Introduce the unit and discuss the objectives with the students.

3. Use the book *A Musical Feast: Recipes from over 100 of the World's Most Famous Musical Artists*, compiled by Wendy Diamond, to share some recipes from famous musical artists.

4. Give students copies of suggested topics.
5. Schedule and accompany classes in the library media center and computer lab.
6. Serve as a resource person to students.
7. Grade student projects.
8. Evaluate unit with library media specialist.

The library media specialist will

1. Prepare and use transparencies to review subject headings and the Dewey decimal classification numbers for nutrition, food, health, and fitness.
2. Assist students in locating print, nonprint, and courseware reference materials.
3. Review search procedures for locating resources.
4. Promote the use of electronic resources such as the Internet and e-mail.
5. Assist students with preparation of graphics or audiovisual aids for projects.
6. Attend student presentations of projects.
7. Evaluate lesson with teacher.

The students will

1. Select a topic.
2. Participate in review of library media skills.
3. Use the library catalogs and the Dewey decimal classification system.
4. Locate resources for topics by using appropriate search procedures.
5. Plan and prepare a project to present to the class.

Evaluative Criteria

The students will successfully locate information and prepare and present a project to the class on a nutrition topic, a food, a food dish, or a health and fitness theme.

Further Suggestions

This lesson can be used as an interdisciplinary unit to accompany the study of countries of the world. Multicultural activities and festivals with foods and fitness programs add a special dimension to student learning and pleasure.

Sample Topics

Nutrition
Food additives
Basic food groups
Milk and milk products
Obesity and nutrition
Fad diets
Vegetarians
Frozen foods
Snacks
Vitamins
Health foods
Foods
Common name of food
Latin name or name of origin
Background information
How food is used

Recipes
Variation of recipes around the world
Preparation and procedures
Serving suggestions
Interesting facts
Health and Fitness
Preservation of mental and physical well-being
Fitness centers and spas
Exercise
Sports medicine
Hygiene
Medical check-ups
Prescription and over-the-counter drugs
Aging
Communicable diseases
Nutrition

Transparency: Subject Headings

Food
see also
COOKERY

Recipes
see also
COOKERY

See also names of foods, e.g.
POTATOES
COCOA
SPINACH

Additional subject headings
Nutrition
Diet
Weight Control

**Transparency for the Selected
Dewey Decimal Classification:
Technology (Applied Sciences)**

600 Technology (Applied Sciences)
630 Agriculture
633 Field and Plantation Crops
640 Home Economics and Family Living
641 Food and Drink
642 Meals and Table Service

LESSON THIRTEEN

Title
Let's Visit Asia!

Overview
The purpose of this unit is to have students locate and use information on a selected Asian country. They will work in groups, select a country, compile information, and prepare a multimedia news program for videotaping or for a live production.

Library Media Skills Objectives
Locate and use print almanacs, atlases, encyclopedias, periodicals, maps, and filmstrips.

Use electronic media.

Use an online catalog.

Use a multimedia format for presentation of information.

Competency Goals and Objectives
1. The learner will engage in a research process to meet information needs and develop a research strategy to access, critique, and use information.
2. The learner will demonstrate knowledge and skills in using computer technology to generate various types of productions.

Subject Area
Social Studies or Interdisciplinary Team.

Learning Strategy
Discussion, practice, and creation of group project and multimedia production.

Resources
List of Asian countries

List of facts for research

Print
Albyn, Carole Lisa, and Lois Sinaiko Webb. 1993. *The Multicultural Cookbook for Students.*
Bloom, Dwila. 1994. *Multicultural Art Activities Kit.*
Burckhardt, Ann L. 1996. *The People of China and Their Food.*
Festivals of the World: China. 1997.
Fox, Mary Virginia. 1991. *Iran.*
Junior Worldmark Encyclopedia of the Nations. 1996. 9 vols.
Lamy, Steven, et. al. 1994. *Teaching Global Awareness with Simulations and Games.*
McNair, Sylvia. 1987. *Thailand.*
Takada, Noriko, and Rita Lampkin. 1997. *The Japanese Way: Aspects of Behavior, Attitudes, and Customs of the Japanese.*
Williams, Suzanne. 1996. *Made in China: Ideas and Inventions from Ancient China.*
Yuan, Juliana Y. 1992. *Our Global Village: China.*

Nonprint and Courseware
Cartopedia. 1995. Dorling Kindersley Multimedia. CD-ROM.
Children of Bali. 1991. Coronet. Videocassette.
The Chinese word for horse. (n.d.). The Media Guild. Videocassette.
Eyewitness history of the world. 1995. Dorling Kindersley Multimedia. CD-ROM.
Faces of Japan I. 1989. Pacific Mountain Network. Videocassette Series.
Microsoft Encarta 96 world atlas. 1995. Microsoft. CD-ROM.
Multimedia workshop. 1996. Davidson. CD-ROM.
Sadako and the thousand paper cranes. 1990. Informed Democracy. Videocassette.
South Korea. 1996. Upbeat Media. Videocassette.
U.X.L. Junior Worldmark. 1997. U.X.L. CD-ROM.
Vietnam. 1993. Upbeat Media. Videocassette.

Magazines and Indexes
National Geographic
Newsweek
Time
U. S. News and World Report

Methods

The teacher will
1. Prepare a selected list of Asian countries for research.
2. Prepare a list of issues for research on a selected country.
3. Divide students into groups of five.
4. Ask each group to choose a country for research.
5. Schedule classes in the library media center and computer lab for research.
6. Schedule groups in production center for videotaping or in large group area for a live production and presentation.
7. Remind students to compare and contrast ideas and to determine cause and effect relationships.
8. Evaluate students' understanding of the issues.
9. Evaluate videotapes or live productions with library media specialist.

The library media specialist will
1. Review the location and use of special reference books.
2. Review search procedures and use of courseware.
3. Assist students in compiling and interpreting data.
4. Rehearse news program with students.
5. If students are making videotapes, assign library media aides or media technician to videotape news programs on each country.

The students will
1. Work cooperatively with assigned group.
2. Select a chairperson of the group.
3. Assign specific areas of research to individual group members.
4. Select an Asian country for research.
5. Locate and use reference sources.
6. Compile data.
7. Analyze data.
8. Utilize data, making sure that all students contribute to group effort.

9. Write script and make assignment of parts and duties.
10. Prepare background scenery and graphics.
11. Use a large map of the country and its flag in background scenery.
12. Have a weatherman describe climate, topography, and natural resources.
13. Use an anchor or chairperson and several reporters to present information on the researched issues.
14. Use phrases or sayings in the various languages of the country.
15. Prepare a storyboard for videotaping or script for a live production of news program.
16. Make a title sign using name of country.
17. Prepare scenery and graphics using clip art, computer-generated graphics, or film clips.
18. Use background music native to the country or from its cultural heritage.
19. Rehearse scenes.
20. Dress in native or festival clothing (optional).
21. Present news program for videotaping or for a live production.

Evaluative Criteria

The students will successfully locate and use information on an Asian country and will produce a videotaped or live production of the news program.

Further Suggestions

If the study is a part of an Interdisciplinary Unit, expand it to include a festival involving students in multicultural activities related to Asian countries in which students and teachers dress in costumes, play games, prepare and eat food, dance, sing, and view or perform in skits and puppet shows.

The resources listed are representative of resources available on many other Asian countries.

LESSON FOURTEEN

Title

Be a Quiz Whiz: Identify Famous People of the World

Overview

The purpose of this lesson is for students to learn about the accomplishments of famous people of the world by locating and using information in various print, nonprint, and courseware resources. Students who choose to do so will compete in a quiz contest on famous people of the world.

Library Media Skills Objectives

Use special dictionaries.

Use an index of special reference sources.

Interpret information found in resources.

Competency Goals and Objectives

The learner will collect information about diverse people and cultures and identify contributions of individuals.

Subject Area

Social Studies or Interdisciplinary Team.

Learning Strategy

Learning centers, computer lab, research, creating product.

Resources

Pictures or study prints of famous people

Quiz

Print

General Reference Books
Biography Index
Current Biography
Dictionary of American Biography
The International Who's Who
McGraw Hill Encyclopedia of World Biography
Webster's New Biographical Dictionary

Individual biographies

Collective biographies
Bragg, Janet Harmon. 1996. *Soaring Above Setbacks: The Autobiography of Janet Harmon Bragg.*
Collective Biographies Series: *African-American Poets.* 1996.
Contemporary African American Series: *Colin Powell.* 1996.
Fleischman, Sid. 1996. *The Abracadabra Kid: A Writer's Life.*
Green, Carol. 1983. *Mother Teresa: Friend of the Friendless.*
Horwitz, Margot F. 1996. *A Female Focus: Great Women Photographers.*
The Importance of Jane Goodall. The Importance of Series. 1997.
Steve Young: NFL Passing Wizard. Millbrook Sports World Series. 1996.

Morey, Janet Nomura, and Wendy Dunn. 1996. *Famous Hispanic Americans.*
Neimark, Anne E. 1996. *Myth Maker*: *J. R. R. Tolkien.*
Saari, Peggy, and Stephen Allison, eds. 1996. *Scientists: The Lives and Works of 150 Scientists.* 3 vols.
Venezia, Mike. 1996. Getting to Know the World's Greatest Artists Series.

Nonprint and Courseware

Eye witness history of the world. 1995. Dorling Kindersley Multimedia. CD-ROM.

Methods

The teacher will

1. Tell students that the library media specialist has prepared a quiz contest on the lives of famous people who have accomplished greatness in their fields. Students who wish to enter the contest may go to the library media center to use the biographical reference materials on reserve.

2. Inform students that this is a voluntary assignment or supplemental activity.

3. Permit individual students or small groups of students to go to the library media center and computer lab to complete the quiz when time is available.

4. Display the winning entry in class area.

The library media specialist will

1. Arrange an attractive display of pictures of famous people in the library media center quiz station or learning center.

2. Place biographical references on reserve in the learning center and in the computer lab.

3. Prepare the quiz questions using the biographical reference sources available in the library media center or computer lab.

4. Grade quiz entries. Place all entries with the correct answers in a box. Draw one entry from the box. Post the name of the winner in the library media center. Return the winning entry to the teacher to display in the classroom.

5. Award a prize to the winner. The prize could be a biography of a famous person on the list.

The students will

1. Use special reference resources to complete the quiz.

2. Enter their answers in the quiz contest.

Evaluative Criteria

The students will successfully complete the quiz and enter it in the quiz contest on famous people.

<u>**Quiz**</u>

Famous People of the World

Name: _____

Teacher: _____

<u>Instructions:</u>
Use the library media center print, nonprint, and electronic media resources to identify these famous people. Use a word processor and a piece of paper to list the nationality, birthdate, main accomplishments, career field, and sources of information for each of the following:

1. Kristi Yamaguchi

2. J. R. R. Tolkien

3. Susan B. Anthony

4. Joe Montana

5. Claire Chennault

6. Jane Goodall

7. Grant Hill

8. Sally K. Ride

9. Gloria Estefan

10. Chiang Kai-shek

11. Sid Fleischman

12. Whitney Houston

13. Queen Elizabeth II

14. Matthew Brady

15. Mary Cassatt

16. Colin Powell

17. Andy Warhol

18. Igor Stravinsky

19. Diego Rivera

LESSON FIFTEEN

Title

Let's Make a Crossword Puzzle

Overview

The purpose of this lesson is for students to work with a partner to make a crossword puzzle based on facts about the life and contributions of an African American vocal or instrumental musician. They will exchange puzzles and solve at least one puzzle. Students will listen to a variety of music performed by African Americans and discuss their contributions and cultural accomplishments.

Library Media Skills Objectives

Locate reference material related to specific subject areas.

Select suitable print, nonprint, and courseware material for a specified topic.

Use an index.

Use computer software.

Make a bibliography.

Competency Goals and Objectives

1. The learner will identify contributions of individuals and cultures.
2. The learner will communicate reading, listening, and viewing experiences from various cultures.

Subject Area

Music and Language Arts or Interdisciplinary Team.

Learning Strategy

Lecture, listening, and creating product.

Resources

Sample Crossword Puzzle

Print

Aretha Franklin: Motown Superstar. 1996. African-American Biography Series.
Barber, Nicola, and Mary Mure. 1996. The World of Music.
Duke Ellington: Giant of Jazz. 1996. African-American Biography Series.
Haskins, James. 1987. Black Music in America: A History Through Its People.
Haskins, James. 1996. The Harlem Renaissance.
La Blanc, Michael, ed. 1992. Contemporary Black Biography: Profiles from the International Black Community.
Phelps, Shirelle, ed. 1996. Who's Who Among African Americans.
Rodgers, Marie E. 1998. The Harlem Renaissance: An Annotated Reference Guide for Student Research.

General Reference Books

Current Biography
Webster's New Biographical Dictionary

Fig. 7-15-1. African American Musicians.

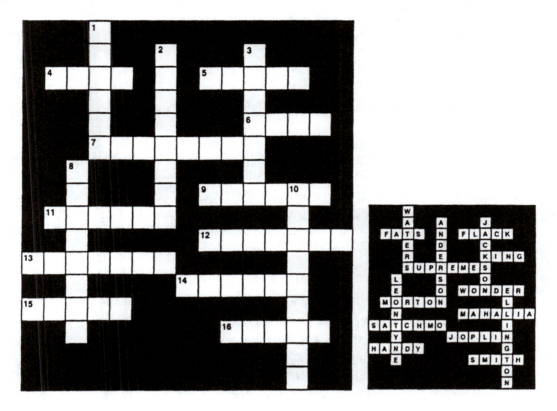

ACROSS CLUES

4. _____ Waller, jazz pianist and composer

5. Roberta _____ , acclaimed at Newport Jazz Festival in 1972

6. Nat _____ Cole, singer who gave a command performance for Queen Elizabeth

7. The _____ , trio who won seven gold records

9. Stevie _____ , singer and pianist blind from birth

11. Jelly Roll _____ , composer or "The Original Jelly Roll Blues"

12. _____ Jackson, outstanding gospel singer

13. Nickname of Louis Armstrong

14. Scott _____ , king of ragtime

15. W. C. _____ , composer of the "St. Louis Blues"

16. Bessie _____ , one of the greatest women blues singers

DOWN CLUES

1. Ethel _____ , celebrated gospel singer

2. Marian _____ , first Black person to sing with the Metropolitan Opera

3. The _____ Five, brothers who formed a successful rock group

8. _____ Price, a great soprano opera star

10. Duke _____ , band leader, pianist, and composer

Nonprint and Courseware

American journey. History in your hands: *The African-American experience*. 1995. Research Publications. CD-ROM.

Crossword magic. 1997. Mindscape. Diskette.

Methods

The teacher will

1. Present a program of recorded music by African American vocal or instrumental musicians.
2. Explain that students will work in pairs to locate information on an African American instrumental or vocal musician and use the information to make a crossword puzzle in the computer lab.
3. Discuss objectives and evaluative criteria.
4. Provide suggestions of names for research assignments such as Charlie Pride, Scott Joplin, Aretha Franklin, Mahalia Jackson, Andre Watts, Louis Armstrong, Bessie Smith, Stevie Wonder, W. C. Handy, Ethel Waters, Eubie Blake, and Miles Davis.
5. Assign partners.
6. Schedule classes in the library media center and computer lab.
7. Evaluate crossword puzzles made by students.
8. Discuss the contributions and cultural accomplishments of African American vocal or instrumental musicians.

The library media specialist will

1. Present a lecture on special reference books in the field of music and biography.
2. Make a sample crossword puzzle for students to solve.
3. Review the answers to the sample puzzle in a large group session.
4. Explain that the sample puzzle is about a number of musicians but that they are to make a crossword puzzle on a single musician.
5. Provide guidance in using a computer program to construct a crossword puzzle.
6. Assist students in constructing a crossword puzzle.
7. Check finished crossword puzzles and clues using the bibliography prepared by students.
8. Give the completed puzzles to the teacher.

The students will

1. Listen to recorded music by African American performers.
2. Work with a partner to solve the sample crossword puzzle.
3. Select the name of an African American instrumental or vocal musician.
4. Locate facts about the musician using reference books and electronic resources such as encyclopedias and magazines.
5. List facts about the life of the musician and the contributions made to music and to American culture.
6. Make a bibliography of the sources used.
7. Construct a crossword puzzle that includes the name of the musician.
8. Make clues that can be answered with facts from reference materials.

9. Turn in the completed assignment pieces to the library media specialist:
    - list of facts and bibliography
    - crossword puzzle with clues
    - solution to crossword puzzle

10. Solve at least one crossword puzzle made by other students.

11. In a class discussion period, discuss contributions and cultural accomplishments of African American musicians.

Evaluative Criteria

Students will successfully make a crossword puzzle about an African American musician and discuss contributions and cultural accomplishments. They will exchange puzzles and solve at least one crossword puzzle.

Skills Lessons for Grade Eight

LESSON ONE

Title
Where to Go...

Overview
The purpose of this lesson is to tell students where to go to find information for a research project. The lesson can serve as a review of library media center information and computer skills. It should be used in conjunction with an actual assignment integrated with the curriculum such as a science, language arts, social studies, or interdisciplinary lesson or unit. All students need to master the essential tools of research in this technological age.

Library Media Skills Objectives
Locate resources using the library catalogs.

Locate print, nonprint, and courseware materials for specific information.

Develop a search strategy by defining and analyzing the task.

Use indexes to locate information on a given topic.

Use print and electronic resources (dictionaries, almanacs, encyclopedias, handbooks, manuals, directories).

Use a variety of computer technologies to access, analyze, interpret, synthesize, apply, and communicate information.

Exhibit ethical behavior in the use of computer technology.

Competency Goals and Objectives
The learner will demonstrate knowledge and skills in using a variety of resources and explore research processes that meet information needs.

Subject Area
Science, Language Arts, Social Studies, or Interdisciplinary Unit.

Learning Strategy
Lecture/discussion, practice, and producing report.

Resources

Dewey Decimal Classification and Relative Index

Handbooks

Indexes

Library catalogs

Newspapers and magazines

Readers' Guide to Periodical Literature

Statistical Abstracts

Vertical file/information file

Print

Ash, Russell. 1996. *The Top 10 of Everything 1997.*

Berkman, Robert I. 1994. *Find It Fast: How to Uncover Expert Information on Any Subject.* 3d ed.

Choron, Sandy, and Harry Choron. 1995. *The Book of Lists for Kids.*

The New York Public Library Student's Desk Reference. 1993.

Tesar, Jenny. 1996. *The New View Almanac: The First All-Visual Resource of Vital Facts and Statistics!*

The World Book Student Information Finder: Language Arts and Social Studies. 1993.

The World Book Student Information Finder: Math and Science. 1988.

General Reference Books

Merriam-Webster Dictionaries: *Webster's Third New International.* 1993, *Merriam-Webster's Collegiate Dictionary.* 10th ed. 1995, *Merriam-Webster's Intermediate Dictionary.* 1994.

Merriam-Webster Hardcover Reference Books: *Webster's New Geographical Dictionary.* 1997. *Merriam-Webster's Biographical Dictionary.* 1995, *Merriam-Webster's School Thesaurus.* 1989, *Merriam-Webster's Encyclopedia of Literature.* 1995.

Nonprint and Courseware

Compton's interactive encyclopedia 1997. 1996. The Learning Company. CD-ROM.

Electric library. 1997. Infonautics. Online.

Grolier multimedia encyclopedia 1997. 1997. Grolier Electronic. CD-ROM.

Infopedia. 1995. Softkey School Unit. CD-ROM.

Info trac/tom. Current. Information Access. CD-ROM.

Microsoft bookshelf. 1996. Microsoft. CD-ROM.

Mindscape student reference library. 1996. Mindscape. CD-ROM.

Picture atlas of the world. 1994. National Geographic Society. CD-ROM.

Professional

AASL electronic library. 1997. American Library Association. CD-ROM.

Methods

The teacher will

1. Select a research topic related to a unit of study and plan the research activities with the library media specialist.

2. Inform the students that for their research project they must submit a written proposal that will be reviewed and returned to them. Next, they will complete a written presentation using a word processor. They may include graphics and illustrations.

3. Check and return written proposals.

4. Explain the objectives.

5. State that the library media specialist will review information sources and assist with locating resources.

6. Remind students that they may also use the learning centers and textbooks in their classrooms.

7. Schedule classes in the library media center and computer lab.

The library media specialist will

1. Introduce the lesson by showing sample reports by students from other years.

2. Ask the students to name some of the steps that were used to produce these reports.

3. Emphasize the importance of collecting, analyzing, interpreting, drawing conclusions, and organizing data.

4. Use transparencies to review library media center information sources. Have a cart of materials and show them with the transparencies.

5. Set up several learning centers with print and nonprint resources for use by students who need guidance.

6. Use the computer program *Infopedia* with a large-screen projection device to introduce its mini-reference collection.

7. Review research procedures: Choose your topic, list search statements by key words, broaden or narrow topic, and use cross-references.

8. Make a student packet of information called "Where to Go..." to distribute after presentation.

9. Assist students in locating resources.

10. Evaluate lesson with teacher.

The students will

1. View sample reports.

2. Discuss some possible procedures, techniques, and research skills that students used in preparing their reports.

3. View, listen, and think about ideas from transparencies on "Where to Go..."

4. Visit learning centers for help in using specific resources.

5. Locate and use print, nonprint, and courseware resources for written presentation.

6. Complete reports.

7. Make a bibliography of resources.

Evaluative Criteria
The students will locate and use data in a written report.

Suggestions for Making Teaching Transparencies

1. Where to Go... to locate information
2. Check these first!
   - Library catalogs
   - Databases
   - Information file/vertical file
3. Can't find subject headings? Try:
   - *Sears List of Subject Headings*
   - *Dewey Decimal Classification and Relative Index*
4. Can't find the right terms? Use:
   - General dictionaries, abridged and unabridged
   - Scientific dictionaries
   - Language dictionaries
   - Thesauruses
5. Excellent sources (general reference books):
   - Almanacs
   - Dictionaries
   - Directories
   - Encyclopedias
   - Manuals
6. Remember to check:
   - Computer software
   - Electronic resources
   - the Internet
   - E-mail
7. Of special note:
   - Indexes
   - Biographical sources
   - Organizations
8. Need current information? Use:
   - Current magazines
   - Newspapers
   - *Facts on File*
9. Need reference help? Use:
   - Guides to reference books
   - *Books in Print*
10. Other sources to check:
    - Public library
    - College library
    - Specialists in the community
11. At any time:
    - Ask your friendly library media specialist!

LESSON TWO

Title
Fun with Math

Overview
The purpose of this lesson is to provide an opportunity for advanced math students to participate in independent research activities in the library media center.

Library Media Skills Objectives
Define a problem for research.

Determine appropriate sources for locating specific information.

Compare two sources of information.

Summarize information from a visual and/or auditory stimulus.

Draw appropriate conclusions based on information presented.

Determine adequacy of information.

Organize to show sequence.

Interpret specialized reference materials to develop and support research.

Utilize organizational skills to produce a research product or media production.

Competency Goals and Objectives
The learner will refine mathematical operational skills, analysis, application, problem-solving skills, and higher order thinking skills through the aid of calculators, measuring tools, and manipulatives.

Subject Area
Math.

Learning Strategy
Independent study, and creating project.

Resources
Print
Franco, Betsy. 1996. *Textile Math.* Multicultural Explorations Through Patterns Series. Grades 6-8.

Kenda, Margaret, and Phyllis E. Williams. 1995. *Math Wizardry for Kids.*

King, Jerry P. 1993. *Art of Mathematics.*

Opie, Brenda, Lory Jackson, and Douglas McAvinn. 1995. *Decimals, Percentages, Metric System, and Consumer Math: Reproducible Skill Builders and Higher Order Thinking Activities Based on NCTM Standards.*

Thornton, Carol A., and Nancy S. Bley, eds. 1994. *Windows of Opportunity: Mathematics for Students with Special Needs.*

Vos Savant, Marilyn. 1993. *World's Most Famous Math Problems.*

Wyler, Rose, and Mary Elting. 1992. *Math Fun with Money Puzzlers.*

Nonprint and Courseware
Comptons's interactive encyclopedia. 1995. Compton's. CD-ROM.

Geometry blaster. 1996. Davidson and Associates. CD-ROM.

Mighty math cosmic geometry. 1996. Edmark. CD-ROM.

Mystery math island. 1995. Lawrence Productions. CD-ROM.

Professional

Glasthal, Jacqueline B. 1996. *American history math: 50 problem-solving activities that link math to key events in U.S. history, grades 4-8.*

Greenberg, Dan. 1996. *Funny and fabulous fraction stories: 30 reproducible math tales and problems to reinforce important reference skills.*

Methods

The teacher will

1. Identify math students who are performing above grade level and have demonstrated the ability and desire to work on an independent math project.
2. Meet with the library media specialist to discuss math topics for research and the availability of resources.
3. Meet with the students to discuss a schedule for conferences.
4. Review progress of students at specified conferences.
5. Evaluate project or report of students.
6. Review and evaluate independent study program with the library media specialist.

The library media specialist will

1. Provide resources to plan math-related activities with the teacher.
2. Discuss research methods with students.
3. Schedule independent study time in library media center with students.
4. Reserve materials and space for students.
5. Assist students with research by locating information, asking questions to clarify ideas, making suggestions, and providing technical assistance on projects.

The students will

Select from the following activities:

1. Review the history of different numeration systems throughout the world and develop own numeration system.
2. Solve interesting mathematical puzzles and make a puzzle for a bulletin board.
3. Choose three famous mathematicians and prepare a biographical sketch about each by producing a photo album, recording, videotape, or booklet.
4. Study the ideas behind the theorems of mathematics. Devise own theorems and present them in an illustrated booklet or a series of charts.
5. Choose one of the branches of mathematics and learn more about it. Locate and use print, nonprint, and courseware materials. Make notes and summarize the information. Compare and contrast the sources of information. Discuss the findings with math teacher.
6. Make a videotape to illustrate a single mathematical concept.

Evaluative Criteria

The students will successfully complete one or more math-related activities.

LESSON THREE

Title
You Be the Judge

Overview
The purpose of this unit is to assist highly able or advanced students in preparing for a debate. They will utilize research and organizational skills, upper level critical thinking skills, and logical, concise presentation skills. They will conduct the debate at a large group meeting or present it on videotape.

Library Media Skills Objectives

Select proper sources for information on specified subjects.

Use vertical file/information file to obtain materials such as pamphlets, pictures, or clippings.

Use *Readers' Guide to Periodical Literature*, print or electronic edition.

Use bibliographies as an aid in locating information.

Use specified reference materials to develop and support research.

Evaluate material for accuracy and/or appropriateness.

Identify unsubstantiated statements or facts.

Use organizational skills: outlining, note taking, etc.

Distinguish between fact and opinion.

Observe copyright laws.

Recognize availability of suitable material in public libraries.

Competency Goals and Objectives

1. The learner will use commercial software to organize and visually display data to draw conclusions.
2. The learner will investigate potential sources of information outside of the school.

Subject Area
Language Arts.

Learning Strategy
Demonstration, lecture, and practice.

Resources

E-mail

The Internet

Public libraries

Vertical file/information file

Print
Carnes, Jim. 1995. *Us and Them: A History of Intolerance in America.*
Current Issues: Critical Issues Confronting the Nation and the World. 1996.
Encyclopedia of Sociology.

Facts on File.
Opposing Viewpoints. 1995-97. American History Series. 10 vols.
Everything You Need to Know About Abusive Relationships. 1996. The Need to
    Know Series.
Readers' Guide to Periodical Literature.
Stewart, Gail B. 1997. *Gangs.* The Other America Series.
Tagliaferro, Linda. 1997. *Genetic Engineering: Progress or Peril?*
Zeinert, Karen. 1995. *Free Speech: From Newspapers to Music Lyrics.*

Magazines
Nofsinger, Bruce, ed. Current. Topics: For and about Teens in Touch with Their
    World. *Topics Magazine.*

Nonprint and Courseware
Animal rights. 1991. GPN. Videocassette.
Grolier multimedia encyclopedia 1997. 1997. Grolier Electronic. CD-ROM.
Sirs discoverer. 1997. Sirs. CD-ROM.

Methods

The teacher will
1. Plan lesson with the library media specialist.
2. Present an overview of the principles, terms, and concepts of debating.
3. Show a videotape of a debate, if available.
4. Lead a discussion on debating techniques focusing on divergent thinking skills and problem-solving strategies.
5. Provide activities to assist students in distinguishing between fact or opinion, identifying and reporting unsubstantiated statements or facts.
6. Ask library media specialist to come to the class to review research skills.
7. Prepare a list of suggested debate topics.
8. Let students decide on debate topics and form debate teams.
9. Schedule classes in the library media center and computer lab.
10. Schedule videotaping sessions or practice session for live presentation.
11. Obtain judges for debate.
12. Evaluate unit with the library media specialist.

The library media specialist will
1. Meet with the teacher to jointly plan the unit.
2. Obtain resources.
3. Review research skills with students.
4. Remind students about the availability of materials in the public library.
5. Assist students with location, research, and organization of resources.
6. Videotape debate or give advice on a live presentation.
7. Evaluate unit.

The students will
1. Learn the techniques of debating.
2. Choose topic.
3. Locate and use resources.
4. Organize notes.

5. Participate in a debate.
6. View and evaluate videotape of debate or evaluate live presentation of debate.

Evaluative Criteria

The students will select a topic for a debate, locate and use resources, organize information, and debate a topic.

Suggested Debate Topics

Euthanasia

Genetic Engineering

Conscription (compulsory enrollment in the armed forces) for Women

Gun Control

Child Abuse

Censorship

Nuclear Weapons

Welfare

Animal Rights

Religion in the Schools

Violence on TV

Abortion

Recycling

Capital Punishment

Tax Reform

Multiculturalism Issues

Grading Systems

Gambling

Information Highway

Free Speech Issues

Gangs

LESSON FOUR

Title
Careers: A Look Ahead

Overview
The purpose of this lesson is to provide research opportunities on careers for students as a part of a careers unit. After completing lessons using decision-making processes to explore interests and aptitudes and relating them to career preferences, students will select at least two careers to investigate. They will complete a job brief on each occupation.

Library Media Skills Objectives
Use all necessary sources that are available to gather information for a specified subject.

Select suitable print, nonprint, and courseware resources for a specified topic.

Paraphrase or summarize material.

Find specific information using visual and audio materials.

Competency Goals and Objectives
The learner will determine usefulness of resources for instructional and personal needs.

Subject Area
Career Exploration or Social Studies.

Learning Strategy
Audiovisual instruction, learning center, and research.

Resources

Career Stations
Folders for each station contain clippings and pamphlets from the vertical file/ information file

Stations reflect career interest categories

Job brief form and interview form

Print
Career Discovery Encyclopedia. 1990.

Careers and Opportunities Series. 1995-96. 10 vols.

Easton, Thomas A. 1996. *Careers in Science.*

Eberts, Marjorie, and Margaret Gisler. 1990. *Careers for Bookworms and Other Literary Types.*

Eberts, Marjorie, and Margaret Gisler. 1991. *Careers for Good Samaritans and Other Humanitarian Types.*

Heitzmann, William R. 1991. *Careers for Sports Nuts and Other Athletic Types.*

Hopke, William E., ed. 1993. *The Encyclopedia of Careers and Vocational Guidance.*

Miller, Louise. 1992. *Careers for Animal Lovers and Other Zoological Types.*

Nonprint and Courseware
Encyclopedia of careers and vocational guidance. 1997. 2d ed. J. G. Ferguson. CD-ROM.

Environmental science and technology. 1991. STV. Videocassette.

Lovejoy's college counselor. 1993. Lovejoy's College Guide. Online.

Set quest: Career discovery in science, engineering, and technology. 1994. COMAP. Videocassettes.

Methods

The teacher will

1. Plan the lesson with the library media specialist. (The guidance counselor will serve as a resource person.)
2. Introduce the "Job Brief Form" and show an example of a completed form. The "Job Brief Form" and "Interview Form" may be adapted for students who expect to apply for part-time employment during their high school years.
3. Explain the procedures for the videotape or audiotape interview.
4. Schedule classes in the library media center and in the computer lab.
5. Accompany the class to the library media center and assist students in locating and interpreting career information.
6. Grade job briefs.
7. View and evaluate videotape of job interviews or listen to the audiotape with the class, the library media specialist, and the guidance counselor.

The library media specialist will

1. Reserve books, nonprint, and courseware resources.
2. For the career interest categories, compile career folders that contain clippings and pamphlets.
3. Make large signs with numbers for the learning centers. Include career folder, print and nonprint resources, and equipment needed for each center. Set up additional centers in the computer lab.
4. Make a directory map showing the location and title of the interest categories.
5. Obtain videos from district technology center and set up viewing areas.
6. Demonstrate use of equipment or electronic resources as needed.
7. Help students use reference books and nonprint materials to locate specific information.
8. Videotape simulated interviews with students applying for jobs or supervise audiotaping.
9. Evaluate unit with teacher and guidance counselor.
10. Assess need for additional resources.

The students will

1. View videotapes and electronic resources, listen to tapes, and read about a number of careers.
2. Explore occupations through the concept of clustering.
3. Select two occupations from an interest inventory.
4. Locate learning center for the two occupations selected. Find information by using resources in center. Complete "Job Brief Form."
5. Use electronic resources to locate additional information on occupations.
6. Work with another student to write script for a simulated interview. Rehearse scenes.
7. Videotape simulated interview or make an audiotape.
8. View interviews with entire class.
9. Discuss strengths and weaknesses of interviews.

Evaluative Criteria

The students will successfully complete at least two job briefs and a simulated video-tape or audiotape interview.

Further Suggestions

Some school systems have instituted a careers exploration course as a regular part of their curriculum. By integrating the basic subjects with the careers exploration courses, students build on academic concepts and apply those concepts to a variety of projects that interest and challenge them. Through this activity-based instruction in many career fields, students are able to form decisions about high school courses of study as well as post-secondary programs of study.

Interview Form

Interviewer will ask the following questions :

1. What job are you applying for?

2. What do you think your duties would be?

3. What are your qualifications?

4. Why are you interested in this job?

5. What salary would you expect?

Job Brief Form

Title of job: _____

Describe the job in a brief statement (typical daily duties): _____

_____

_____

_____

Education and training required: _____

_____

Skills and aptitudes: _____

_____

Pay: _____

Job opportunities: _____

_____

Advantages: _____

_____

Disadvantages: _____

_____

Sources of information: _____

_____

_____

LESSON FIVE

Title

Let's Get Poetic!

Overview

The purpose of this unit is to give students in-depth learning experiences with poetry. They will review a variety of poetic forms, read many poems, use a poetry index, and complete a creative activity.

Library Media Skills Objectives

Recognize a variety of poetic forms.

Use an index to locate material.

Select reading material relevant to interests and purposes.

Prepare a media presentation that expresses a mood or feeling.

Produce audiovisual project.

Competency Goals and Objectives

1. The learner will use language for the acquisition, interpretation, and application of information.
2. The learner will respond to the effects of rhyme, rhythm, and sensory imagery.

Subject Area

Language Arts or Reading.

Learning Strategy

Audiovisual instruction, demonstration, practice, and creating project.

Resources

List of activities ("Let's Get Poetic!")

Camera and photographic supplies

Transparencies of sample entries (subjects, authors, titles, first lines)

Print

Adoff, Arnold. 1979. *Eats.*

Frankovich, Nicholas, ed. 1997. *The Columbia Granger's Index to Poetry in Anthologies.* 11th ed.

Hopkins, Lee Bennett, sel. 1996. *Opening Days: Sports Poems.*

Livingston, Myra Cohn. 1997. *Cricket Never Does: A Collection of Haiku and Tanka.*

Livingston, Myra Cohn. 1991. *Poem-Making: Ways to Begin Writing Poetry.*

Ryan, Margaret. 1991. *How to Read and Write Poems.*

Yolen, Jane. 1996. *Sacred Places.*

Nonprint and Courseware

The Columbia Granger's world of poetry 1995. 1995. Columbia. CD-ROM.

In my own voice. 1996. Sunburst. CD-ROM.

Poetry, a beginner's guide. 1986. Coronet. Videocassette.

Skills for writers. 1997. Pierian Springs Software. CD-ROM.

Professional

How to read and understand poetry. 1995. Clearview. CD-ROM.
Wooldridge, Susan. G. 1996. *Poemcrazy: Freeing your life with words.*

Methods

The teacher will

1. Plan the unit with the library media specialist.
2. Divide responsibilities.
3. Explain the objectives to the students.
4. Use selections from *How to Read and Understand Poetry* and *Skills for Writers* to review poetic forms.
5. Select and read poems to illustrate humorous verse.
6. Let students practice writing such forms as haiku, diamante, tanka, cinquain, and limericks.
7. Schedule classes in the library media center.
8. Accompany class to the library media center and assist students with activities.
9. Grade and evaluate activities with library media specialist.

The library media specialist will

1. Review use of poetry indexes.
2. Prepare transparencies of sample entries for subjects, authors, titles, and first lines.
3. Have a collection of poetry books on reserve. Allow students to spend one period reading at least 10 poems.
4. Prepare list of activities ("Let's Get Poetic!").
5. Distribute list of activities and discuss with students.
6. Let each student choose one activity.
7. Assist students with use of poetry indexes and location of poems, if necessary.
8. Give technical assistance as needed.
9. Grade and evaluate activities with the teacher.

The students will

1. Review poetic forms.
2. Practice writing poetry using various forms.
3. Review skills for using a poetry index.
4. Select and read at least 10 poems.
5. Choose an activity from list "Let's Get Poetic!"
6. Complete activity.

Evaluative Criteria

The students will select and read at least 10 poems and will successfully complete an activity.

Further Suggestions

How to Read and Understand Poetry is an advanced program. It is suggested for use as a teaching tool. National Poetry Month is celebrated each April. Resources may be obtained from: The Academy of American Poets, 584 Broadway, Suite 1208, New York, NY 10012.

Let's Get Poetic!

Choose one of the following activities:

1. Compile an anthology of poetry on a specific theme such as wildlife, seasons, holidays, African Americans, or cities. Neatly copy each poem or use a word processor.
    a. Use a print or electronic index to poetry.
    b. Give the source of the poem in correct bibliographic format.
    c. Make an interesting cover for the anthology.

2. Compile an anthology of poetry on a specific theme as suggested above, but instead of writing the poems, record the poems using a cassette recorder.
    a. Practice reading each poem several times before recording.
    b. Background music or sound effects may be added.
    c. State the source of each poem.

3. Write several poems using one form of poetry: cinquain, haiku, diamante, narrative, or limerick.
    a. Draw illustrations for each poem using one of these mediums: watercolor, pen and ink, or pencil.
    b. Combine poetry and illustrations into a booklet.

4. Using several sources, choose poems. Illustrate each poem by designing write-on slides or by taking photographs using slide film.
    a. Select and record background music.
    b. Record poems.
    c. Show production to class.

5. Write a poem or select one from a book of poems.
    a. Design a wall hanging.
    b. Use calligraphy to copy the poem.

6. Another activity may be selected, but a written statement must be presented describing the activity to the library media specialist for approval.

LESSON SIX

Title
Literary Literature

Overview
The purpose of this lesson is to assist students in using important reference sources in the field of literature. Most of the references used are in the print collection.

Library Media Skills Objectives
Determine the most appropriate reference for a particular purpose.

Use information in preface, foreword, and notes to locate and interpret information.

Identify the organization of a particular reference format.

Use guide words to locate appropriate page or location.

Use appropriate search techniques for electronic sources.

Interpret information.

Competency Goals and Objectives
The learner will identify, select, and use information.

Subject Area
Language Arts, Reading, or Interdisciplinary Team.

Learning Strategy
Lecture, discussion, demonstration, and practice.

Resources
Important Reference Sources in the Field of Literature Worksheets

Transparencies of sample pages (index, guide words, and key to symbols)

Transparencies of search techniques for electronic sources (author, title, subject, key word, first line, last line, topic, date, nationality, and geography)

Print

Andrews, William L., Frances Smith Foster, and Trudier Harris, eds. 1997. *The Oxford Companion to African American Literature.*

Bartlett, John. 1990. *Familiar Quotations.* 16th ed.

Brunvand, Jan Harold, ed. 1996. *American Folklore: An Encyclopedia.*

Drabble, Margaret, ed. 1995. *The Oxford Companion to English Literature.* rev. ed.

Evans, Ivor H. 1981. *Brewer's Dictionary of Phrase and Fable.*

Frankovich, Nicholas, ed. 1997 *The Columbia Granger's Index to Poetry in Anthologies.* 11th ed.

Jones, Alison. 1995. *Larousse Dictionary of World Folklore.*

Kaplan, Justin, ed. 1992. *Bartlett's Familiar Quotations.* 16th ed.

Leach, Maria, and Jerome Fried. eds, 1984. *Funk and Wagnalls Standard Dictionary of Folklore, Mythology, and Legend.*

Manguel, Alberto, and Gianni Guadalupi. 1987. *The Dictionary of Imaginary Places.*

Opie, Iona, and Peter Opie, eds. 1951. *The Oxford Dictionary of Nursery Rhymes.*

Perkins, George, Barbara Perkins, and Phillip Leininger. 1991. *Benét's Reader's Encyclopedia of American Literature.*

Siepman, Katherine Baker, ed. 1987. *Benét's Reader's Encyclopedia.* 3d ed.

Nonprint and Courseware

Bartlett's familiar quotations. 1995. Time Warner. CD-ROM.

The Columbia Granger's world of poetry 1995. 1995. Columbia. CD-ROM.

The teacher will

1. Plan with the library media specialist for the lesson to be taught to complete a literature unit that requires a literary report.
2. Schedule the library media specialist to come to the classroom.
3. Reinforce the skills taught as the students use the reference books and electronic sources for their literary report.
4. Evaluate the unit with the library media specialist.

The library media specialist will

1. Write questions and prepare worksheets.
2. Make copies of sample pages (index, guide words, and key to symbols) from several reference books listed on the worksheet. It is permissible under the copyright laws to make a copy of these pages if they are to be used in direct instruction with students.
3. Make transparencies of search techniques for electronic sources.
4. Put the reference books listed in the resources on a cart for reserve use in the classroom.
5. Put electronic sources on reserve either in the classroom or in the computer lab.
6. Go to the classroom and give a brief overview of each reference book on the cart.
7. Use transparencies to demonstrate how to use an index to locate a poem or a quotation.
8. Make transparencies to demonstrate search procedures using electronic sources.
9. Divide students into six groups.
10. Give each group a set of questions.
11. Instruct the group members to work together to answer the questions.
12. After all groups have completed the assignment, ask students to share answers with the entire class.
13. Leave books in the classroom for students to use for their literary report.
14. Evaluate the unit with the teacher.

The students will

1. Learn how to use special reference books and electronic sources by taking part in the demonstration lesson by the library media specialist.
2. Work with a group to answer questions on the worksheet "Important Reference Sources in the Field of Literature."
3. Use suggested resources in preparing literary report.

Evaluative Criteria

The students will successfully answer the questions given to their group by using the assigned reference sources.

Text continues on page 173.

Important Reference Sources in the Field of Literature

Directions: Use the suggested reference sources in each category to answer questions.

Section One: General Literary References

The Oxford Companion to African American Literature.
The Oxford Companion to English Literature.

Identify and list two facts about the following:

1. *The Drinking Gourd*

_____

_____

2. *Swiss Family Robinson*

_____

_____

3. *The Cricket on the Hearth*

_____

_____

4. Arna Bontemps

_____

_____

5. Langston Hughes

_____

_____

6. Edward Lear

_____

_____

7. Platonic love

_____

_____

8. Chowder

_____

_____

From *Media Skills for Middle Schools.* © 1999 Lucille W. Van Vliet. Libraries Unlimited. (800) 237-6124.

Continued on page 170.

Important Reference Sources in the Field of Literature

Section Two: Poetry

The Columbia Granger's Index to Poetry in Anthologies.
Columbia Granger's World of Poetry. CD-ROM.

Use title, first line, last line, or subject indexes to identify the following:

1. "Autumn wind blows across the sea in the deepening twilight."

_____

2. "And never get up at all."

_____

3. "Don't talk to me of love. I've had an earful."

_____

4. "Gums hurt, teeth ache—the ills and woes of age."

_____

5. Lunch

_____

6. Dating

_____

7. Charms

_____

8. *Fog*

_____

Section Three: Quotations

Familiar Quotations.
Bartlett's Familiar Quotations. CD-ROM.

Identify the author and work in which the following statements appear:

1. "Mr. Watson, come here." _____

2. "different drummer" _____

3. "buried hatchet" _____

4. "One small candle may light a thousand."

_____

5. "Praise the Lord and pass the ammunition."

_____

6. "Early to bed and early to rise, makes a man healthy, wealthy, and wise."

_____

7. "In the faces of men and women I see God."

_____

8. "The report of my death was an exaggeration."

_____

Important Reference Sources in the Field of Literature

Section Four: Literary Dictionaries and Encyclopedias
  Benét's Reader's Encyclopedia of American Literature.
  Benét's Reader's Encyclopedia.
  Brewer's Dictionary of Phrase and Fable.
Find the meaning or background of the following:

1. Hoosier
_____

2. Broadway
_____

3. Goody-goody
_____

4. clodhopper
_____

5. Glen Rounds
_____

6. Ogden Nash
_____

7. *The Face That Launched a Thousand Ships*
_____

8. *Show Boat*
_____

Section Five: Folklore
  American Folklore: An Encyclopedia.
  Funk and Wagnalls Standard Dictionary of Folklore, Mythology and Legend.
  Larousse Dictionary of World Folklore.
Identify the following:

1. Baba Yaya _____
2. cakewalk _____
3. dead man's hand _____
4. talking trash _____
5. tall tale _____
6. mummers _____
7. wagtail _____
8. folk drama _____

Continued on page 172.

Important Reference Sources in the Field of Literature

Section Six: Nursery Rhymes
The Oxford Dictionary of Nursery Rhymes.
Locate and quote a couple of lines from the following:

1. "For want of a nail . . ."

_____

2. "He loves me . . ."

_____

3. "Here is the church, and here is the steeple . . ."

_____

4. "Goosey, goosey, gander . . ."

_____

5. "London Bridge . . ."

_____

6. ". . . Boy Blue . . ."

_____

7. "Hush-a-bye-baby . . ."

_____

8. "Mary had a little lamb . . ."

_____

Section Seven: Imaginary Places
The Dictionary of Imaginary Places.
Identify the following places:

1. Camelot _____
2. Middle Earth _____
3. Kargad Empire _____
4. Prydain _____
5. Thieves City _____
6. Enchanted Ground _____
7. Oz _____
8. Greedy Island _____

LESSON SEVEN

Title
Step-by-Step

Overview
The purpose of this lesson is to assist students with the planning and construction of a mural depicting the geography, history, culture, and symbols of their state.

Library Media Skills Objectives
Select suitable source of information for a specified subject.

Infer facts and ideas from maps and charts.

Use appropriate audiovisual equipment for selected presentation.

Competency Goals and Objectives
1. The learner will determine the location of physical and cultural aspects of places in their state.
2. The learner will identify and assess the role of prominent figures and ethnic groups.
3. The learner will demonstrate knowledge and skills in using computer technology.

Subject Area
Art and Social Studies or Interdisciplinary Team.

Learning Strategy
Research, practice, and designing art project.

Resources
Library Media Center's collection of books on individual states

Opaque projector

Maps of states

Print
Capek, Michael. 1996. *Murals: Cave, Cathedral, to Street.*
National Geographic Picture Atlas of Our Fifty States. 1991.
National Parks of North America. 1995.
The World Almanac and Book of Facts. 1997.

Nonprint and Courseware

E-mail

Web sites of individual states

Historical Sites

State History

American History

Current Events

Government

Important People

Maps

African Americans, Hispanic Americans, and Native Americans

Kuralt, Charles, and Loonis McGlohon. 1991. *North Carolina is my home.* Research Triangle Park: N.C. Public Television Foundation. Videocassette.
Murals in perspective. 1990. Ti-In. Videocassette.
Old Salem. 1990. A Video Tours, Inc. Production. Videocassette.
TripMaker. 1996. Rand McNally. CD-ROM.
World Book 1997 multimedia encyclopedia. 1996. IBM. CD-ROM.

Methods

The teacher will

1. Tell the students that they are going to plan and construct a mural depicting the geography, history, culture, and symbols of their state.
2. As an example of the types of pictorial displays that they may want to include in the mural, show excerpts from the *TripMaker* CD-ROM. *TripMaker* vividly features photos, panoramic city views, historical sites, and state and national parks.
3. Demonstrate the techniques and purposes of murals.
4. Schedule reference sessions in the library media center and computer lab.
5. Critique students' mural designs, which are drawn on large sheets of paper.
6. Select best designs for actual mural paintings on wall of school or on a large canvas that can be rolled and stored when not in use.
7. If the mural is on a wall in the school, hold a dedication or unveiling ceremony. Plan a special program presented by the students with exhibits and memorabilia on display. Use the state symbols, flag, and song. Invite parents, school administrators, state officials, and members of the community to the reception.

The library media specialist will

1. Reserve books and nonprint materials.
2. Assist students in locating symbols, maps, historical data, and pictures of famous people of their state.
3. Show examples of types of resources available about their state. For the state of North Carolina, for instance, show the videocassettes of *Old Salem* and *North Carolina Is My Home.*
4. Demonstrate use of opaque projector.
5. Evaluate lesson with the art teacher.
6. If there is a ceremony and reception, assist with the planning and preparations.

The students will

1. View pictures and slides of murals.
2. Practice drawing designs of murals.
3. Locate pictures and descriptions of historical background, people, culture, industries, and state symbols.
4. Use computer graphics to draw symbols and topography of state.
5. Draw design of mural using large sheets of paper or use opaque projector or overhead projector to trace designs.
6. Transfer design on wall by using opaque projector or overhead projector.
7. If there is a ceremony and reception, assist with the planning, preparations, and presentation.

Evaluative Criteria

The students will plan and construct a mural depicting geography, history, culture, and symbols of their state.

Further Suggestions

In place of a mural, students could construct a frieze on heavy paper, laminate it, and make a border around the classroom.

LESSON EIGHT

Title
P/S Sources

Overview
The purpose of this lesson is to familiarize students with two sources of data: primary and secondary.

Library Media Skills Objective
Identify primary and secondary sources.

Competency Goals and Objectives
The learner will identify and apply strategies to evaluate and communicate information for learning, decision making, and problem solving.

Subject Area
Language Arts or Social Studies.

Learning Strategy
Discussion and practice.

Resources
Worksheet

Dictionaries

Print

Newspapers

Magazines

Diaries

Letters

Contracts

Historical novels

History books

Editorials

Photographs

Vertical file/information file

Nonprint and Courseware

American journey: History in your hands. 1994-96. Primary Source. CD-ROM.

Eye witness encyclopedia of space and the universe. 1996. Dorling Kindersley Multimedia. CD-ROM.

Eye witness history of the world. 1995. Dorling Kindersley Multimedia. CD-ROM.

Landmark documents in American history. 1995. Facts on File. Diskettes.

Methods

The teacher will

1. Invite the library media specialist to come to the classroom to discuss primary and secondary sources of data.
2. Record completion of worksheet without assigning a grade.
3. Evaluate lesson and review worksheet.

The library media specialist will

1. Gather samples of primary and secondary sources.
2. Ask students to define primary and secondary sources. Use dictionaries to confirm answers.
3. Discuss the space shuttle as a topic for research. Ask questions, such as: What are some primary sources you could use? What are some secondary sources?
4. Tell students that when they do a research paper, it is important to understand the difference between primary and secondary sources. Primary sources are direct and firsthand. Secondary sources are derived from something original, primary, or basic. They are of second rank.
5. Show examples of primary and secondary sources. Show excerpts from *American Journey: History in Your Hands* and *Landmark Documents in American History.* Discuss types of sources portrayed.
6. Give out worksheets.
7. Correct worksheets with students and discuss answers. Clarify any questions students may raise.

The students will

1. Define primary and secondary sources. Use qualifiers such as source of information, evidence, and documents.
2. Discuss applications of primary and secondary sources.
3. Complete worksheets.
4. Discuss answers.

Evaluative Criteria

The students will correctly identify primary and secondary sources.

P/S Sources of Data

Write **P** if primary source, **S** if secondary source of data

_____ Memoirs

_____ Certificate

_____ History book

_____ Deed

_____ Bible commentary

_____ Will

_____ Textbook

_____ Charter

_____ Government documents

_____ Editorial

_____ Laws

_____ Historical novel

_____ Contracts

_____ Letters

_____ Newspaper accounts

_____ Time capsules

_____ Magazine accounts

_____ Diaries

_____ Pictures

_____ Constitution

_____ Electronic encyclopedia accounts

_____ Eyewitness accounts

_____ Prima facie evidence

_____ Documentary

_____ Interviews

Can you make your own list of primary and secondary sources on a separate piece of paper?

LESSON NINE

Title
To Copy or Not to Copy

Overview
The purpose of this lesson is to inform students about the meaning and purpose of the copyright law of the United States. The aim is to suggest guidelines for student use of copyrighted materials.

Library Media Skills Objectives
Locate and interpret copyright symbols.

Learn the basics of copyright laws and the meaning of "fair use."

Know that copyright statutes are federal law.

Observe copyright guidelines for students.

Competency Goals and Objectives
1. The learner will understand important issues of copyright and will exhibit ethical behavior in the use of information.
2. The learner will credit sources used in communicating experiences.

Subject Area
Social Studies or Interdisciplinary Team.

Learning Strategy
Discussion, reading, and practice.

Resources
Federal Copyright Statute, U.S. Public Law 94-533. 90 Stat. 2541, as amended

Transparencies

"To Copy or Not to Copy" worksheet

Print

Copyright Law of the United States. 1996. In *The World Almanac and Book of Facts 1997*.

Jensen, Mary Brandt. 1996. *Does Your Project Have a Copyright Problem? A Decision-Making Guide for Librarians*.

Kurz, Raymond A., with Bart G. Newland, Steven Lieberman, and Celine M. Jimenez. 1996. *Internet and the Law: Legal Fundamentals for the Internet User*.

Li, Xia, and Nancy Crane. 1993. *Electronic Style: A Guide to Citing Electronic Information*.

Simpson, Carol Mann. 1997. *Copyright for Schools: A Practical Guide*. 2d ed.

Methods

The teacher will

1. Plan the lesson with the library media specialist.
2. Include the lesson as a part of a research project.
3. Include questions from the lesson on a unit test.
4. Schedule the class in the library media center.

The library media specialist will

1. Have the primary responsibility for teaching the lesson.
2. Make transparencies listing the exclusive rights and limitations of copyright owners.
3. Introduce the lesson by asking students to brainstorm ideas about the purpose and use of copyright laws.
   - List students' ideas on transparencies.
   - Incorporate students' ideas into the discussion.
   - Give a brief history of copyright laws.
   - Summarize copyright law U.S. Public Law 94-533.
   - Discuss criteria for fair use.
   - Define public domain, plagiarism, and royalties.
   - Give a summary of the copyright regulations concerning audiovisuals, computer software, and the Internet.
   - Discuss penalties for infringement of copyrighted materials.
   - Show samples of requests for permission to use copyrighted materials.
   - Discuss the school and district policies on the use of copyrighted materials.
4. Ask students to complete the "To Copy or Not to Copy" worksheet.
5. Let students check their answers as each question is discussed.
6. Ask students to put their corrected copy of the worksheet in their school handbook.
7. Evaluate lesson with the teacher.

The students will

1. Brainstorm ideas about copyright laws.
2. Discuss the meaning and purpose of copyright laws.
3. Complete the "To Copy or Not to Copy" worksheet.
4. Correct and discuss answers to the worksheet.
5. Include corrected copy of the worksheet in school handbook.

Evaluative Criteria

The students will complete the "To Copy or Not to Copy" worksheet and will check all answers to ensure that they are correct.

Further Suggestions

When creating multimedia productions, the best advice, according to Carol Mann Simpson in her book *Copyright for Schools: A Practical Guide*. 2d ed. is to "invest in clip art, music, and video sold expressly for multimedia productions or create your own" (1997, 46).

Many excellent ideas on promoting copyright concerns to the school faculty and staff were presented by Eve Keller, media specialist at Trindale Elementary School, Archdale, North Carolina, and Sue Spencer, director of Media Services, Randolph County Schools, North Carolina, at the North Carolina Association for Educational Communications and Technology (NCAECT) annual conference on March 5, 1997. Using props complete with costume and parasol, Keller presented "Walking the Copyright Wire: How One County Keeps Its Balance." She asked, "If we fall, where is the net?"

Keller continued: "Randolph County Media Specialists formed a committee in 1995-96 to address ongoing copyright concerns, particularly video questions. Their work resulted in a copyright brochure for the faculty and staff and a notebook for media specialists. These materials and the experience gained in their creation may help others find their balance on the copyright wire!"

The Board of Education of Randolph County Schools issued a policy statement that every employee would know and obey copyright laws. In Randolph County Public Schools, one faculty meeting per year addresses copyright issues.

At Trindale Elementary School, Keller keeps the faculty informed about copyright policies and rules using innovative techniques and humorous dialogues and reminders. She states the real reason for obeying the copyright laws is to "do it, because it is right."

Answer Key for To Copy or Not to Copy: 1 yes, 2 yes, 3 no, 4 yes, 5 yes, 6 no, 7 no, 8 yes, 9 no, 10 yes, 11 yes, 12 yes, 13 yes, 14 no, 15 no, 16 yes.

To Copy or Not to Copy

Under the copyright law of the United States, students may or may not lawfully use copyrighted material in the following ways: (State Yes or No)

_____ 1. Copy a photograph from a magazine for use in a social studies report.

_____ 2. Make a single copy of an article from a CD-ROM encyclopedia for personal research.

_____ 3. Perform musical work at a school dance when compensation is paid to performers.

_____ 4. Use opaque projector to trace a single map for class project.

_____ 5. Use a paragraph in direct quotes from a reference book including a notice of copyright.

_____ 6. Make an off-air recording of a commercial television program and bring the videotape to school to show to a class.

_____ 7. Copy a compact disc belonging to a friend.

_____ 8. Make a single copy of a cartoon for use on a poster for a language arts class.

_____ 9. Copy a computer software program from the school computer lab to take home to complete an assignment.

_____10. Use copyrighted material owned by the library media center in a multimedia production for a class instructional unit, as long as the material is not modified or changed.

_____11. Perform a play for which a royalty has been paid.

_____12. Copy video clips for use in a school newscast as long as the video is not altered in any way.

_____13. Record stories, poems, or songs in the public domain.

_____14. Copy several pages of information from the Internet to use in a school report, if the Internet source is copyrighted.

_____15. Use a recording as background music for a student video production to be performed at a state film festival.

_____16. Make slides from a book of photographs after obtaining permission from copyright owner.

LESSON TEN

Title

Is the Medium the Message?

Overview

The purpose of this unit on visual literacy is to help students understand the messages of visuals, develop visual skills, and communicate their own ideas through a visual and literary medium.

Library Media Skills Objectives

Identify and use all parts of a book.

Infer facts and ideas from reading.

Evaluate material for appropriateness.

Locate specific information using electronic resources.

Summarize information from a visual and/or auditory stimulus.

Compare two sources of information.

Select suitable modes of production for presentations.

Competency Goals and Objectives

The learner will appreciate various visual forms, compare and contrast visual images, and formulate a personal response to visual messages.

Subject Area

Language Arts, Art, or Interdisciplinary Team.

Learning Strategy

Audiovisual instruction, lecture, learning centers, art, and creation of project.

Resources

Learning centers

Visual literacy project guidelines

Print

California Media and Library Educators Association. 1994. *From Library Skills to Information Literacy: A Handbook for the 21st Century.*

Cumming, Robert. 1995. *Annotated Art.*

Cummings, Pat, ed. 1995. *Talking with Artists II.*

Davidson, Rosemary. 1993. *Take a Look: An Introduction to the Experience of Art.*

Dorling Kindersley Ultimate Visual Dictionary. 1994.

Dorling Kindersley Visual Encyclopedia. 1995.

Friedhoffer, Bob. 1996. *Magic and Perception: The Art and Science of Fooling the Senses.*

Locker, Thomas, with Candace Christiansen. 1995. *Sky Tree: Seeing Science Through Art.*

Manguel, Alberto, and Gianni Guadalupi. 1987. *The Dictionary of Imaginary Places.*

Porter, Eliot, sel. 1967. *From Henry David Thoreau: "In Wildness Is the Preservation of the World."*

Simon, Hilda. 1983. *Sight and Seeing: A World of Light and Color.*

Stubbs, Charles B. 1994. *Art Is Elementary: Teaching Visual Thinking Through Art Concepts.* rev. ed.

Winters, Nathan. 1986. *Architecture Is Elementary: Teaching Visual Thinking Through Architectural Concepts.*

Wood, A. J. 1996. *Nicki Palin's Hidden Pictures.*

Journal Articles

Amatenstein, Sherry. 1995. What you see is what you get. *Mademoiselle*, October, 101, 156-159. WilsonDisc, *Readers' Guide* Abstracts. Mega Ed. Version 3:3.

Field of dreams. 1996. *Psychology Today*, September/October, 29, 26. Wilson-Disc, *Readers' Guide* Abstracts. Mega Ed. Version 3:3.

Neimark, Jill. 1997. When hearing is believing. *Psychology Today*, May/June, 30, 20. WilsonDisc, *Readers' Guide* Abstracts. Mega Ed. Version 3:3.

Pirisi, Angela. 1997. Eye-catching advertisements. *Psychology Today*, January/February 30, 14. WilsonDisc, *Readers' Guide* Abstracts. Mega Ed. Version 3:3.

Wenger, Win, and Richard Poe. 1995. The Einstein factor. *Success*, November, 42, 55-62. WilsonDisc, *Readers' Guide* Abstracts. Mega Ed. Version 3:3.

Nonprint and Courseware

Images of the world. 1995. National Geographic Society. Posters.

Thoreau's Walden: A video portrait. 1996. Photovision. Videocassette.

Visual illusions. 1990. Ti-In. Videocassette.

Vizability. 1996. PWS. CD-ROM.

The world our minds invent. 1987. Wilton. Videocassette.

Yes? No? Maybe? Decision-making skills. 1990. Sunburst.

Professional

von Wodtke, Mark. 1993. *Mind over media: Creative thinking skills for electronic media.*

Methods

The teacher will

1. Plan activities for a visual literacy program designed to equip students with the knowledge and experience to interpret visual representations in this complex world.

2. Use excerpts from the CD-ROM program *Vizability* to introduce the culture of art and visual interpretation as a means of visual communication.

3. Lead students in a discussion of the elements of a visual vocabulary, the types of visual expression, and the influences on vision and perception.

4. Arrange for the library media specialist to explain to the students the procedures for completing the learning center activities in the library media center.

5. Divide the class into five groups.

6. Accompany the students to the library media center and rotate to each activity to give supervision.

7. Review and discuss the completed learning center activities with the library media specialist to determine grades for students.

8. Read the proposals for projects by students and discuss details with students. Projects may include graphic displays, photographs, charts, diagrams, advertisements, cartoons, paintings, picture books, video, and computer productions.

9. Allow students to meet with the library media specialist for assistance with photography, video, and computer productions.
10. Plan with the art teacher for incorporating art activities with language arts skills.
11. View and evaluate projects with the art teacher and the library media specialist.

The library media specialist will

1. Plan and develop the entire unit with the teacher.
2. Divide responsibilities with the teacher.
3. Write activities for learning centers.
4. Set up centers with necessary resources.
5. Share supervision with the teacher of students who are working at the centers by asking questions, reviewing answers, and guiding activities.
6. After the students have completed the learning center activities over a period of five days, invite the class to come to the media center for a multimedia program on creative expression planned jointly with the art teacher. The program will introduce the following ideas for student projects:
   - Make slides by using pictures from books and magazines. Include slides of words, such as: War, peace, hate, love, wealth, and poverty. Play selected music while showing the slides.
   - Show hand-drawn slides made by students or show pictures drawn on write-on slides that have been prepared ahead of time.
   - Show a series of enlarged and mounted photographs that express some aspect of nature, such as life at the seashore.
   - Ask the art teacher to show examples of cartoons, paintings, posters, models, and graphic displays.
7. Demonstrate the use of the photographic equipment, including camcorders, digital cameras, and digital photo printers to the students who select photography projects.
8. Give technical assistance to these students in selecting the correct equipment, using the elements of composition, and making good use of light.
9. View and evaluate projects with the classroom and art teachers.
10. Review and evaluate entire unit with teacher. Revise unit as necessary.

The students will

1. Complete five learning centers.
2. Work in groups. Each group will spend one class period at each center on a rotating schedule.
3. After completing the learning center activities and still working as a group, communicate their own ideas through an art, photography, or computer project portraying a literary theme.

Evaluative Criteria

Students will complete the learning center activities and create and present a group project portraying a literary theme. The project will be evaluated on originality of theme, organization, artistic value, composition, literary merit, and general effectiveness.

Further Suggestions

Substitute available resources for use in the learning centers.

Learning Centers: Visual Literacy Theme

Center 1:

A. Read the preface, foreword, or introduction to the following book to determine the purpose of the author, Eliot Porter, in writing *From Henry David Thoreau: "In Wildness Is the Preservation of the World."* Look at the photographs and read the text. The photographer has captured the message of Henry David Thoreau. If Porter's book is not available, use the videocassette *Thoreau's Walden: A Video Portrait.* Write a short, descriptive paragraph explaining the message.

Look carefully at the photographs in the National Geographic Society poster set *Images of the World.* These photographs were produced by National Geographic photographers who have something to communicate. Write a paragraph describing impressions of these images.

Center 2:

A. At a computer station, view the section on "Imaging" in the *Vizability* program. Brainstorm with group to imagine the world as it could be. Write a synopsis of the group's ideas.

B. View the section on "Seeing" in the *Vizability* program. Discuss ways to interpret critical details, patterns, and motion through the interactive activities. Make an outline of key points.

Center 3:

A. Use the *Dorling Kindersley Visual Encyclopedia* to research ideas in the arts and media section. Combine illustrations and facts and react to the statement "Visuals are more valuable when related to subject matter and explained by text." Compare and contrast visual and print information.

B. Browse through the *Dorling Kindersley Ultimate Visual Dictionary* to find illustrations on science and technology. Determine the author's viewpoint about what is included or excluded in the field of science and technology. Summarize the group's personal response to the visual messages in this section.

Center 4:

A. View the videocassette *Visual Illusions*, which is on the topic of optical illusions. Discuss with the group the illustration and demonstration of how we can be visually deceived. Write a summary of the group's discussion. Illustrate an example of optical illusions.

Look at the book *Nicki Palin's Hidden Pictures.* Find the camouflaged creatures. Apply insights and strategies to become more aware of visual messages. Share experiences about identifying relevant details in visual presentations.

Center 5:

A. Use the book *Annotated Art* by Robert Cumming as a guide to viewing paintings and to learn about the basic elements of art. Pick out several paintings and read about the symbolism, perspective, and other artistic elements. Ask each member of the group to annotate the information on one painting.

B. Using the *Dictionary of Imaginary Places* by Manguel and Guadalupi, select several imaginary places. Visualize what you perceive the places to look like.

Draw illustrations to portray your visualization or write a short description that will enable others to visualize the places.

Visual Literacy Project Guidelines

Work as a group to express yourself through a visual project and a literary medium. Projects may include graphic displays, photographs, charts, diagrams, advertisements, cartoons, paintings, picture books, video, and computer productions.

Ideas for literary mediums

- Poetry.
- Quotations.
- Short Stories.
- Illustrators.
- Authors.
- Fictional characters.

Ideas for photography

- Use a 35-mm camera, indoors and outdoors, for taking prints or slides.
- Use write-on slides to draw pictures.
- Use prepared slides from the library media center collection.
- Use a digital camera.
- Use a camcorder.

Ideas for art projects

- Make a booklet.
- Make a model.
- Make a book of cartoons.
- Illustrate advertisements.
- Use computer graphics as illustrations.

Plan your project

1. Start with an idea.
2. Select the visual medium to use.
3. Select the literary medium to use.
4. Plan objective (what you want to accomplish).
5. Make a storyboard or design a layout.
6. Prepare visuals and written commentary.
7. Combine visuals with literary medium.
8. Use the talents of everyone in the group.
9. Complete the project.
10. View and evaluate.
11. Did you accomplish your purpose?

LESSON ELEVEN

Title

Know Your State

Overview

The purpose of this lesson is to learn about the personalities, localities, and events of individual states that have given the state a distinctive place in the nation. Students will research the past and present major events, personalities, social, economic, and political changes in their state. They will work in assigned groups on assigned topics and produce a booklet about their state.

Library Media Skills Objectives

Interpret maps.

Infer facts from charts and maps.

Use specialized reference materials to develop and support research.

Identify sequence of events.

Select relevant topics.

Use information from many sources.

Use primary and secondary sources.

Competency Goals and Objectives

1. The learner will become proficient in the use of different kinds of maps and historical documents.
2. The learner will acquire knowledge about historic personalities and events and make judgments about social phenomena.

Subject Area

Social Studies or Interdisciplinary Team.

Learning Strategy

Research, discussion, lecture, and practice.

Resources

State maps and maps of largest cities

Brochures on state attractions

Newspaper clippings

Diaries

Pamphlets on state government agencies

Collection of books written by native authors

Resource files of business and industries

Illustrations of state symbols

Lists of ethnic groups

Special collection of books and materials related to the state (sociology, geography, history, the arts, fiction, and biographies)

Print

    Brodie, Carolyn S., ed. 1994. *Exploring the Plains States Through Literature.* Exploring the United States Through Literature Series.

    Discover America! A Scenic Tour of the Fifty States. 1989.

    Doll, Carol A., ed. *Exploring the Pacific States Through Literature.* 1994. Exploring the United States Through Literature Series.

    Historical Atlas of the United States. 1993.

    Kids Explore America's African-American Heritage. 1993.

    Kids Explore America's Hispanic Heritage. 1992.

    National Geographic Picture Atlas of Our Fifty States. 1991.

    Veltze, Linda, ed. 1994. *Exploring the South-East States Through Literature.* Exploring the United States Through Literature Series.

Nonprint and Courseware

    America alive. 1994. Media Alive. CD-ROM.

    Chronicle of the 20th century. 1996. Dorling Kindersley Multimedia. CD-ROM.

    Discovering multicultural America. 1996. Gale Research. CD-ROM.

    Map 'n' go. 1997. DeLorme. CD-ROM.

    The map room. 1996. Edunetics. CD-ROM.

    Skytrip America. 1996. Discovery Channel. CD-ROM.

    Where in the USA is Carmen Sandiego? 1997. 3d ed. 1997. Broderbund. CD-ROM.

Methods

The teacher will

1. Define the objectives.
2. Explain to students that this study will involve learning about their state, its historical perspective, and its role in American history from its founding to the present.
3. State that the study will be an in-depth study over a period of time. It will involve many interesting activities with field trips, guest speakers, research, artifacts, crafts, games, music, and food.
4. Tell students that they will have opportunities to work in the library media center and in the computer lab using the electronic databases, online catalogs, the Internet, and e-mail.
5. Explain that fun activities will be interspersed throughout the unit of study culminating in a festival.
6. Inform students that they will make an illustrated booklet that they can keep. It will contain significant facts and interesting anecdotes concerning their state.

The library media specialist will

1. Entertain students with a lively multimedia presentation of state history, geography, personalities, and customs.
2. Introduce the students to the wide variety of resource materials available.
3. Relate legends, folktales, and fictional literature to state history.
4. Remind the students that the library media specialist is a resource person who will assist them in their research and projects.
5. Provide the teachers with resource assistance.

The students will

1. Research and learn state history and geography through the use of print, nonprint, and courseware.
2. Make a time line of the state's history.
3. Conduct recorded interviews.
4. Learn about state and local governments.
5. Identify geographic features, historic sites, natural resources, products, businesses, and industries.
6. Appreciate the diverse cultures, values, and beliefs of past and present inhabitants.
7. Participate in field trips, performances, art projects, and festivals.
8. Learn about state symbols and songs.
9. Make a personal illustrated booklet of their state.

Evaluative Criteria

Students will participate in research activities, field trips, listen to guest speakers, share artifacts and games, create artistic projects, make a personal booklet about their state, and take part in festivals.

Further Suggestions

This unit of study lends itself to an interdisciplinary team approach involving the entire curriculum areas, parents, and the community. As an added attraction, hold a culminating activity with music, games, food, dance, guest performers, state personalities, and displays of student productions.

LESSON TWELVE

Title
"Singing the Black Bug Blues"

Overview
The purpose of this lesson is to give students an opportunity to work independently on a science project based on their own interests. One example of a research project is a slide/tape or videotape presentation on how to make an insect collection. The library media specialist will provide the instruction and guidance in photography. The science teacher will supervise the scientific research. The production will be entered in the local science fair.

Library Media Skills Objectives
Interpret specialized reference materials to develop and support research.

Use organizational skills to produce a multimedia presentation.

Organize to show sequence.

Produce a multimedia presentation that contains specific subject matter.

Competency Goals and Objectives
The learner will develop the ability to use science process skills and demonstrate the ability to experiment.

Subject Area
Science.

Learning Strategy
Discussion, research, independent study, and completing a project.

Resources

Independent study guide for science classes

Print
Bombaugh, Ruth. 1990. *Science Fair Success.*
Dorros, Arthur. 1995. *Ciudades de Hormigas.*
Ehrlich, Robert. 1996. *What If You Could Unscramble an Egg?*
Familiar Insects and Spiders. 1995. A National Audubon Society Pocket Guide.
Mound, Laurence A. 1990. *Insects.* Eyewitness Books.
Raintree Steck-Vaughn Illustrated Science Encyclopedia. 1997. rev. ed.
Vecchione, Glen. 1995. *100 Amazing Make-It-Yourself Science Fair Projects.*

Nonprint and Courseware
Chemistry: Leafcutting ants, nature's chemists. 1988. Allegro. Videocassette.
Insect. 1994. Eyewitness Video Series. New York: Dorling Kindersley. Videocassette.
Insects. 1995. Bill Nye the Science Guy Series. Disney. Videocassette.
Insects. 1990. Tell Me Why Video Series. TMW Sales. Videocassette.
Insects. 1996. Junior Nature Guide Series. Integrated Communications and Entertainment. CD-ROM.
Learning about insects. 1995. Queue. CD-ROM.
Multimedia bugs. 1996. Inroads Interactive. CD-ROM.
An odyssey of discovery: Science. 1996. Pierian Spring Software. CD-ROM.

Production

35-mm camera, film, processing mailers

Digital camera

Camcorder

Hyperstudio. 1995. Roger Wagner. CD-ROM.
Kid pix studio. 1995. Broderbund. CD-ROM.
Mediaweaver. 1996. Humanities Software. CD-ROM.
The print shop press writer. 1997. Broderbund. CD-ROM.

Professional

Haven, Kendall. 1996. *Great moments in science: Experiments and readers theatre*.

Methods

The teacher will

1. Explain the worksheet "Independent Study Guide for Science Classes."
2. Discuss requirements and expectations.
3. Review and approve independent research topics such as "How to Make an Insect Collection."
4. Meet with the library media specialist to plan strategies for working with students who are on independent study.
5. Meet with students at a scheduled time to discuss and review activities.
6. Evaluate the multimedia presentation with the library media specialist.
7. Enter qualified productions in the local science fair.

The library media specialist will

1. Meet with students to determine media-related needs.
2. Assist with obtaining and using resources.
3. Show the *Learning About Insects* program as a motivating example.
4. Guide students in planning production "How to Make an Insect Collection."
5. Give instruction in photography (use of 35-mm camera, digital camera, camcorder, composition techniques, and special effects).
6. Assist with production.
7. Accompany students to the local science fair.
8. Evaluate multimedia production with teacher and students.

The students will

1. Select topic for research such as "How to Make an Insect Collection."
2. Meet with the science teacher and library media specialist to discuss topic and strategies.
3. Locate and use resources.
4. Prepare a storyboard or script.
5. Get special instruction and guidance from the library media specialist on photographic techniques.
6. Take photographs during collection, storing, classifying, mounting, labeling, and organizing insect collection.
7. Write script.
8. Make graphics of titles and credits.

9. Select or create musical background. Work with music teacher to compose and perform original music such as "The Black Bug Blues."

10. Preview and evaluate program with the teacher and library media specialist.

11. Enter qualified productions in the local science fair.

Evaluative Criteria

The students will select a topic for independent study and will successfully complete a multimedia production.

Further Suggestions

If a teacher or staff member who enjoys teaching photography would like an opportunity to work with students on an independent study project, encourage them to do so. A guidance counselor assisted the student with the photography in this lesson. A science teacher composed and performed the music "Singing the Black Bug Blues." The slide/tape program won an award at the county and state film festivals. The production became a part of the library media circulating collection.

The translated version of *Ciudades de Hormigas* "Cities of Ants" could be used as an instructional resource by a second language teacher. It includes making an ant colony for a science fair project.

Independent Study Guide for Science Classes

Work independently or in small groups to:

1. Identify a topic for study.

2. Pose questions of inquiry related to topics.

3. Hypothesize answers.

4. Carry out an investigation or research to verify hypothesized answers.

5. Plan a media presentation to effectively share your investigation.

6. Organize and produce a multimedia production.

LESSON THIRTEEN

Title
Celebrating Earth Day

Overview
The purpose of this lesson is to focus on environmental issues through a celebration of Earth Day, April 22, a day set aside to promote ecology, encourage respect for life on Earth, and highlight the problem of pollution. The library media center will provide a sampling of resources on this multifaceted topic. Classes will be invited to visit the library media center in advance of Earth Day to view displays, collection of books, videotapes, and electronic sources containing information about ecology topics and environmental issues. Students will be encouraged to make posters and contribute to the display. They will discuss their role in protecting the environment through prevention and preservation and the impact that environmental issues have on their future.

Library Media Skills Objectives
Infer facts and ideas from resource materials.

Select proper resources for information on specified subjects.

Use resources to form opinions.

Competency Goals and Objectives
1. The learner will develop an understanding of the relevance of current environmental issues.
2. The learner will investigate how human activities affect ecosystems.

Subject Area
Science, Social Studies, or Interdisciplinary Team.

Learning Strategy
Viewing, reading, discussion, and practice.

Resources
Print
Gardner, Robert. 1992. *Celebrating Earth Day.*

Hoff, Mary, and Mary M. Rodgers. 1992. *Our Endangered Planet: Life on Land.*
———. 1991. *Our Endangered Planet: Oceans.*

Howard, Tracy Apple, with Sage Alexandra Howard. 1992. *Kids Ending Hunger: What Can WE Do?*

Markle, Sandra. 1991. *The Kid's Earth Handbook.*

Maynard, Caitlin, and Thane Maynard. 1996. *Rain Forests and Reefs: A Kid's-Eye View of the Tropics.*

O'Neill, Mary. 1991. *Nature in Danger.*

Pfiffner, George. 1995. *Earth-Friendly Holidays: How to Make Fabulous Gifts and Decorations from Reusable Objects.*

Sirch, Willow Ann. 1996. *Eco-Women: Protectors of the Earth.*

Temple, Lannis, ed. 1993. *Dear World: How Children Around the World Feel About Our Environment.*

Nonprint and Courseware

Bill Nye the Science Guy Series. 1996. Disney Educational Productions. Videocassettes.

Earth explorer. 1996. Sunburst Communications. CD-ROM.

Endangered animals: Survivors on the brink. 1997. National Geographic Society. Videocassette.

Environment: Conservation. 1995. Mentorom Multimedia. CD-ROM.

Environment: Dwindling resources. 1995. Mentorom Multimedia. CD-ROM.

Environment: Land and air. 1995. Mentorom Multimedia. CD-ROM.

Environment: Water. 1995. Mentorom Multimedia. CD-ROM.

GTV: Planetary manager. 1992. National Geographic Society. Videodisc.

Healing the Earth. 1995. National Geographic Society. Videocassette.

Manatees and how they live. 1995. AIMS Media. Videocassette.

Our environment. 1996. Edunetics. CD-ROM.

Science and the environment. 1995. Voyage. CD-ROM.

Web Sites: National Audubon Society. http://www.audubon.org/ (Accessed June 20, 1998). http://www.audubon.org/directory/ (Accessed June 20, 1998).

Professional

Simpson, Martha Seif. 1995. *Environmental awareness activities for librarians and teachers: 20 interdisciplinary units for use in grades 2-8.*

Methods

The teacher will

1. Introduce the unit and tell the students that they will be discussing the topic of ecology in different classes.
2. Obtain resources from the library media specialist.
3. Use the interdisciplinary environmental lessons from Simpson's *Environmental Awareness Activities for Librarians and Teachers*.
4. Schedule classes in the library media center.
5. Involve the students in planning special activities for Earth Day.

The library media specialist will

1. Obtain resources from many sources.
2. Set up learning centers and displays for Earth Day.
3. Assist students with research.
4. Plan a special program for Earth Day.
5. Exhibit student work.
6. Hold an open house on Earth Day. Invite parents and community members.

The students will

1. Study the relationship between organisms and their environment.
2. Study the detrimental effects of modern civilization on the environment and learn ways in which conservation can reverse trends through prevention and preservation.
3. Research a topic of special interest in the library media center or in the computer lab.
4. Contribute a poster or exhibit to the display in the library media center.
5. Observe Earth Day with a special activity.

Evaluative Criteria

The students will gather information on ecology topics and environmental issues through research and class discussion. They will observe Earth Day by participating in special activities as determined in class discussions. They will visit the library media center to view displays and resource materials.

LESSON FOURTEEN

Title
For Novel Lovers

Overview
The purpose of this lesson is to allow students to select one or more novels to read for pleasure. The students will evaluate the books for the media center's reading guidance file "Novels: To Read or Not to Read."

Library Media Skills Objectives
Select reading as a leisure time activity.

Explore fiction genre.

Utilize reading guidance resources.

Competency Goals and Objectives
1. The learner will use language for personal response.
2. The learner will express reactions and personal opinions to a selection.

Subject Area
Reading, Language Arts, or Interdisciplinary Team.

Learning Strategy
Booktalk, reading, and creating a product.

Resources
Guidelines for reading guidance file
Print
Cadnum, Michael. 1996. *Zero at the Bone*.
Cooney, Caroline B. 1995. *Flash Fire*.
Dessen, Sarah. 1996. *That Summer*.
Doherty, Berlie. 1995. *The Snake-Stone*.
Farmer, Nancy. 1997. *A Girl Named Disaster*.
Halecroft, David. 1992. *Benched!*
Hesse, Karen. 1996. *The Music of Dolphins*.
Jicai, Feng. 1995. *Let One Hundred Flowers Bloom*. Translated by Christopher Smith.
Lowry, Lois. 1993. *The Giver*.
Miller, Dorothy Reynolds. 1996. *The Clearing: A Mystery*.
Nixon, Joan Lowery. 1997. *Murdered, My Sweet*.
Nolan, Han. 1996. *Send Me Down a Miracle*.
Pausewang, Gudrun. 1996. *The Final Journey*. Translated by Patricia Crampton.
Peck, Richard. 1993. *Bel Air Bambi and the Mall Rats*.
Plummer, Louise. 1995. *The Unlikely Romance of Kate Bjorkman*.
Sleator, William. 1995. *Dangerous Wishes*.
Wallace, Rich. 1997. *Shots on Goal*.
Yumoto, Kazumi. 1996. *The Friends/Natsu no niwa*. Translated by Cathy Hirano.

Reading Guidance

Immell, Myra, ed. 1992. *The Young Adult Reader's Adviser.* Vol. 1.
Spencer, Pam. 1994. *What Do Young Adults Read Next? A Reader's Guide to Fiction for Young Adults.*

Nonprint and Courseware

Book brain. 1996. Version 1.0. Grade Level 7-9. Oryx Press. CD-ROM.
What do I read next? 1996. Gale Research. CD-ROM.

Professional

Herald, Diana Tixier. 1997. *Teen genreflecting.*
Jones, Patrick. 1992. *Connecting young adults and libraries: A how-to-do-it manual.*
McCarthy, Tara. 1996. *Teaching genre: Exploring 9 types of literature to develop lifelong readers and writers.*
Shipley, Roberta Gail. 1995. *Teaching guides for 50 young adult novels.*
Van Vliet, Lucille W. 1992. *Approaches to literature through genre.*

Methods

The teacher will

1. Introduce the lesson.
2. Use ideas and activities from the professional reading guidance books by Herald, McCarthy, and Van Vliet for promoting reading as a lifelong venture.
3. Tell the students that they may select one or more novels to read for pleasure. They will not be required to write a book report.
4. Schedule a booktalk with the library media specialist to introduce a number of fiction books from the library media center.
5. Accompany the class to the media center for the booktalk.
6. Read and review reading guidance cards with the library media specialist.

The library media specialist will

1. Select and purchase a variety of fiction books, including a large number of paperback books and follow the approved selection policy.
2. Select personal choices of previously read fiction books and prepare a booktalk. Include humor, fantasy, romances, mysteries, science fiction, historical fiction, animal stories, realistic fiction, sports stories, and adventures. As an added attraction, try the theme: "Books to Cry By."
3. Present a lively, exciting booktalk using props, illustrations, and catchy themes.
4. Show students a sample reading guidance card.
5. Ask students to complete the card after they have read one or more novels. Tell them that the cards will be reviewed by the teacher and library media specialist and that selected cards will be included in the card file "Novels: To Read or Not to Read." The card file will be used by students looking for reading suggestions.
6. Place a sign in the media center next to a 4" x 6" card file that states:

Novels: To Read or Not to Read
Compiled by Students for Students

7. Review reading guidance cards and evaluate with reading teacher.
8. Select cards to be included in the card file of the library media center.

The students will
1. Listen to booktalk.
2. Select and read one or more novels.
3. Utilize print and electronic reading guidance sources.
4. Complete reading guidance card.

Evaluative Criteria

The students will select and read one or more novels and correctly complete a reading guidance card.

Sample Reading Guidance Card

Novels: To Read or Not to Read

Author: _____

Title: _____

Brief summary:

_____

_____

Recommended (brief reason):

_____

_____

Or

Not recommended: (brief reason):

_____

_____

Submitted by: _____

LESSON FIFTEEN

Title

Moving On!

Overview

The purpose of this lesson is to prepare students to celebrate the arrival of the new century. They will participate in research activities and use their imaginations to predict future trends in many fields. They will plan schoolwide celebration activities.

Library Media Skills Objectives

Define a problem for research.

Select reading and viewing as means of acquiring information.

Interpret specialized reference materials.

Draw appropriate conclusions.

Competency Goals and Objectives

1. The learner will use language for acquisition, interpretation, critical analysis, and evaluation.
2. The learner will apply insights and strategies to formulate a personal response to messages about the future.

Subject Area

Interdisciplinary Team.

Learning Strategy

Research, lecture, displays, and completion of group projects.

Resources

Print

Bader, Bonnie, and Tracey West. 1996. *Countdown to 2000: A Kid's Guide to the New Millennium.*

Chandler, Gary, and Kevin Graham. 1996. *Making a Better World Series: Alternative Energy Sources; Guardians of Wildlife; Kids Who Make a Difference; Natural Foods and Products; Protecting Our Air, Land, and Water; Recycling.*

Darling, David. 1995. *Computers of the Future.*

Jones, Lawrence. 1996. *Job Skills for the 21st Century: A Guide for Students.*

Stearns, Michael, ed. 1995. *A Starfarer's Dozen: Stories of Things to Come.*

Tracy, Steve. 1995. *L5: Behind the Moon.*

Weiss, Ann E. 1996. *Virtual Reality: A Door to Cyberspace.*

Nonprint and Courseware

Virtual reality. 1994. Films for the Humanities and Science. Videocassette.

Professional

Carnegie Council on Adolescent Development. Task Force on Education of Young Adolescents. 1989. *Turning points: Preparing American youth for the 21st century: The report of the task force on education of young adults.* Washington, D.C.: Carnegie Council on Adolescent Development.

Page, Susan. 1997. Clinton lays plans for millennium festivities. *USA Today,* 15 August, 1A.

Methods

The teacher will

1. Collaborate with teachers in all subject areas to make this an interdisciplinary unit.

2. Study or review *Turning Points: Preparing American Youth for the 21st Century: The Report of the Task Force on Education of Young Adults.* Use information in making plans for the schoolwide celebration.

3. Review plans that President Clinton proposed on launching a federal effort to spark nationwide celebrations in 2000 to mark the millennium. President Clinton's theme is: "Honor the Past, Imagine the Future." In an article entitled "Clinton Lays Plans for Millennium Festivities," Susan Page reported that "Clinton will outline three broad goals: preserving U.S. culture and history, encouraging creativity and exploration, and extending the bonds of international understanding." Plans are to have activities that last throughout the year. This is in deference to the debate over whether the millennium starts at the beginning of 2000 or 2001. A Web site will be posted at the White House at www.whitehouse.gov covering the festivities.

4. Plan long-term and short-term goals.

5. Include students in the planning stages.

6. Use resources such as Chandler and Graham's *Making a Better World Series* and Bader and West's *Countdown to 2000: A Kid's Guide to the New Millennium.*

7. Plan with the library media specialist for special collections of resources, display areas, research activities, productions, and use of the library media center and computer lab.

The library media specialist will

1. Collaborate with the interdisciplinary team, administration, students, parents, and community leaders in setting short-term and long-term goals.

2. Obtain resources, including print, nonprint, and courseware.

3. Use the Vertical file/information File to store clippings, pamphlets, and community information.

4. Assist in planning for field trips and for guest speakers.

5. Make facilities, resources, and own expertise available as needed.

The students will

1. Plan with interdisciplinary team to take part in the new millennium festivities.

2. Define millennium and study the calendar's definition.

3. Think and dream about the future.

4. Use available resources including the Internet and e-mail.

5. Write down many ideas and suggestions.

6. Enthusiastically take part in the festivities.

Evaluative Criteria

The students will participate in research activities and use their imaginations to predict future trends in many fields. They will assist in planning and carrying out schoolwide millenium celebration activities.

PART THREE

Introduction

Profiles of two exemplary middle schools are included here as examples that reflect the vision, fundamental principles, and implementation of the middle grade philosophy. Research on the development and learning of early adolescents has been incorporated into the student-centered, curriculum-rich, technology-based projects and program. There is a schoolwide approach to provide middle grade students with high performance instruction, increased attention to these adolescents' special needs, and a focus on active learning in which students can participate in a variety of learning experiences. These schools support the students' effective use of technology as a tool to enhance and extend their learning. The learning environment is structured to ensure that middle grade students are taught the necessary information literacy skills to prepare them for the twenty-first century. The integration of the library media program with the school's instructional program provides an atmosphere of teamwork, collaboration, and articulation of effective instruction.

Elkridge Landing Middle School in Howard County, Maryland, provides an example of an established middle school program that was instituted with the opening of a model middle school in 1969. Many changes have taken place there, ranging from creation of open space facilities, curricular innovations, teaching strategies, and student learning styles, to the current technological revolution. Using the knowledge of past middle school successes and failures, the Elkridge Landing Middle School program is a consolidation of these findings. It is featured here as an exemplary middle school that facilitates and models effective integration of the library media program and the instructional program.

West Pine Middle School in Moore County, North Carolina, provides an example of an agent of change from a traditional elementary/middle school program to an innovative program based on the tenets of middle level educational philosophy and goals. It has the strong support of its parents and community. The effective leadership of school administrators has affected educational reform. New paradigms were created and teachers and staff members were empowered with the necessary tools and facilities. The administrators, library media specialist, teachers, and staff are collaboratively working to preview and select print, nonprint, and courseware to support the instructional program. It is featured here as an example of a newly established middle school to encourage other schools to make the necessary changes to provide an environment that meets the needs of young adolescents.

CHAPTER NINE

Profiles of Exemplary Middle Schools

Elkridge Landing Middle School

Elkridge Landing Middle School, 7085 Montgomery Road, Elkridge, Maryland 21227

410-313-5040, 410-313-5045 FAX

Kenneth T. Gill, Principal
Kathy McKinley, Assistant Principal
Alfreda Martino, Library Media Specialist
H. Thomas Walker, Supervisor of Media Services, Howard County, Maryland

ELKRIDGE LANDING MIDDLE SCHOOL

Elkridge Landing Middle School in Howard County, Maryland, is a prototype of a twenty-first century school with its use of extensive technology throughout the school. The exemplary use of technology is demonstrated in the schoolwide instructional agenda. Communications is a high priority item. The Home/School Communication Service is an information system that increases parent/teacher, home/school interaction. It is an inbound/outbound automated message system providing school information from a touch-tone telephone. The service is available 24 hours a day, seven days a week. It includes Safe-to-School and Homework Hotline telephone numbers.

Elkridge Landing Middle School, a beautiful, spacious, well-planned new facility, was opened in the 1995-96 school year. Its media center facilities and program add a special dimension to this technology-oriented school. It was a challenge to the new library media specialist to establish an innovative library program while working with a new school administration, staff, and facility. The library media specialist, media assistant, and the G/T teacher, who teaches in the

Gifted/Talented program, spent time managing the 100 computers in the school. This included unpacking and setting up the equipment, loading software, troubleshooting and repairing problems, and instructing staff members in the use of the computers and software. The media center houses 47 computers, including: The computerized circulation system, 12 networked computers used for accessing the Intelligent Catalog and CD-ROM resources, 29 computers in the media center lab, one in the media specialist's office, one in the media center workroom, and three file servers. The networking was completed by the end of the year. A special recognition was given to Celeste Smalkin and the media technical services staff who deserve much credit and thanks for the work they do to set up new media centers. The computer network and repair group were invaluable for the time and support they provided with the computer equipment, especially the Mac LC 630.

The following information about the Media Center appears in the Faculty Handbook:

"The media center offers a large variety of computer software, videos, books, magazines, newspapers, and equipment for use by staff, students, and community. The media center is open during the school day for those who wish to utilize the array of print and nonprint knowledge. A computerized Intelligent Catalog lists materials available for lending, and these materials and equipment can be borrowed by following the procedure established by the media center staff using the circulation computer. A video distribution system allows dial-in access from the classrooms to view prearranged videotapes. Staff members must plan with the media specialist to schedule the use of the media center or computer labs to ensure equitable use of the facilities and materials. Prompt return of borrowed items allows other staff and students the opportunity of using the resources."

The excellent print, nonprint, and software collection provided resources for the numerous projects and activities planned between the media specialist and the teachers. For example, the eighth grade Language Arts students used the computerized resources and print materials to gather and use information for a research activity on contemporary topics. The students' outlines were then prepared using the computer software program Inspiration. A seventh-grade reading assignment had students use resources such as the computerized program MacGlobe and print resources such as Culturegrams to create a travel brochure on a European country. The brochure was designed and printed on the computer using the program Student Writing Center.

In the 1996-97 school year, 520 students were enrolled in the school. The media center budgets were: Print/Nonprint, $5,995; Media Supplies, $590; AV Supplies, $1,250; Computer Supplies, $720. The computerized circulation system is maintained by Library Corp. (Bibliofile). Macintosh LC 630 computers (12) are used for Intelligent Catalog and Tom Jr. (Infotrac) magazine database with full text articles (DOS side) and Macintosh site licensed software such as MacGlobe, World Geograph, and CD-ROM encyclopedias such as Grolier, Compton's, Encarta, World Book, and Encyclopedia Americana (Mac side). Resources also include an extensive list of software with site licenses. Power Macintosh 5200/75LC computers (30) are located in the computer lab and in each classroom, with Ethernet connections to the school's file server; Internet. World Wide Web access is available through Netscape Gold. Internal e-mail is available through Eudora Lite and the school's file server. A Web page was designed by the students of Terry Sullivan, G/T teacher.

Statistical data from the Maryland State Department of Education Public School Annual Library Media Center Report 1996-97 includes:

Staffing
number with state library
    media certification   1
number of paid Tech./Cler./Aides   1

Library Media Collection
books   12,253
number of periodical
    subscriptions   22
video materials   691
microcomputer software   147
CD-ROMs   171
other audiovisual materials   138

Services
Information technology services provided through the library media center

Technology Services (Stand-alone or Networked)
Circulation system, public access catalog, CD-ROMs.

Computer Lab
Managed by LMC staff, networked to LMC

Reference Resources
Connection to Sailor/Internet

Television
School closed circuit

Instruction/scheduling
Flexibly scheduled classes

Some events of note at the school during the last school quarter were:

Pirates of Penzance performance with dessert theatre

Midsummer Night's Dream performance

Spring Concert—Band and Strings

Field trips to Walters Art Gallery, Holocaust Museum, Music Festival in Hershey, Pennsylvania

Sixth grade-Outdoor Education Program

Eighth grade-Farewell Social

A visit from Maryland Governor Parris N. Glendening

The media center was the winner of a $750 grant from Maryland Instructional Computer Coordinators Association, Inc., for "Multimedia Student Portfolios: Stepping Towards Our Future."

The library media specialist, Alfreda Martino, has 25 years of experience in elementary and middle school media centers. She has been an exemplary user of technology over the years. Her ability to work with teachers, students, administrative staff, and parents qualifies her as an instructional partner and codesigner of instruction for this twenty-first century school. In 1997, Alfreda Martino received the Mae I. Graham Award from the Maryland Educational Media Organization for Outstanding Media Program of the year.

West Pine Middle School

West Pine Middle School, 144 Archie Road, West End, North Carolina 27376

910-673-1464

Joan Frye, Principal
Jeff Maples, Assistant Principal
Vickie McKenzie, Media Coordinator
Peggy Olney, Media Services Director, Moore County Public Schools, North Carolina

WEST PINE MIDDLE SCHOOL

West Pine Middle School in Moore County, North Carolina, is a prototype of a new middle school facility in the county. Prior to the opening of West Pine Middle School and New Century Middle School in the fall of 1997, middle schools served grades four through eight and kindergarten through eight in some schools with a generally traditional curriculum. In 1986, Kaye Richards-Beale, Ph.D., was appointed director of Middle Grades Education for Moore County, Carthage, North Carolina. Richards-Beale worked at the implementation of the middle school concept as far as feasible in the kindergarten through eighth-grade environment. In 1991, a middle school study commission was appointed. In 1995, the Moore County Board of Education recommended the adoption and implementation of the middle school grades six through eight plan. It was Richards-Beale's vision that middle schools would be organized to serve grades six through eight with an interdisciplinary team organization, flexible scheduling, high technology, and state-of-the-art lab facilities. She states:

"There is little that is unique in what Moore County Schools believes about middle school students and the type of program that best meets their needs. We have tried to do what most others who embrace the middle school philosophy have tried to do:

- staff the schools we build with people who understand and appreciate the complexity of early adolescence;

- provide an academic program that challenges and supports students' intellectual development;

- give students opportunities to explore their interests;

- organize both people and time in ways that allow students and teachers to deepen their understandings of each other and their academic subjects; [and]

- promote the grouping and scheduling flexibility that will enable us to meet the needs of the students and the demands of the curriculum.

Our unique contribution to the cause, if there is one, is in the way we have furthered the notion of connecting students to people and ideas through building and program design. We expect students to gather information and explore ideas using a variety of human and material resources. Therefore, we have provided access to those resources through physical and instructional structures that are developmentally appropriate for young adolescents."

Peggy Olney, media services director, promoted the inclusion of state-of-the-art technology equipment and resources not only in the media center but throughout the school. A Middle School Planning Committee worked with the administrators of Moore County Public Schools and the Board of Education to plan, design, and implement their goals and objectives by the time the first two new middle schools were constructed in the county in the fall of 1997.

The principal of West Pine Middle School, Joan Frye, was awarded a national $25,000 Excellence in Education Award from the Milken Family Foundation in 1997. State Superintendent Mike Ward came to the school by helicopter to make the surprise award. He complimented Frye on the exceptional job of consolidating Pinehurst and West End Schools into one powerful new middle school.

The faculty and staff of West Pine are committed to the middle school philosophy. An ongoing staff development program is an important part of their commitment. They have flexible scheduling and interdisciplinary teams with a core academic program of communication skills, math, science, and social studies. A 90-minute team-planning time each day allows interdisciplinary teaching collaboration, as well as time to discuss students and their achievements and behavior, to share notes, and to call parents. Students have 90 minutes each day for their explorative elective program of Encore Classes: art, music, band, orchestra, physical education, and career exploration. The career exploration curriculum enables students to increase self-awareness and examine educational and occupational opportunities in the world of work. In career explorations, students are able to form decisions about high school courses and post-secondary programs of study. Students develop basic technical literacy through application of principles, processes, and skills. The integration of language, math, science, social studies, and arts allows students to build on aca-demic concepts and apply those concepts to a variety of projects that interest and challenge the adolescent. Students experience decision-making, problem-solving, and creative-thinking skills through activity-based instruction.

The use of technology is evident throughout the school. All teachers have computers on their desks. There are four computer labs: one in each of the three interdisciplinary team areas, and one in the career exploration lab. The library media center houses five computers. This arrangement allows for greater use of the computers by students. Teachers have special training in computer technology and accompany their classes to the lab. Computer usage is integrated with the curriculum. The media coordinator, Vickie McKenzie, assists teachers in the labs as needed and provides in-service training. The hub is in the media center. The media center has an open-door policy and flexible scheduling. It is attractive and inviting. Student projects and art are on display. Resources include a beginning collection of reference, fiction, and nonfiction books. Nonprint and courseware materials are being selected to accompany the developing curriculum. The media center includes a student production lab. A theatre room is available in the school for student and guest productions.

McKenzie and her full-time assistant, Bonnie Reeves, are fostering collaboration with the interdisciplinary teams, which is necessary for the successful integration of library media and information skills into curricular instruction. McKenzie has a Masters Degree in the education field and taught in the classroom for 16 years. She recently completed a Masters of Library Science degree with a specialty in technology. Her preparation, dedication, and skills have prepared her for a key role in leading students, teachers, and administrators into the information-rich twenty-first century.

Skills Lessons Bibliography: Print

Aaseng, Nathan. 1995. *Autoimmune diseases.* New York: Franklin Watts.

——. 1988. *The inventors: Nobel Prizes in chemistry, physics, and medicine.* Minneapolis: Lerner.

Adoff, Arnold. 1979. *Eats.* New York: Mulberry Books.

African-American poets. 1996. Collective Biographies Series. Springfield, N.J.: Enslow.

Albyn, Carole Lisa, and Lois Sinaiko Webb. 1993. *The multicultural cookbook for students.* Phoenix, Ariz.: Oryx Press.

Aliki. *How a book is made.* 1986. New York: HarperCollins.

American Medical Association family medical guide. 1994. rev. ed. New York: Random House.

Ames, Sandra, ed. 1995. *Teaching electronic information skills: A resource guide, grades 6-8.* Chicago: Follett Software.

Andrews, William L., Frances Smith Foster, and Trudier Harris, eds. 1997. *The Oxford companion to African American literature.* New York: Oxford University Press.

Aretha Franklin: Motown superstar. 1996. African-American Biography Series. Springfield, N.J.: Enslow.

Arnold, Nick. 1995. *Voyages of exploration.* New York: Thomson Learning.

Ash, Russell. 1996. *The top 10 of everything 1997.* New York: Dorling Kindersley.

Atelsek, Jean. 1993. *All about computers.* Emeryville, Calif.: Ziff-Davis Press.

Avi. 1996. *Beyond the Western Sea. Book one: The escape from home.* New York: Orchard.

Bader, Bonnie, and Tracey West. 1996. *Countdown to 2000: A kid's guide to the new millennium.* Salt Lake City, Utah: Gibbs Smith.

Bangura, Abdul Karim. 1994. *The Heritage Library of African peoples: Kipsigis.* New York: Rosen.

Barber, Nicola, and Mary Mure. 1996. *The world of music.* Morristown, N.J.: Silver Burdett/Simon & Schuster.

Barron, Ann. 1997. *How to create great school Web pages.* Classroom Connect. Lancaster, Pa: Wentworth Worldwide Media.

Bartlett, John. 1990. *Familiar quotations.* 16th ed. Boston: Little, Brown.

Bender, Lionel. 1991. *Invention.* New York: Alfred A. Knopf.

Berger, Sandy. 1997. *How to have a meaningful relationship with your computer.* Fairfield, Iowa: Sunstar.

Berkman, Robert I. 1994. *Find it fast: How to uncover expert information on any subject.* 3d ed. New York: HarperCollins.

Berman, Matt. 1996. *What else should I read? Guiding kids to good books.* Vol. 2. Englewood: Colo.: Libraries Unlimited.

Bever, Edward. 1996. *Africa*. Phoenix, Ariz.: Oryx Press.

Bielak, Mark. 1995. *Television production today*. 3d ed. Lincolnwood, Ill.: National Textbook.

Bloom, Dwila. 1994. *Multicultural art activities*. Denver, Colo.: University of Denver, Center for Teaching International Relations.

Blos, Joan W. 1994. *Brooklyn doesn't rhyme*. New York: Charles Scribner's Sons.

——. 1994. *A gathering of days: A New England girl's journal, 1830-32*. New York: Charles Scribner's Sons.

Bombaugh, Ruth. 1990. *Science fair success*. Springfield, N.J.: Enslow.

Bragg, Janet Harmon. 1996. *Soaring above setbacks: The autobiography of Janet Harmon Bragg*. Edited by Marjorie M. Kriz. Washington, D.C.: Smithsonian.

Branley, Franklyn. 1987. *Raining cats and dogs: All kinds of weather and why we have it*. Boston: Houghton Mifflin.

Brantley, C. L. 1995. *The Princeton Review writing smart junior: The art and craft of writing*. New York: Random House.

Breen, Karen. 1988. *Index to collective biographies for young readers*. 4th ed. New York: R. R. Bowker.

Brodie, Carolyn S., ed. 1994. *Exploring the Plains states through literature*. Exploring the United States Through Literature Series. Phoenix, Ariz.: Oryx Press.

Brownstone, David, and Irene Franck. 1997. *People in the news*. New York: Simon & Schuster.

Brunvand, Jan Harold, ed. 1996. *American folklore: An encyclopedia*. New York: Garland.

Burckhardt, Ann L. 1996. *The people of Africa and their food*. Mankato, Minn.: Capstone Press.

——. 1996. *The people of China and their food*. Mankato, Minn.: Capstone Press.

——. 1996. *The people of Mexico and their food*. Mankato, Minn.: Capstone Press.

——. 1996. *The people of Russia and their food*. Mankato, Minn.: Capstone Press.

Burnett, Gail Lemley. 1996. *Muscular dystrophy*. Parsippany, N.J.: Crestwood House.

Burnford, Sheila. 1961. *The incredible journey*. New York: Bantam Books.

Byrnes, Ronald S., and Peter Downing, with Carol Vogler. 1995. *Teaching about Africa: A Continent of complexities*. Denver, Colo.: University of Denver, Center for Teaching International Relations.

Cadnum, Michael. 1996. *Zero at the bone*. New York: Penguin USA.

Calishain, Tara. 1996. *Official Netscape guide to Internet research*. Chapel Hill, N.C.: Ventana Press.

Caney, Steven. 1985. *Invention book*. New York: Workman.

Capek, Michael. 1996. *Murals: Cave, cathedral, to street*. Minneapolis: Lerner.

Career discovery encyclopedia. 1990. Chicago: J. G. Ferguson.

Careers and opportunities series. 1995-96. 10 vols. New York: Rosen.

Carnes, Jim. 1995. *Us and them: A history of intolerance in America*. New York: Oxford University Press.

Cary, Alice. 1996. *Jean Craighead George.* Santa Barbara, Calif.: The Learning Works.

Chandler, Gary, and Kevin Graham. 1996. Making a Better World Series: *Alternative energy sources; Guardians of wildlife; Kids who make a difference; Natural foods and products; Protecting our air, land, and water; Recycling.* New York: Charles Scribner's Sons.

Charlesworth, Liza, and Bonnie Sachatello-Sawyer. 1995. *Dinosaurs.* New York: Scholastic.

The Chicago manual of style. 1993. 14th ed. Chicago: University of Chicago Press.

Children's atlas of world history. 1988. Skokie, Ill.: Rand McNally.

Choron, Sandy, and Harry Choron. 1995. *The book of lists for kids.* Boston: Houghton Mifflin.

Christmas in Spain: Christmas around the world from world book. 1983. Chicago: World Book.

Clapp, Patricia. 1968. *Constance: A story of early Plymouth.* New York: Beech Tree Books.

Cleary, Beverly. 1983. *Dear Mr. Henshaw.* New York: William Morrow.

Cleary, Frances. 1995. *American home cooking.* New York: Anness.

Clements, Gillian. 1993. *The picture history of great inventors.* New York: Alfred A. Knopf.

Cohen, Daniel. 1987. *Dinosaurs.* New York: Doubleday.

Colborn, Candy. 1994. *What do children read next? A reader's guide to fiction for children.* Detroit: Gale Research.

Colin Powell. 1996. Contemporary African American Series. Chatham, N.J.: Raintree/Steck-Vaughn.

Coombes, Allen J. 1992. *Trees.* New York: Dorling Kindersley.

Cooney, Caroline B. 1995. *Flash fire.* New York: Scholastic.

Cooper, Kay. 1990. *Where in the world are you? A guide to looking at the world.* New York: Walker.

Copyright law of the United States. 1996. In *The world almanac and book of facts 1997.* Mahwah, N.J.: World Almanac Books.

Crampton, William. 1989. *Flag.* New York: Alfred A. Knopf.

Cumming, Robert. 1995. *Annotated art.* New York: Dorling Kindersley.

Cummings, Pat, ed. 1995. *Talking with artists II.* Old Tappan, N.J.: Macmillan.

Current issues: Critical issues confronting the nation and the world. 1996. Denver, Colo.: University of Denver, Center for Teaching International Relations.

Darling, David. 1995. *Computers of the future.* Morristown, N.J.: Silver Burdett Press.

Davidson, Rosemary. 1993. *Take a look: An introduction to the experience of art.* New York: Viking.

Denenberg, Barry. 1996. *When will this cruel war be over? The Civil War diary of Emma Simpson, Gordonville, Virginia.* New York: Scholastic.

Dessen, Sarah. 1996. *That summer.* New York: Orchard/Watts.

Dewey decimal classification and relative index. 1989. 20th ed. Albany, N.Y.: Forest Press.

Diamond, Wendy, comp. 1995. *A musical feast: Recipes from over 100 of the world's most famous musical artists.* New York: Global Liaisons.

Dietz, Joan. 1986. *You mean I have to stand up and say something?* New York: Atheneum.

Discover America! A scenic tour of the fifty states. 1989. Washington, D.C.: National Geographic Society.

Doherty, Berlie. 1995. *The snake-stone.* New York: Orchard Books.

Doll, Carol A., ed. 1994. *Exploring the Pacific states through literature.* Exploring the United States Through Literature Series. Phoenix, Ariz.: Oryx Press.

Donavin, Denise Perry, ed. 1992. *American Library Association best of the best for children.* New York: Random House.

Dorling Kindersley ultimate visual dictionary. 1994. New York: Dorling Kindersley.

Dorling Kindersley visual encyclopedia. 1995. New York: Dorling Kindersley.

Dorling Kindersley world reference atlas. 1994. New York: Dorling Kindersley.

Dornberg, John. 1995. *Central and Eastern Europe.* Phoenix, Ariz.: Oryx Press.

———. 1996. *Western Europe.* Phoenix: Oryx Press.

Dorros, Arthur. 1995. *Ciudades de hormigas.* Translated by Daniel Santa Cruz. Let's Read-and-Find Out Series. New York: HarperCollins.

Drabble, Margaret, ed. 1995. *The Oxford companion to English literature.* rev. ed. New York: Oxford University Press.

Duden, Jane. 1992. *Men's and women's gymnastics.* New York: Crestwood House.

Duke Ellington: Giant of jazz. 1996. African-American Biography Series. Springfield, N.J.: Enslow.

Easton, Thomas A. 1996. *Careers in science.* VGM Career Horizons. Lincolnwood, Ill.: National Textbook.

Eberts, Marjorie, and Margaret Gisler. 1990. *Careers for bookworms and other literary types.* Lincolnwood, Ill.: National Textbook.

———. 1991. *Careers for Good Samaritans and other humanitarian types.* Lincolnwood, Ill.: National Textbook.

Educator's Internet companion: Classroom connect's complete guide to educational resources on the Internet. 1995. Lancaster, Pa.: Wentworth Worldwide Media.

Ehrlich, Robert. 1996. *What if you could unscramble an egg?* New Brunswick, N.J.: Rutgers University Press.

Eureka! Scientific discoveries and inventions that shaped the world. 1995. 6 vols. Detroit, Mich.: UXL.

Evans, Ivor H. 1981. *Brewer's dictionary of phrase and fable.* Centenary ed., rev. New York: Harper & Row.

Everything you need to know about abusive relationships. 1996. The Need to Know Series. San Diego, Calif.: Lucent Books.

Facaros, Dana, and Michael Parks. 1992. *Spain.* 3d ed. Cadogan Guides. Old Saybrook, Conn.: Globe Pequote.

Familiar insects and spiders. 1995. A National Audubon Society Pocket Guide. New York: Alfred A. Knopf.

Farmer, Nancy. 1997. *A girl named disaster.* New York: Richard Jackson/Orchard.

Festivals of the world: China. 1997. Milwaukee, Wis.: Gareth Stevens.

Festivals of the world: Germany. 1997. Milwaukee, Wis.: Gareth Stevens.

Fleischman, Sid. 1996. *The abracadabra kid: A writer's life.* New York: Greenwillow Books/William Morrow.

Fleischman, Paul. 1991. *The borning room.* New York: HarperCollins.

Fodor's exploring Spain. 1995. New York: Fodor's Travel Publications.

Forbes, Esther. 1943. *Johnny Tremain.* Boston: Houghton Mifflin.

Fox, Mary Virginia. 1991. *Iran.* Chicago: Childrens Press.

Fox, Paula. 1973. *The slave dancer.* New York: Bradbury Press.

Franco, Betsy. 1996. *Textile math.* Multicultural Explorations Through Patterns Series. Grades 6-8. Orlando, Fla.: Creative.

Frankovich, Nicholas, ed. 1997. *The Columbia Granger's index to poetry in anthologies.* 11th ed. New York: Columbia University Press.

Fraser, Linda, consultant ed. 1996. *Best-ever chicken: 200 step-by-step chicken recipes.* New York: Smithmark.

Freedman, Alan. 1995. *The computer glossary: The complete illustrated dictionary.* 7th ed. New York: American Management Association.

Freeman, Judy. 1990. *Books kids will sit still for.* 2d ed. New York: R. R. Bowker.

Friedhoffer, Bob. 1996. *Magic and perception: The art and science of fooling the senses.* New York: Franklin Watts.

Fritz, Jean. 1994. *Around the world in a hundred years: From Henry the Navigator to Magellan.* New York: G. P. Putnam's Sons.

———. 1967. *Early thunder.* New York: Penguin Books.

Galperin, Ann. 1990. *Nutrition.* New York: Chelsea House.

Ganeri, Anita. 1992. *Germany and the Germans.* New York: Glouster Press.

———. 1992. *France and the French.* New York: Glouster Press.

Gardner, Robert. 1992. *Celebrating earth day.* Brookfield, Conn.: Millbrook Press.

Gibbons, Gail. 1992. *Stargazers.* New York: Holiday House.

Gillespie, John T., and Corinne J. Naden. 1996. *The Newbery companion: Booktalk and related materials for Newbery medal and honor books.* Englewood, Colo.: Libraries Unlimited.

Gilster, Paul. 1995. *The mosaic navigator: The essential guide to the Internet interface.* New York: John Wiley.

Glasthal, Jacqueline B. 1996. *American history math: 50 problem-solving activities that link math to key events in U.S. history, grades 4-8.* New York: Scholastic.

Gold, John Coopersmith. 1996. *Heart disease.* Parsippany, N.J.: Crestwood House.

Gold, Susan Dudley. 1996. *Alzheimer's disease.* Parsippany, N.J.: Crestwood House.

Goldsmith, Donald. 1996. When worlds and comets collide. In *World Book science year 1996*. World Book. 211-19.

Graham, Billy. 1997. *Just as I am: The autobiography of Billy Graham*. San Francisco: HarperCollins Worldwide.

Grant, Neil. 1992. *The great atlas of discovery*. New York: Alfred A. Knopf.

Green, Carol. 1983. *Mother Teresa: Friend of the friendless*. Chicago: Childrens Press.

Green, Rayna. 1992. *Native American women*. New York: Chelsea House.

Greenberg, Dan. 1996. *Funny and fabulous fraction stories: 30 reproducible math tales and problems to reinforce important reference skills*. New York: Scholastic.

Gregory, Kristiana. 1997. *The winter of the red snow: The revolutionary diary of Abigail Jane Stewart*. New York: Scholastic.

Gutman, Dan. 1996. *Gymnastics*. New York: Viking/Penguin Books USA.

Hahn, Mary Downing. 1996. *The gentleman outlaw and Me-Eli: A story of the old west*. Boston: Houghton Mifflin.

Halecroft, David. 1992. *Benched!* New York: Penguin.

Hansen, Barbara J., and Philip English Mackey. 1993. *Your public schools: What you can do to help them*. North Haven, Conn.: Catbird Press.

Harrington, Diane, and Laurette Young. 1993. *Everything you need to know to guide your child through today's schools*. New York: Noonday Press.

Harris, Jacqueline L. 1993. *Communicable diseases*. New York: Twenty-First Century Books.

Hartman, Donald K., and Greg Sapp. 1994. *Historical figures in fiction*. Phoenix, Ariz.: Oryx Press.

Haskins, James. 1987. *Black music in America: A history through its people*. New York: HarperCollins.

———. 1996. *The Harlem Renaissance*. Brookfield, Conn.: Millbrook Press.

Haven, Kendall. 1996. *Great moments in science: Experiments and readers theatre*. Englewood, Colo.: Teacher Ideas Press.

Hawkes, Nigel. 1994. *New technology: Communications*. New York: Twenty-First Century Books.

Haycock, Kate. 1991. *Olympic sports: Gymnastics*. Morristown, N.J.: Silver Burdett Press.

Heitzmann, William R. 1991. *Careers for sports nuts and other athletic types*. Lincolnwood, Ill.: National Textbook.

Heneghan, James. 1997. *Wish me luck*. New York: Farrar, Straus, & Giroux.

Herald, Diana Tixier. 1997. *Teen genreflecting*. Englewood, Colo.: Libraries Unlimited.

Herz, Sarah K., with Donald R. Gallo. 1996. *From Hinton to Hamlet: Building bridges between young adult literature and the classics*. Westport, Conn.: Greenwood Press.

Hesse, Karen. 1996. *The music of dolphins*. New York: Scholastic.

Historical atlas of the United States. 1993. Washington, D.C.: National Geographic Society.

Hoff, Mary, and Mary M. Rodgers. 1992. *Our endangered planet: Life on land.* Minneapolis: Lerner Group.

———. 1991. *Our Endangered Planet: Oceans.* Minneapolis: Lerner Group.

Hopke, William E., ed. 1993. *The encyclopedia of careers and vocational guidance.* Chicago: J. G. Ferguson.

Hopkins, Lee Bennett, sel. 1996. *Opening days: Sports poems.* San Diego, Calif.: Harcourt Brace Jovanovich.

Horwitz, Margot F. 1996. *A female focus: Great women photographers.* New York: Franklin Watts/Grolier.

How to create successful Internet projects. 1997. Classroom Connect. Lancaster, Pa.: Wentworth Worldwide Media.

Howard, Tracy Apple, with Sage Alexandra Howard. 1992. *Kids ending hunger: What can we do?* Kansas City, Mo.: Andrews and McMeel.

Howe, Harold, II. 1993. *Thinking about our kids.* New York: Free Press.

Hunt, Irene. 1964. *Across five Aprils.* Chicago: Follett.

Immell, Myra, ed. 1992. *The young adult reader's adviser.* Vol. 1. New Providence, N.J.: R. R. Bowker.

The importance of Jane Goodall. 1997. The Importance of Series. San Diego, Calif.: Lucent Books.

"It Only Hurts When I Land." 1996. *Zillions* 7:1 July/August, 17-20.

Iwago, Mitsuaki. 1986. *Serengeti: Natural order of the African plain.* San Francisco: Chronicle Books.

Jeffrey, Laura S. 1996. *American inventors of the 20th century.* Springfield, N.J.: Enslow.

Jensen, Mary Brandt. 1996. *Does your project have a copyright problem? A decision-making guide for librarians.* Jefferson, N.C.: McFarland.

Jicai, Feng. 1995. *Let one hundred flowers bloom.* Translated by Christopher Smith. New York: Penguin Books USA.

Jones, Alison. 1995. *Larousse dictionary of world folklore.* New York: Larousse.

Jones, Lawrence. 1996. *Job skills for the 21st century: A guide for students.* Phoenix, Ariz.: Oryx Press.

Jones, Patrick. 1992. *Connecting young adults and libraries: A how-to-do-it manual.* New York: Neal-Schuman.

Junior worldmark encyclopedia of the nations. 1996. 9 vols. Detroit: UXL/Gale Research.

Kaplan, Justin, ed. 1992. *Bartlett's familiar quotations.* 16th ed. Boston: Little, Brown.

Karnes, Frances A., and Suzanne M. Bean. 1995. *Girls and young women inventing: Twenty true stories about inventors plus how you can be one yourself.* Minneapolis: Free Spirit.

Kavanagh, Jack. 1992. *Sports great Larry Bird.* Springfield, N.J.: Enslow.

Kehret, Peg. 1996. *Small steps: The year I got polio.* Morton Grove, Ill.: Whitman.

Keith, Harold. 1957. *Rifles for Watie.* New York: Crowell.

Keller, Charles. 1989. *Driving me crazy: Fun on wheels jokes.* New York: Pippin Press.

Kenda, Margaret, and Phyllis E. Williams. 1995. *Math wizardry for kids.* Hauppauge, N.Y.: Barron's Educational Series.

Kids explore America's African-American heritage. 1993. Santa Fe, N. Mex.: John Muir Publications.

Kids explore America's Hispanic heritage. 1992. Santa Fe, N. Mex.: John Muir.

King, Jerry P. 1993. *Art of mathematics.* New York: Fawcett.

Klepper, Nancy. 1990. *Our global village: Africa.* St. Louis, Mo.: Milliken.

Kneidel, Sally Stenhouse. 1993. *Creepy crawlies and the scientific method: Over 100 science experiments for children.* Golden, Colo.: Fulcrum.

Kohen, Elizabeth. 1992. *Spain.* New York: Marshall Cavendish.

Konigsburg, E. L. 1996. *The view from Saturday.* New York: Jean Karl/Atheneum.

Korman, Gordon. 1996. *The chicken doesn't skate.* New York: Scholastic.

Kurz, Raymond A., with Bart G. Newland, Steven Lieberman, and Celine M. Jimenez. 1996. *Internet and the law: Legal fundamentals for the Internet user.* Rockville, Md.: Government Institutes.

La Blanc, Michael, ed. 1992. *Contemporary Black biography: Profiles from the international Black community.* Detroit: Gale Research.

Ladson, Gloria. 1994. *The dreamkeepers: Successful teachers of African American children.* San Francisco: Jossey-Bass.

Laird, Elizabeth. 1991. *Kiss the dust.* New York: Penguin Books USA.

Lamy, Steven, et. al. 1994. *Teaching global awareness with simulations and games.* Denver, Colo.: University of Denver, Center for Teaching International Relations.

Langley, Andrew. 1990. *Twenty explorers.* New York: Marshall Cavendish.

Lasky, Kathryn. 1996. *A journey to the new world: The diary of Remember Patience Whipple, Mayflower, 1620.* New York: Scholastic.

Lass, Abraham, David Kiremidjian, and Ruth M. Goldstein. 1987. *Dictionary of classical, Biblical, and literary allusions.* New York: Fawcett.

Lauber, Patricia. 1996. *Flood: Wrestling with the Mississippi.* Washington, D.C.: National Geographic Society.

———. 1996. *Hurricanes: Earth's mightiest storms.* New York: Scholastic.

Leach, Maria, and Jerome Fried, eds. 1984. *Funk and Wagnalls standard dictionary of folklore, mythology, and legend.* San Francisco: Harper.

Leinwand, Gerald. 1996. *Heroism in America.* New York: Franklin Watts.

Lents, P. J. 1992. *Our global village: Germany.* St. Louis, Mo.: Milliken.

Lessem, Don. 1996. *Dinosaur worlds: New dinosaurs, new discoveries.* Honesdale, Pa.: Boyds Mills Press.

Li, Xia, and Nancy Crane. 1993. *Electronic style: A guide to citing electronic information.* Westport, Conn.: Mecklermedia.

Lightman, Alan. 1994. *Time for the stars: Astronomy in the 1990's.* New York: Warner Books.

Lipson, Michelle, and friends. 1994. *The fantastic costume book: 40 complete patterns to amaze and amuse.* New York: Sterling.

Livingston, Myra Cohn. 1997. *Cricket never does: A collection of haiku and tanka.* New York: McElderry/Simon & Schuster.

——. 1991. *Poem-making: Ways to begin writing poetry.* New York: HarperCollins.

Locker, Thomas, and Candace Christiansen. 1995. *Sky tree: Seeing science through art.* New York: HarperCollins.

Lomask, Milton. 1984. *Exploration: Great lives.* New York: Charles Scribner's Sons.

——. 1991. *Great Lives: Invention and technology.* New York: Charles Scribner's Sons.

Lowry, Lois. 1993. *The giver.* New York: Bantam Dell Books for Young Readers.

Macaulay, David. 1977. *Castle.* Boston: Houghton Mifflin.

MacLachlan, Patricia. 1985. *Sarah, plain and tall.* New York: HarperCollins.

Macnow, Glen. 1993. *Sports great Cal Ripken, Jr.* Springfield, N.J.: Enslow.

Manguel, Alberto, and Gianni Guadalupi. 1987. *The dictionary of imaginary places.* San Diego, Calif.: Harcourt Brace Jovanovich.

Markle, Sandra. 1991. *The kid's Earth handbook.* New York: Atheneum.

Martin, John. 1994. *In-line skating.* Minneapolis: Capstone Press.

Martin, Judith. 1997. *Miss Manners' basic training: Communication.* New York: Crown.

Maynard, Caitlin, and Thane Maynard. 1996. *Rain forests and reefs: A kid's-eye view of the tropics.* New York: Franklin Watts/Grolier.

McCarthy, Tara. 1996. *Teaching genre: Exploring 9 types of literature to develop lifelong readers and writers.* New York: Scholastic.

McKeever, Susan, ed. 1993. *The Dorling Kindersley science encyclopedia.* New York: Dorling Kindersley.

McKissack, Patricia, and Frederick McKissack. 1994. *African-American scientists.* Brookfield, Conn.: Millbrook Press.

McLain, Tim, and Gregory Giagnocavo. 1996. *The Internet homework helper.* Upper Saddle River, N.J.: Prentice Hall.

McMillan, Bruce. 1991. *The weather sky.* New York: Farrar, Straus & Giroux.

McNair, Sylvia. 1987. *Thailand.* Chicago: Childrens Press.

McVey, Vicki. 1991. *The Sierra Club book of weather wisdom.* Boston: Little, Brown.

Miles, Betty. 1981. *The secret life of the underwear champ.* New York: Alfred A. Knopf.

Miller, Dorothy Reynolds. 1996. *The clearing: A mystery.* New York: Atheneum/Simon & Schuster.

Miller, Louise. 1992. *Careers for animal lovers and other zoological types.* Lincolnwood, Ill.: National Textbook.

Mitchell, Barbara. 1986. *A pocketful of goobers: A story about George Washington Carver.* Minneapolis: Carolrhoda Books.

——. 1986. *Shoes for everyone: A story about Jan Matzeliger.* Minneapolis: Carolrhoda Books.

Morey, Janet Nomura, and Wendy Dunn. 1996. *Famous Hispanic Americans.* New York: Cobblestone/Penguin USA.

Mound, Laurence A. 1990. *Insect.* Eyewitness Books. New York: Alfred A. Knopf.

Muirden, James. 1993. *Stars and planets.* Danbury, Conn.: Grolier Encyclopedia Educational Corp.

Munsart, Craig A. 1997. *American history through earth science.* Englewood, Colo.: Teacher Ideas Press/Libraries Unlimited.

Murray, Jacelyn. 1993. *Africa.* New York: Facts on File.

National Geographic picture atlas of our fifty states. 1991. Washington, D.C.: National Geographic Society.

National parks of North America. 1995. Washington, D.C.: National Geographic Society.

Needler, Toby, and Bonnie Goodman. 1991. *Exploring global art.* Denver, Colo.: University of Denver, Center for Teaching International Relations.

Neimark, Anne E. 1996. *Myth maker: J. R. R. Tolkien.* San Diego, Calif.: Harcourt Brace.

The New York public library student's desk reference. 1993. New York: Prentice Hall General Reference.

Nicolson, Iain. 1991. *The illustrated world of space.* New York: Simon & Schuster.

Nixon, Joan Lowery. 1992. *Land of hope.* New York: Bantam Books.

———. 1997. *Murdered, my sweet.* New York: Delacorte Press.

Nofsinger, Bruce, ed. Current topics: For and about teens in touch with their world. *Topics Magazine.*

Nolan, Han. 1996. *Send me down a miracle.* San Diego, Calif.: Harcourt Brace.

Norman, David. 1996. *Dinosaurs.* London: Salamander Books.

Norton, Donna E. 1991. *Through the eyes of a child: An introduction to children's literature.* 3d ed. Columbus, Ohio: Merrill.

NTC's beginner's Spanish and English dictionary. 1992. Lincolnwood, Ill.: National Textbook.

Odean, Kathleen. 1997. *Great books for girls: More than 600 books to inspire today's girls and tomorrow's women.* New York: Ballantine Books.

O'Hara, Shelley, Jennifer Fulton, and Ed Guilford. 1995. *The big basics book of windows 95.* Indianapolis, Ind.: Macmillan.

Oleksy, Walter. 1995. *Science and medicine.* New York: Facts on File.

O'Neill, Mary. 1991. *Nature in danger.* Mahwah, N.J.: Troll.

Opie, Brenda, Lory Jackson, and Douglas McAvinn. 1995. *Decimals, percentages, metric system, and consumer math: Reproducible skill builders and higher order thinking activities based on NCTM standards.* Reston, Va.: National Council of Teachers of Math.

Opie, Iona, and Peter Opie. eds. 1951. *The Oxford dictionary of nursery rhymes.* New York: Oxford University Press.

Opposing viewpoints. 1995-97. American History Series. 10 vols. San Diego, Calif.: Greenhaven Press.

Palmer, Edward. 1988. *Television and America's children: A crisis of neglect.* New York: Oxford University Press.

Parker, Steve. 1994. *How the body works.* Pleasantville, NY: Reader's Digest Association.

———. 1992. *Marie Curie and radium.* New York: HarperCollins.

Parsons, Larry. 1990. *A funny thing happened on the way to the school library: A treasury of anecdotes, quotes, and other happenings.* Englewood, Colo.: Libraries Unlimited.

Patent, Dorothy Hinshaw. 1992. *Nutrition: What's in the food we eat.* New York: Holiday House.

Paterson, Katherine. 1974. *Of nightingales that weep.* New York: Harper & Row.

Pausewang, Gudrun. 1996. *The final journey.* Translated by Patricia Crampton. New York: Viking.

Peck, Richard. 1993. *Bel Air Bambi and the mall rats.* New York: Bantam Dell Books for Young Readers.

Perkins, George, Barbara Perkins, and Phillip Leininger. 1991. *Benét's reader's encyclopedia of American literature.* New York: HarperCollins.

Pfiffner, George. 1995. *Earth-friendly holidays: How to make fabulous gifts and decorations from reusable objects.* New York: John Wiley.

Phelps, Shirelle, ed. 1996. *Who's who among African Americans.* 9th ed. Detroit: Gale Research.

Plummer, Louise. 1995. *The unlikely romance of Kate Bjorkman.* New York: Delacorte Press.

Porter, Eliot, sel. 1967. *From Henry David Thoreau: "In wildness is the preservation of the world."* New York: Ballantine Books.

Porter, Pat Lowery. 1992. *I am an artist.* Brookfield, Conn.: Millbrook Press.

Raintree Steck-Vaughn illustrated science encyclopedia. 1997. rev. ed. Chatham, N.J.: Raintree/Steck-Vaughn.

Rathbone, Andy. 1994. *Multimedia and CD-ROMs for dummies.* San Mateo, Calif.: IDG Books Worldwide.

Reiss, Johanna. 1972. *The upstairs room.* New York: Crowell.

Robinson, Dindy. 1996. *World cultures through art activities.* Englewood, Colo.: Teacher Ideas Press/Libraries Unlimited.

Rodgers, Marie E. 1998. *The Harlem Renaissance: An annotated reference guide for student research.* Englewood, Colo.: Libraries Unlimited.

Rodriguez, Consuelo. 1991. *Cesar Chavez.* New York: Chelsea House.

Ryan, Margaret. 1991. *How to read and write poems.* New York: Franklin Watts.

Saari, Peggy, and Stephen Allison, eds. 1996. *Scientists: The lives and works of 150 scientists.* 3 vols. San Diego, Calif.: Harcourt Brace Jovanovich.

Saari, Peggy, and Daniel B. Baker. 1995. *Explorers and discoverers: From Alexander the Great to Sally Ride.* New York: UXL.

Salzman, Marian, and Robert Pondisco. 1995. *Kids on-line: 150 ways for kids to surf the net for fun and information.* New York: Avon Camelot Books.

Schenk de Regniers, Beatrice, et al. 1988. *Sing a song of popcorn.* New York: Scholastic.

Schmitt, Lois. 1989. *A young consumer's guide: Smart spending.* New York: Charles Scribner's Sons.

Schnyder, Sandy Eddy, David Haskin, and Ed Guilford. 1995. *The big basics book of Word for Windows 95.* Indianapolis, Ind.: Macmillan.

Selby, Anna. 1994. *Spain.* Chatham, N.J.: Raintree/Steck-Vaughn.

Semple, Carol McCormick. 1996. *Diabetes.* Parsippany, N.J.: Crestwood House.

Seymour, Simon. 1994. *Comets, meteors, and asteroids.* New York: Morrow Junior Books.

Shakespeare, William. 1996. *Romeo and Juliet.* Wishbone Classics. Retold by Billy Aronson. New York: HarperCollins.

Shapes and structure. 1991. Science in our World. Vol. 11. Danbury, Conn.: Grolier, Atlantic Europe.

Shapiro, Lee T., ed. 1997. Astronomy and calendar. In *The world almanac and book of facts 1997*, Vols. 440-80. Mahwah: N.J.: World Almanac Books.

Shapiro, Lillian L., and Barbara L. Stein. 1992. *Fiction for youth.* 3d ed. New York: Neal-Schuman.

Shelley, Mary Wollstonecraft. 1996. *Frankenstein.* Wishbone Classics. Retold by Michael Burgan. New York: HarperCollins.

Shipley, Roberta Gail. 1995. *Teaching guides for 50 young adult novels.* New York: Neal-Schuman.

Siepman, Katherine Baker, ed. 1987. *Benét's reader's encyclopedia.* 3d ed. New York: Harper & Row.

Silverman, Jerry, ed. 1994. *African roots.* New York: Chelsea House.

Simon, Hilda. 1983. *Sight and seeing: A world of light and color.* New York: Philomel.

Simpson, Carol Mann. 1997. *Copyright for schools: A practical guide.* 2d ed. Worthington, Ohio: Linworth.

Simpson, Martha Seif. 1995. *Environmental awareness activities for librarians and teachers: 20 interdisciplinary units for use in grades 2-8.* Jefferson, N.C.: McFarland.

Sirch, Willow Ann. 1996. *Eco-women: Protectors of the Earth.* Golden, Colo.: Fulcrum.

Skinner, David. 1992. *You must kiss a whale.* New York: Simon & Schuster.

Sleator, William. 1995. *Dangerous wishes.* New York: E. P. Dutton.

Speare, Elizabeth George. 1961. *The bronze bow.* Boston: Houghton Mifflin.

———. 1958. *The witch of Blackbird Pond.* New York: Laurel Leaf Books.

Spencer, Pam. 1994. *What do young adults read next? A reader's guide to fiction for young adults.* Detroit: Gale Research.

Spero, Robert. 1980. *The duping of the American voter: Dishonesty and deception in presidential television advertising.* New York: Lippincott and Crowell.

Sreenivasan, Jyotsna. 1997. *Aruna's journeys.* St. Louis, Mo.: Smooth Stone Press.

St. George, Judith. 1992. *Dear Dr. Bell . . . Your friend, Helen Keller.* New York: G. P. Putnam's Sons.

Stearns, Michael, ed. 1995. *A starfarer's dozen: Stories of things to come.* San Diego, Calif.: Harcourt Brace.

Steve Young: NFL passing wizard. 1996. The Millbrook Press Sports World Series. Brookfield, Conn.: Millbrook Press.

Stevenson, Robert Louis. 1947. *Treasure Island.* Illustrated Junior Library. New York: Grosset & Dunlap.

Stewart, Gail B. 1997. *Gangs.* The Other America Series. San Diego, Calif.: Lucent Books.

Stubbs, Charles B. 1994. *Art is elementary: Teaching visual thinking through art concepts.* rev. ed. Salt Lake City, Utah: Gibbs Smith.

Sullivan, Helen, and Linda Sernoff. 1996. *Research reports: A guide for middle and high school students.* Brookfield, Conn.: Millbrook Press.

Sutcliff, Rosemary. 1976. *Blood feud.* New York: Dutton.

Symynkywicz, Jeffrey B. 1996. *Germany: United again.* Parsippany, N.J.: Dillon.

Tagliaferro, Linda. 1997. *Genetic engineering: Progress or peril?* Minneapolis: Lerner Group.

Takada, Noriko, and Rita Lampkin. 1997. *The Japanese way: Aspects of behavior, attitudes, and customs of the Japanese.* Lincolnwood, Ill.: Passport Books/National Textbook.

Tanner, Fran A. 1996. *Creative communication: Projects in acting, speaking, and oral reading.* 5th ed. Lexington, Ky.: Clark.

Taylor, Mildred. 1976. *Roll of thunder, hear my cry.* New York: Dial Press.

Temple, Lannis, ed. 1993. *Dear world: How children around the world feel about our environment.* New York: Random House.

Tesar, Jenny. 1996. *The new view almanac: The first all-visual resource of vital facts and statistics!* Woodbridge, Conn.: Blackbirch Press.

Thomas, Peggy. 1997. *Medicines from nature.* New York: Twenty-First Century Books.

Thornton, Carol A., and Nancy S. Bley, eds. 1994. *Windows of opportunity: Mathematics for students with special needs.* Reston, Va.: National Council of Teachers of Mathematics.

Tobias, Sheila. 1993. *Overcoming math anxiety.* New York: W. W. Norton.

Tracy, Steve. 1995. *L5: Behind the moon.* Indianapolis, Ind.: Silver Books.

Trevor, William. 1991. *Juliet's story.* New York: Simon & Schuster.

Tucker, Tom. 1995. *Brainstorm! The stories of twenty American kid inventors.* New York: Farrar, Straus & Giroux.

Turner, Megan Whalen. 1996. *The thief.* New York: Greenwillow Books.

Van Leeuwen, Jean. 1996. *Blue sky, butterfly.* New York: Dial Books for Young Readers.

Van Vliet, Lucille W. 1992. *Approaches to literature through genre.* Phoenix, Ariz.: Oryx Press.

———. 1985. "Historical Hat Parade! A Single-Camera Video Production." *School Library Media Activities Monthly* 1:9 May, 38-39, 42, 45.

Vecchione, Glen. 1995. *100 amazing make-it-yourself science fair projects.* New York: Sterling.

Veltze, Linda, ed. 1994. *Exploring the south-east states through literature.* Exploring the United States Through Literature Series. Phoenix, Ariz.: Oryx Press.

Venezia, Mike. 1996. Getting to Know the World's Greatest Artists Series. Chicago: Childrens Press/Grolier.

Voigt, Cynthia 1982. *Dicey's song.* New York: Atheneum.

von Wodtke, Mark. 1993. *Mind over media: Creative thinking skills for electronic media.* New York: McGraw-Hill.

Vos Savant, Marilyn. 1993. *World's most famous math problems.* New York: St. Martin's Press.

Wallace, Joseph. 1994. *The American Museum of Natural History's book of dinosaurs and other ancient creatures.* New York: Simon & Schuster.

Wallace, Rich. 1997. *Shots on goal.* New York: Alfred A. Knopf/Random House.

Webb, Farren, et al. 1995. *The world wise consumer: Consumer strategies in an age of scarcity.* Denver, Colo.: University of Denver, Center for Teaching International Relations.

Webb, Lois Sinaiko. 1996. *Holidays of the world cookbook for students.* Phoenix, Ariz.: Oryx Press.

Weiss, Ann E. 1996. *Virtual reality: A door to cyberspace.* New York: Twenty-First Century Books/Henry Holt.

West, Delno C., and Jean M. West. 1996. *Braving the North Atlantic: The Vikings, the Cabots, and Jacques Cartier voyage to America.* New York: Atheneum/Macmillan.

White, Ron. 1995. *How computers work.* 2d ed. Emeryville, Calif.: Ziff-Davis Press.

Wilder, Laura Ingalls. 1953. *Little house on the prairie.* New York: Harper & Row.

Williams, Bard. 1995. *The Internet for teachers.* San Mateo, Calif.: IDG Books Worldwide.

Williams, Suzanne. 1996. *Made in China: Ideas and inventions from ancient China.* Berkeley, Calif.: Pacific View Press.

Williams, Trevor I. 1987. *The history of invention.* New York: Facts on File.

Winn, Marie. 1987. *Unplugging the plug-in drug.* New York: Viking Penguin.

Winpenny, Patricia G., and Katherine W. Caldwell, with Louise Cadwell. 1995. *Teaching Russian studies: History, language, culture and art.* Denver, Colo.: University of Denver, Center for Teaching International Relations.

Winters, Nathan. 1986. *Architecture is elementary: Teaching visual thinking through architectural concepts.* Salt Lake City, Utah: Gibbs Smith.

Wood, A. J. 1996. *Nicki Palin's hidden pictures.* Brookfield, Conn.: Millbrook Press.

Wood, Frances M. 1996. *Becoming Rosemary.* New York: Delacorte Press.

Wooldridge, Susan G. 1996. *Poemcrazy: Freeing your life with words.* New York: Crown.

The world almanac and book of facts. 1997. Mahwah, N.J.: World Almanac Books.

The world book student information finder: Language arts and social studies. 1993. Chicago: World Book.

The world book student information finder: Math and science. 1988. Chicago: World Book.

Wyler, Rose, and Mary Elting. 1992. *Math fun with money puzzlers.* New York: Messner.

Yolen, Jane. 1996. *Sacred places.* San Diego, Calif.: Harcourt Brace Jovanovich.

Yuan, Juliana Y. 1992. *Our global village: China.* St. Louis, Mo.: Milliken Press.

Yumoto, Kazumi. 1996. *The friends/Natsu no niwa.* Translated by Cathy Hirano. New York: Farrar, Straus & Giroux.

Zeinert, Karen. 1995. *Free speech: From newspapers to music lyrics.* Springfield, N.J.: Enslow.

Index